CANOEING

CANOEING

Prepared by
The American National Red Cross
With 367 Illustrations

First Printing 1977

DOUBLEDAY & COMPANY, INC.
GARDEN CITY, NEW YORK

ACKNOWLEDGMENTS

The American National Red Cross acknowledges with appreciation the contributions made by Joseph L. Hasenfus and the late Waldemar Van Brunt Claussen, former assistant directors of its Water Safety Services. Their efforts toward the advancement of safe and skilled canoeing have contributed greatly to the development of this book.

Special acknowledgment and thanks are extended to the following members of the Canoeing Text Advisory Committee, who have given guidance, advice, and direction in the preparation of this text: Al Beletz, American Canoeing Association poling chairman; John Berry, boatbuilder, former national C-1 and C-2 slalom and wildwater champion and member of the first U.S. team in world competition; Jack Buchannan, educator, coach, and American Red Cross volunteer instructor; Ramone S. Eaton, canoeist and retired American Red Cross Senior Vice President; Jay Evans, former national K-1 champion and coach for the 1972 Olympic Whitewater Team; John Hunsucker, Ph.D., educator and American Red Cross volunteer instructor; Louis Matacia, author, guide, and canoeing outfitter; Robert McNair, author and canoeing educator; and John Sweet, Ph.D., former national C-1 slalom and wildwater champion and adviser to the Penn State Outing Club.

Appreciation for special assistance is extended to the following persons whose experience, interest, and suggestions were invaluable in the preparation of this textbook: Ernst K. Goetz, Pierre Pulling, John Komp, Donald R. Jarrell, Glorianne Perrier, and Betty Walters.

In addition to the individuals mentioned above, the Red Cross extends special appreciation to the Pennsylvania State University Outing Club, the Boy Scouts of America, the American Canoeing Association, the American Camping Association, the American Whitewater Affiliation, the U.S. Canoe Association, and the many Red Cross volunteers and paid staff members whose advice and cooperation have contributed greatly to the preparation of this text.

Robert F. Burnside, director of the American Red Cross Small Craft Program, was responsible for the coordination of materials and the development of this textbook. Raymond P. Miller II, program specialist, Small Craft Program, was responsible for the writing of the text material and the selection of illustrative material.

This book was illustrated by Richard Guy.

INTRODUCTION

Since the early 1920's, the American Red Cross has included canoeing instruction in its water safety programs at National Aquatic Schools. Training received by water safety instructor candidates at the schools includes instruction in safe canoe handling, self-rescue, and ways of helping others in or on the water. The amount of time devoted to the subject of canoeing at these schools was limited but was sufficient to enable the instructor to include canoe-safety instruction in his junior and senior lifesaving courses and in other training.

Since 1948, the Red Cross has conducted National Small Craft Schools, where canoeing instruction is one of the major subjects. This training prepares canoeing instructors to teach the Red Cross Basic Canoeing course and to conduct canoe-safety demonstrations. Thousands of these courses and demonstrations have been conducted through the years, reaching large numbers of people with canoe-safety information. Canoeing instructors are also trained in Red Cross chapters and at selected National Aquatic and First Aid Schools.

The American Red Cross has prepared this textbook in response to popular demand and in recognition of the need for it as support for the programs described above. Use of the book should help to prevent loss of life in canoeing activity throughout the country. This text contains all the information required for Red Cross canoeing programs, from the basic level through the instructor level.

The information in this book extends into all areas of canoeing activity. The book therefore contains information on specialized forms of activity such as canoe trips, river canoeing, competition, poling, sailing, and other activities. It also gives information on how to care for canoes and equipment and how to make repairs to the various types. Chapter 1 explains the history and development of canoes. Chapter 2 contains information on modern canoes. Chapters 3 and 4 cover information on paddles and other equipment and canoe transportation. For all canoeists, from the beginner to the very proficient, the book contains information of value.

As canoeing knowledge and skill increase, safety increases. The end result is a decrease in accidents and deaths, among beginners and among those who have special skills but have formerly lacked essential safety and self-rescue information.

CONTENTS

CANOEING

1

CANOE HISTORY

The canoe is an incredibly significant product of human workmanship. In the earliest ages of man, there was a time when he did not have the cultural advancement to make any object or to use any tool more refined than a club. Then gradually, over a long period of time, he developed the simplest of tools and made the simplest of objects to use in his struggle to survive. If he lived near the water, one of these objects was a dugout canoe. This first vessel was not much of a craft, but its contribution to the course of man's history and its influence on that history are immeasurable. All the vessels that man has used on the waters of the earth, through the countless centuries to the present, have evolved from the dugout canoe. It is fascinating to compare the parent craft with its evolving descendants, from the galley to the modern ocean liner and the warship, but greater meaning lies in the fact that there would be no civilization as we know it today without water transportation, which started with the dugout canoe. Added to this fact, and making it all the more remarkable, is the fact that in some areas of the earth the dugout canoe has never evolved to higher types of craft. It exists today as it did in the beginning. It has served its basic purpose relatively unchanged in essential form for thousands of years and has never needed improving.

How man first got afloat is, to a degree, a matter of supposition. However, basing their assumptions upon accumulated knowledge of early man and contemporary primitive people, historians generally agree that primordial man probably ventured into and onto the water merely because of his proximity to it. His venture in this direction may have been hastened or intensified by the need to get food for himself and his family or to escape from a predatory enemy.

A log was probably the first floating support that man used. At first he held onto it, supporting himself and swimming it along wherever he wished to go. Later he lay on it and hand-paddled it, and then sat up astride the log and poled it along in shallow-water areas. These latter two skills were rather diffi-

cult, so that when members of his family group on other logs floated close to his log, he welcomed the greater stability resulting when they held the logs together. It was then a natural step to lash the logs together with vines or root fibers to make a

raft. When the raft got out of shallow water, at first accidentally, poling had to give way to paddling with the pole until the bottom could be reached again. The paddling activity suggested the flattening of a stick for better purchase in the water. This was the birth of the paddle, which permitted trips far from shore.

THE DUGOUT CANOE

After the raft, the dugout—a product of man's development of primitive tools and his discovery of firemaking—came on the scene. The first vessel may have been suggested by nature. Surely lightning caused fires then as now, and logs partially burned out could have been found, experimented with, and further hollowed out with fire and stone tools. Greater stability and increasingly shallow draft developed as the hollowing deepened and extended fore and aft. The next step was shaping the ends to lessen resistance, thus making the craft speedier and

more maneuverable. Afterward, suitably sized logs were selected and hollowed out, and a "home industry" of canoe building was inaugurated.

Since this explanation of log, raft, hollow log, and dugout canoe suggests such a natural evolutionary process, probably taking a very long time, it is logical to assume that it took place independently in many places over the earth, at the same time and at different times. In some instances, of course, primitive people who had developed canoes may have migrated over land or water and taught their new art to others.

As the art of making dugout canoes developed, regional variety in sizes and designs resulted. Some canoes were small and simple in construction like that of the Pamunkey Indians of Eastern Virginia. Simple dugouts of this type are used today in parts of Africa and elsewhere. At the present time, a much longer and more graceful dugout is used by natives in Central America and by Seminole Indians in Florida.

A crude but rather unique dugout is that from Fortuna Island, a French possession north of the Fiji Islands. The dugout of the Bushnegro of Dutch Guiana combines good design with

decorative carving. Decorative pattern is carried to a high degree of excellence in the ceremonial and sacred canoe of the Santa Cruz Islands of the British Solomons. Canoes used in the Pacific Islands have outriggers to provide stability. Sizes range from small canoes for children to large war canoes. Many are equipped with sails.

Indian tribes of the Northwestern coastal regions of North America have made dugouts of excellent design and with elaborate totemic decorations. They were made of cedar logs, some of giant sizes, often as long as 60 feet, for use on the ocean and sometimes for hunting whales, a remarkably courageous canoeing adventure. Canoes of very large sizes have been used on nearly every continent and in the Pacific Islands. An interesting and elaborately decorated one had been used by the King of Siam in state processions.

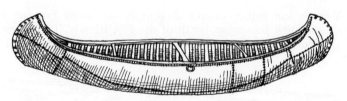

A rather rare primitive canoe has been made by sewing thinly hewed planks together with root fibers or rawhide.

The dugout canoe is the type that evolved into larger craft. As men progressed with canoe building, some of them enlarged the canoes to transport goods for trade with neighboring tribes or groups. To get more freeboard than the dugout could provide, boards were added to extend above the normal gunwale level. Progressive people continued this process until the original dugout became little more than the keel. The planks, first added for extra freeboard to keep out the splashing waves, became the planking of the hull. During this time, oars and sails were invented for use with larger craft. These craft evolved into the galleys of early history, which in turn led to larger ships of subsequent centuries.

FRAME-AND-SKIN CRAFT

Where trees were scarce, frame-and-skin canoes were made. One interesting type is the bull boat, or circular canoe, which had a circular framework of sticks covered with animal skin.

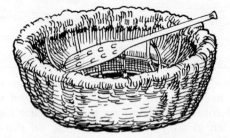

In the early days of the West, the Plains Indians made these craft with buffalo hides. After about 1885, cowhide was used. In the British Isles, a craft of this type, still in use, is called a coracle. In the region of the Tigris and Euphrates Rivers, a craft of the same shape is woven of basket material and made watertight with pitch. Another unusual type of craft propelled by paddles or poles is the balsa raft, or grass boat, which could also be called a grass canoe.

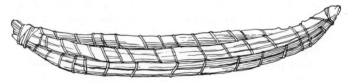

A type of primitive craft about which few people have heard is a canoe made by Northeastern American Indian hunters out of the hides of the moose they killed. They built a frame consisting of gunwales, keel, and ribs, sewed two or more moose hides together, and shaped and secured the hides tightly over the frame. After the seams were waterproofed with pitch and melted moose tallow, the canoe was ready to load with moose meat to be taken downriver to the home village.

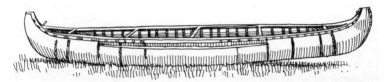

The Eskimos, who inhabit the Arctic coasts of the North American continent, mainly Alaska and Greenland, make the kayak and the umiak. (Both "kayak" and "umiak" are spelled in several ways, but the currently preferred spelling is given here.) In parts of Alaska the kayak is called a bidarke, bidarkee, or baiderka, and the umiak is called a bidar, bidarra, or bidadara, but "kayak" and "umiak" are more widely used.)

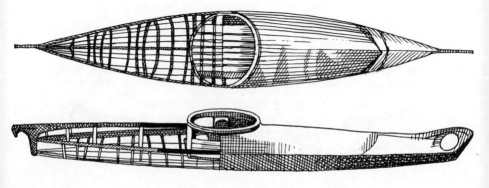

The kayak is made by constructing a wooden framework and stretching sealskin over the frame, bottom and top, leaving only the cockpit opening. The wooden framework is usually made of driftwood pieces held together with rawhide-thong lacings and ties. The skin covering is similarly held in place with rawhide.

The kayak is usually paddled with a double-bladed paddle, although a single blade is also used. It is typically a one-place craft, although larger kayaks are sometimes manned by several people, who paddle with single-bladed paddles often more than 7 feet long.

The umiak is also constructed on a wooden framework, of driftwood pieces or other wood covered with the skin of seals or walruses. The upper edges of the covering are stretched tightly over the gunwales and held in place by a rawhide lacing passing through holes in the skin covering and over and under, or around, a riband (longitudinal strip of wood) a few inches below the gunwale. The typical size is about 30 feet long by 8 feet at the widest point.

THE BIRCHBARK CANOE

Primitive canoe building reached its highest form with the birchbark canoe made by the North American Indians, who inhabited the forest regions where the paper birch tree (also

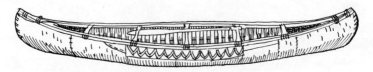

called canoe birch and white birch of the north) grew in great numbers. This canoe deserves special consideration because of its remarkable frame-and-bark construction and because it has a very special place in American and Canadian history.

When the discoverers, explorers, missionaries, merchants, and settlers from Europe and the British Isles came to North America, they found the greatest primeval forest area on earth—literally impenetrable except on foot on land or afloat on the countless thousands of rivers, lakes, and streams. The American Indian used the birchbark canoe to facilitate his travel in regions to be known as Canada and northern parts of the United States. In fact, so many of the Indian's activities depended upon the birchbark canoe that some people have called his way of life a "canoe culture." His canoe had good lines for speed and maneuverability on the water and was lightweight for ease in carrying between bodies of water. It was made of a size to suit its owner, in accordance with the use for which it was being built. The portability of this canoe made long-distance travel practical on extensive water routes throughout the northeastern regions of North America.

Some one-man birchbark canoes were as short as 12 or 13 feet, with beams ranging from 26 to 35 inches. Variations of design in these and larger canoes were relatively minor for the most part but included differences in shape of ends, amount of sheer, depth of craft in respect to length and beam, tribal decorations, and quality of workmanship. Many were of a size similar to the popular canoes of the present day, for which they were, of course, the prototypes. These longer canoes ranged in

length from about 14 feet to approximately 20 feet, with beams varying from 32 inches to about 47 inches. Some very large canoes were built for war; later, in times of the white man, for trade. They ranged up to 30 feet and longer. It is probable that the very longest were made after the coming of the white man and that the typical war canoe of the Indian was somewhat less than 30 feet.

The birchbark canoe was significant in man's exploration and development of the northern portions of North America. Today, the birchbark canoe has disappeared from nearly all the rivers and lakes on which it was once used, and the art of making one is now known and practiced by relatively few Indians and fewer white men.

Some years ago, Waldemar Van Brunt Claussen, famous canoeist and a pioneer in small craft safety, wrote a letter in which he gave the details of making a birchbark canoe. He based his notes on his experience of having assisted a Maine guide several times in this fascinating project. The guide had learned his art from the Indians of Maine.

OTHER FRAME-AND-BARK CANOES

In areas where birch trees did not grow, other barks were used in the making of bark canoes. Basswood bark canoes and elm bark canoes were made by the Iroquois Indians in regions south of the birch forests.

Interestingly enough, frame-and-bark canoes have been made in other parts of the world also, such as the one made by the Goldi tribe of the Lower Amur River in eastern Asia. Canoes of bark, usually pine or spruce, closely resembling this design, were found in the Kootenay region of British Columbia and in the northwestern United States. In view of the fact that aboriginal North Americans are known to have migrated from Asia to the American continent, a relationship can be assumed between the canoes of these two groups. Another bark canoe of interest is that of the Indians of Tierra del Fuego, at the extreme southern projection of the continent of South America. This craft is of frame-and-bark construction, rather large (25 feet long), but of less refinement than the birchbark canoes of North American Indians.

Upon his arrival on the North American continent, the white man made almost immediate use of the birchbark canoe in his exploration, missionary work, fur trading, and settlement. Every schoolchild reads of the explorers and missionaries having used birchbark canoes, employing the Indians to help them. In fact, the canoe was the chief means of travel to unexplored areas for a couple of centuries.

Perhaps the most romantic of all the chapters in the story of canoes is that concerning the *coureur de bois* and the *voyageur*. During the early settlement period of Canada, many of the French found that clearing the land and farming it was less inviting than the more adventurous life of hunting and trapping for fur. Canoes were essential in this latter occupation and were obtained on short notice from the Indian canoe builders. The mobility involved in the work brought the Frenchmen the romantic name of coureurs de bois, or bushrangers. They came in close contact with the Indians, and many married Indian women. A great amount of their activity during the seventeenth century involved transporting large quantities of merchandise by canoe into remote areas of the wilderness to trade with Indian tribes for beaver and other furs. By the eighteenth century, most of the coureurs de bois had changed from being independent hunters, trappers, and traders to being hired canoemen called voyageurs. They were French Canadians, half-breeds, and, sometimes, pure-blooded Indians. They worked for merchants licensed to trade in fur and for explorers famous in history.

The prowess of the voyageur as a canoeman and a *portageur* apparently reached an extremely high level, especially in terms of his ability to paddle rapidly for hours on end and to carry very heavy loads on portages. His character is legendary in

Canadian folklore and history. The Canadian poet William
Henry Drummond has immortalized the voyageur in such poems
as "The Voyageur," * which, like much of his work, is written
in the French-Canadian dialect. Some selected lines are given
below.

> Gone he is now, an' de beeg canoe
>
> . . . .
>
> Ax' heem de nort' win' w'at he see
> Of de Voyageur long ago,
> An' he'll say to you w'at he say to me,
>
> . . . .
>
> "I see de track of hees botte sau-vage
> On many a hill an' long portage
> Far, far away from hees own vill-age
>
> . . . .
>
> . . . I meet heem singin' hees lonely way
> De happies' man I know—
> I cool hees face as he's sleepin' dere
> Under de star of de Red Riviere,
>
> . . . .
>
> De blaze of hees camp on de snow, I see
> An' I lissen hees 'En Roulant'
> On de lan' w'ere de reindeer travel free,
> Ringin' out strong an' clear—
> Offen de grey wolf sit before
> De light is come from hees open door,
> An' caribou foller along de shore
> De song of de Voyageur."
> So dat's de reason I drink tonight
> To de man of de Grand Nor' Wes',
> For hees heart was young, an' hees heart was light
>
> . . . .
>
> I'm proud of de sam' blood in my vein
> I'm a son of de Nort' Win' wance again.

THE TRANSITION TO MODERN MATERIALS

The period of transition from the birchbark to the all-wood
and the canvas-covered canoe is not well recorded; therefore, an
explanation of it will have to be partially assumptive. For ex-

* *The Poetical Works of William Henry Drummond.* New York: G. P.
Putnam's Sons, The Knickerbocker Press, 1912, p. 259.

ample, the Indian, no doubt, used the white man's tools, as he did his weapons, as soon as they were made available. This usage could have resulted in some improvement in the birchbark canoe. An occasional effort was made by an individual, either Indian or white man, to use materials other than bark, roots, and pitch, or hollowed log, to make a canoe. There are two famous examples: about 1865, John McGregor made the famous Rob Roy, a decked canoe patterned somewhat after the Eskimo kayak; and a few years later, Nathaniel H. Bishop had a canoe made for him out of paper pulp mixed with glue. Both of these sportsmen made voyages in their canoes and wrote accounts of them. Other efforts of this sort were, no doubt, made in many more utilitarian and unpublicized circumstances.

In Peterborough, Ontario, about 1870, John Stevenson made an all-wood canoe of rib-and-plank construction. He worked with Col. J. Z. Rogers in the perfection of this canoe, and in 1879 a canoe company was founded in Peterborough for its production. Only a few years later, in Old Town, Maine, men were considering the possibility of making canoes of rib, plank, and canvas construction. This forward thinking was the result of known success in patching birchbark canoes with canvas or cloth. Beginning in the 1880's, canoe companies were founded in Old Town and elsewhere for building canvas-covered canoes, which ultimately became famous throughout the world.

A later development was a canoe of double-plank construction with a waterproof cloth lining between the layers of planking. In recent times, canoes of molded plywood have been made—a few in the United States but most in Europe. In common with other watercraft of molded plywood, they combine strength, lightness, and easy upkeep.

The aluminum canoe also has come on the scene. It has achieved popularity because of its relative ruggedness combined with light weight and easy upkeep.

The *pirogue* (pē-rōg) is a craft similar to a canoe. It was originally a dugout but now is nearly always made of 1/4-inch plywood over a hardwood frame. Its overall length is approximately 14 feet, and the beam is about 3 feet. It is constructed much the same way in which a small, flat-bottomed rowboat or skiff is made but with very low gunwales (approximately 9 inches amidships). Pirogues are popular craft in southern parts of the United States, and many homemade ones are still in use today.

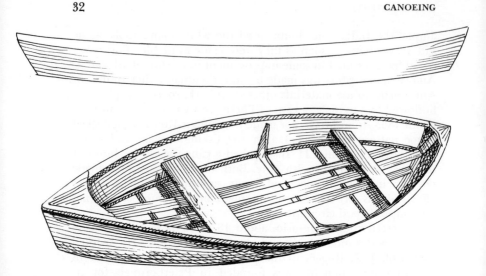

MODERN CANOEING—FOR RECREATION AND SPORT

A dominant feature of modern canoeing activity is that it has been largely for recreational purposes. This type of canoeing has led to the establishment of canoe clubs, outing clubs with special interest in some form of canoeing, and canoeing programs within various organizations. A pioneer and leading organization in canoeing has been the American Canoe Association (established in 1880 at Crosbyside Park, Lake George, New York) to unite canoeists for various forms of recreational canoeing. This organization gives leadership in such canoeing activities as racing, cruising, sailing, and poling.

Other organizations, such as the American Whitewater Affiliation and the United States Canoe Association, have also become recognized as leaders in promoting all aspects of canoeing and kayaking.

The XIth Olympiad, in Berlin in 1936, saw canoeing introduced as an official game. The F-1 or F-2 (folding kayak), the K-1 or K-2 (rigid kayak), and the C-1 (Canadian canoe) were all used for competition. All of the preceding craft were raced over distances of 1,000 and 10,000 meters.

The canoe and the kayak are both of North American origin, but the sport of whitewater racing originated in Europe and was developed there. The basic boats were modified to meet the demands of steeply descending rocky rivers and rough water. The races are a natural outgrowth of man's competitive urge. The sport was introduced in the late thirties and enjoyed rapid growth after World War II. A slalom world championship was held at Geneva in 1949 and has been held every 2 years since. The Thirteenth Slalom and the Eighth Wildwater World Championships were held in Switzerland in 1973. In 1972, for the first time, the slalom was part of the Olympic Games, in Germany.

The North American slalom debut was in 1953, on the Brandywine Creek near Wilmington, Delaware. This race was repeated the following year, and movies taken there helped popularize the sport across the country. The first slalom national championship was held on the West River in Vermont in 1958.

In those early days, and, in fact, until 1962, standard cruising canoes were used. Some were equipped with spray decks to keep out some water, but these decks did not make them any more maneuverable.

The next milestone of the sport was the introduction of a one-man fiberglass slalom canoe. These boats, designed for maneuverability, fully decked, and built to the minimum dimensions allowed, revolutionized the sport.

Kayaks and kayak techniques were improving simultaneously. Early kayaks were of the folding variety, not always built to minimum dimensions or with maximum maneuverability. Later, rigid fiberglass construction and improved designs were introduced. Paul Bruhin, a Swiss kayakist, was instrumental in improving kayak technique in the Eastern United States, and Erich Seidel, a former German champion, introduced and popularized the sport in Colorado.

In 1962 there were two major slalom races in the eastern United States. Today, slaloms are numerous all over this nation. The present slalom courses are far more difficult than the early courses, reflecting the increased ability of today's paddlers and boats.

Meanwhile, as the slalom advanced rapidly, wildwater racing was dragged along like a little brother. The maneuverable slalom boats are not suited for wildwater, where straight speed is required, but were used for want of anything else. However, in 1964 and 1965, special wildwater boats began to appear. At present, although still lagging behind slalom, wildwater racing is beginning to advance on its own. In 1968, separate rankings were determined for the top wildwater paddlers in all classes for the first time.

Improved techniques and training have kept pace with the

equipment developments. In the early days, river running was adequate training for racing, and the sport was a leisure-time activity. Some paddlers began to take it more seriously, practice became important, and soon physical fitness entered the picture. Now, serious competitors train virtually year round as in any other highly competitive sport. Weekly practice sessions in pools, using gates suspended from ropes or wires, give experts a chance to sharpen their skills. Beginners use this pool time to learn basic techniques, especially Eskimo rolls (see chapter 7); hence these workouts are called rolling sessions. These practice sessions lead to the indoor pool slalom. Generally held in February or early March, just prior to the whitewater season, these races provide a jump on the season without the dangers of cold weather and ice-choked rivers.

2

MODERN CANOES

This chapter will give the reader information about the kinds of construction used in the manufacture of modern canoes. It is planned so that the novice can learn in logical sequence those things necessary for him to get started as a canoeist.

NOMENCLATURE

As is true with other specialized activities, some words and phrases used in canoeing are quite foreign to noncanoeists—parts or features of the canoe, for example, and terminology relating to its use. Every canoeist should learn correct terminology as it is used in this text and throughout the paddling fraternity. However, where local tradition and usage create a conflict in terminology, there is no reason why local usage should not prevail.

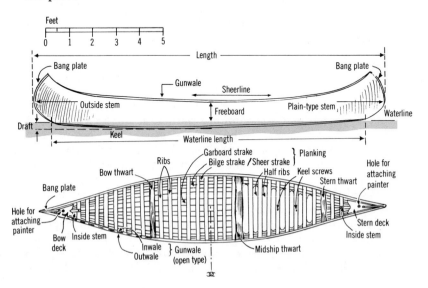

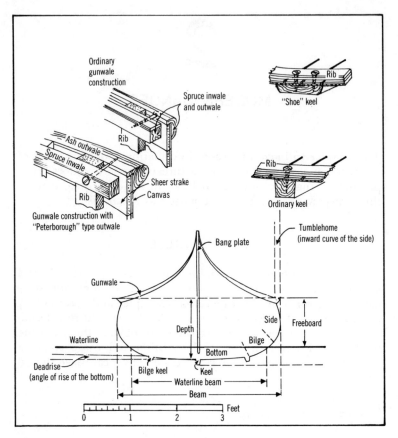

SELECTION OF A CANOE

There is no uniform opinion regarding relative merits of the various canoes available on today's market, any more than there is in the area of automobile selection. Recommendations regarding selection of a canoe will not be made in this manual, but the reader will be able to make up his own mind on the basis of the fundamental information given and can relate it to the purpose of the craft.

As pointed out above, there are variations among the types of canoes—in their sizes, types of construction, and materials. Obviously these varieties of canoes have proved satisfactory to users. Otherwise, lack of demand for some of them would have

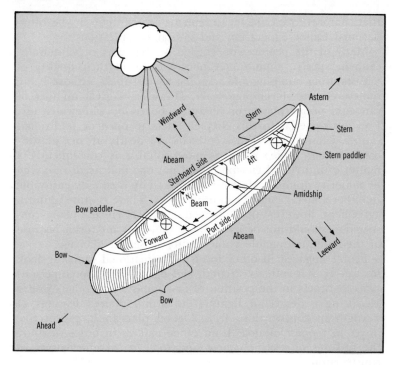

led to discontinuance of their production. Their diversification is based on the variety of activities and conditions in which canoes are used—for example, leisurely paddling on quiet water near centers of population, fishing on local waters, day cruising, camping trips, running river rapids (whitewater), summer camp use, racing, and wilderness trips. All these activities are recreational. In addition, in northern Canada, the canoe is still used for freighting and water transportation in wild, undeveloped regions.

Men who use canoes commercially for transportation and hauling goods select them on the basis of the size load that it is practical to haul in the regions in which they operate. If portages are not involved, they may wisely use large canoes that could well be equipped with an outboard motor. Furthermore, if the canoe does not have to be carried, excessive weight is not a disadvantage; therefore, greater strength may be built into it. If portages are involved, smaller canoes of lighter construction are preferred.

People who participate in formalized canoe racing use canoes that conform to specific measurements agreed upon by the International Canoe Federation and similar organizations.

Many of the people who engage in the sport of whitewater canoeing prefer aluminum canoes because of their quality of withstanding bumping and scraping against rocks without being punctured and developing leaks. However, a great number of canoeists prefer plastic or fiberglass boats for whitewater use. Previous material in this chapter refers to open or traditional canoes. Closed or decked-over boats are nearly all of "plastic" construction. Which canoe is most suitable is consequently a matter of individual viewpoint and not one that needs resolving by majority opinion. Most canoeing activity is equally enjoyable in either a metal canoe or in other types. There is quite uniform agreement, however, that all-wood canoes of rib-and-plank construction should not be used where they may hit rocks, because of their unquestionable vulnerability to serious damage.

People engaged in other forms of recreational canoeing look for canoes that embody strength and light weight. Some persons place lightness in the position of first importance; others prefer sacrificing a degree of lightness to attain desired features of strength in construction. It is a good plan for a prospective buyer to request catalogs from canoe makers in order to study the features of specific canoes and to learn of alternatives in construction.

The following information applies to open-canoe selection, although many of the factors mentioned may be utilized in selecting closed boats.

The size of a canoe for general recreational use is an important consideration. If it is too big, a canoe will be hard to carry and launch, and in some cases it will be difficult to handle on the water. The 16-foot canoe is regarded as the most suitable size for solo paddling, but on trips where gear is taken, a 17-foot canoe would be preferred by many canoeists. If the trip were extended, requiring the added weight of food and gear, or if a third person were added, some canoeists would elect to use an 18-foot canoe for ease of handling with the added load. For adult solo paddling and for either solo or tandem paddling for youngsters, the 15-foot canoe is popular. Its lightness makes it desirable for youth programs. Canoes of even shorter length, especially when of good proportions, are easy for children to carry, launch, and paddle.

The canoeist has a choice of selecting a canoe without a keel or one with a standard tapered keel or a shoe keel. Because the canoe without a keel is very maneuverable owing to its smooth bottom, it is excellent for use in a fast stream or in slalom competition and for smart handling, as when among other craft or coming alongside a dock. The same canoe with a standard keel will be less maneuverable, but on open water will hold a steadier course because the keel projecting down into the water tends to prevent the canoe from swinging off course in response to the paddling strokes and from being blown sideward by the wind. The keel also provides some protection for the bottom of the canoe in the event of accidentally running aground or running onto an underwater obstruction such as a rock. The shoe keel is a good compromise for a river canoe. It provides rigidity to the bottom of the canoe, and because of its flatness, the shoe keel does not lessen maneuverability to as great a degree as a conventional keel.

Following are some of the items relating to design that might be considered in selecting a canoe:

- A canoe that is wide and consequently quite flat-bottomed is relatively very stable. The farther forward and aft the fullness of the bottom is carried, the more stable the canoe will be. Such a canoe will not be fast, and although it will handle nicely with a tandem crew, it will be relatively cumbersome for solo paddling.
- Any canoe that has the fullness of the bottom carried well fore and aft toward the ends will ride with the waves of a lake or river rather than knife dangerously into them as a canoe with more pointed ends would do.
- A canoe that has a slight longitudinal, rockerlike curve to its bottom will be more maneuverable than a canoe with a straighter bottom line. This feature will also help its ends to rise and fall with the waves, especially in solo paddling, and also somewhat in tandem paddling, when the crew members move closer together near amidships.
- Narrow canoes are rounder of bottom. Their narrowness makes them easier to paddle solo. If the longitudinal bottom line of a narrow canoe is straight, the canoe will be fast. If it is a long canoe, it will be still faster. If, in addition, it has nicely shaped, narrow, knifelike ends, it will be the fastest of its type. It will, however, be the least maneuverable of canoes and will be gripped firmly by currents rather than being able to slide over them.
- Canoes with higher-than-typical sides (deeper) and high ends will be noticeably more affected by the wind but in high waves will be less likely to take in water.
- Hardwood gunwales are structurally important and they are

desirable in any case (except, of course, for aluminum canoes and closed boats) because of the protection they afford.

The following illustrations show three views of most canoe and kayak designs. These silhouettes identify the prominent features of the craft, ranging from traditional canoes of history to the highly specialized flatwater kayaks used in world competition today.

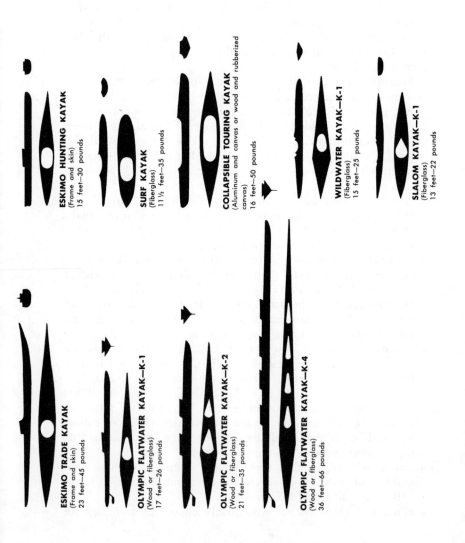

ESKIMO HUNTING KAYAK
(Frame and skin)
15 feet—30 pounds

SURF KAYAK
(Fiberglass)
11½ feet—35 pounds

COLLAPSIBLE TOURING KAYAK
(Aluminum and canvas or wood and rubberized canvas)
16 feet—50 pounds

WILDWATER KAYAK—K-1
(Fiberglass)
15 feet—25 pounds

SLALOM KAYAK—K-1
(Fiberglass)
13 feet—22 pounds

ESKIMO TRADE KAYAK
(Frame and skin)
23 feet—45 pounds

OLYMPIC FLATWATER KAYAK—K-1
(Wood or fiberglass)
17 feet—26 pounds

OLYMPIC FLATWATER KAYAK—K-2
(Wood or fiberglass)
21 feet—35 pounds

OLYMPIC FLATWATER KAYAK—K-4
(Wood or fiberglass)
36 feet—66 pounds

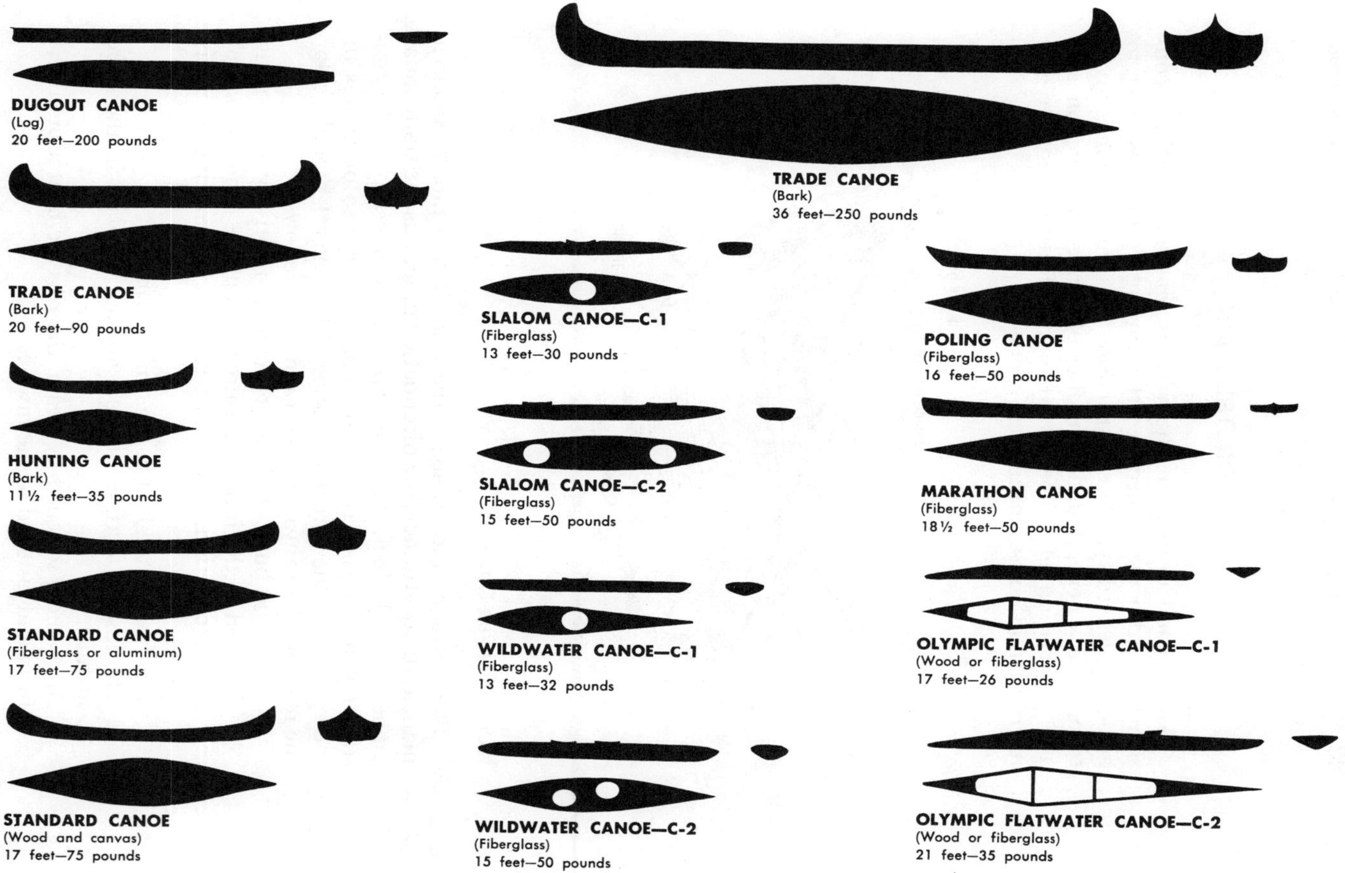

TRADE CANOE
(Bark)
36 feet—250 pounds

POLING CANOE
(Fiberglass)
16 feet—50 pounds

MARATHON CANOE
(Fiberglass)
18½ feet—50 pounds

OLYMPIC FLATWATER CANOE—C-1
(Wood or fiberglass)
17 feet—26 pounds

OLYMPIC FLATWATER CANOE—C-2
(Wood or fiberglass)
21 feet—35 pounds

SLALOM CANOE—C-1
(Fiberglass)
13 feet—30 pounds

SLALOM CANOE—C-2
(Fiberglass)
15 feet—50 pounds

WILDWATER CANOE—C-1
(Fiberglass)
13 feet—32 pounds

WILDWATER CANOE—C-2
(Fiberglass)
15 feet—50 pounds

DUGOUT CANOE
(Log)
20 feet—200 pounds

TRADE CANOE
(Bark)
20 feet—90 pounds

HUNTING CANOE
(Bark)
11½ feet—35 pounds

STANDARD CANOE
(Fiberglass or aluminum)
17 feet—75 pounds

STANDARD CANOE
(Wood and canvas)
17 feet—75 pounds

CONSTRUCTION

This section deals with the various materials used for construction. Also mentioned are the various techniques used to achieve a desired type of construction. This information is given to provide a general understanding of canoe construction and an appreciation of canoe qualities and features, not to give instruction in how to make these canoes.

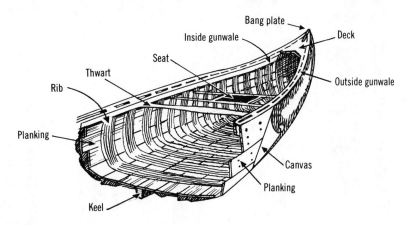

Wood, Canvas-Covered

The canvas-covered canoe is the traditional canoe of modern man, as its forerunner, the birchbark canoe, was the traditional canoe of the Indian. There is expert craftsmanship in the construction of the canvas-covered canoe, as there so often was in the making of the birchbark canoe. The general procedure for the making of a canvas-covered canoe is as follows:

1. A form is built. It is a permanent, relatively solid mold designed to the inside measurements of the canoe to be put into production. It will last through the making of many canoes, for years.
2. The inwales are laid in the canoe forms.
3. The inside stems, preshaped, are put in place in the same manner.
4. After being softened by steam, the ribs are bent around the form and fastened to the inwales.

5. The ribs and stems are then faired up (smoothed) by plane, and the planking is laid on.
6. Only the bottom planks are fastened to the inside stem while the canoe is still on the form. This method allows the canoe to be spread enough to be taken off the form. This spreading is necessary because of the tumblehome in the canoe at the sides and of the curve at the ends.
7. When the canoe is taken off the form, the breast plates are attached to the inwales and the stems. The ends of the planking also are attached to the stems.
8. The rest of the planking is put on, and the thwarts are put in place to give the canoe strength and to maintain its shape.
9. The canvas is put on, and then filler and finish are applied. Then the outwales, outside stems, and keel (if any) and bang plates are put on, and all wooden parts are finished with varnish or some other appropriate finish.

Some characteristics of canvas-covered canoes are as follows:
- *Ribs* are nearly always made of white cedar, $\frac{5}{16}$ inch thick (sometimes $\frac{1}{4}$ inch thick on lightweight canoes), from $1\frac{1}{2}$ to $2\frac{1}{4}$ inches wide, and spaced from $1\frac{1}{2}$ to $2\frac{1}{4}$ inches apart. On freight canoes, the ribs are wider, thicker, and closer together.
- *Planking* is generally of red cedar, from $\frac{5}{32}$ to $\frac{3}{16}$ inch thick and from $3\frac{1}{2}$ to 4 inches wide. In lightweight canoes, the planking is sometimes $\frac{1}{8}$ inch thick.
- *Gunwales* are made of mahogany, spruce, oak, or ash.
- *Breast plates* are small, more or less triangular, pieces of wood about an inch thick, fastened in the ends of the canoe to the stems and inwales. They are usually formed from mahogany or oak and are structural supports. They have been known as "decks," but this terminology is incorrect inasmuch as they are inside the canoe and do not cover the gunwale.
- *Decks* are any material running across the craft from gunwale to gunwale with the express purpose of keeping out water.
- *Stems* are made of oak or ash.
- *Bang plates* are formed from corrosion-resistant metal.
- *Thwarts* are made of mahogany, oak, ash, or spruce.
- *Exterior keels* are usually a part of canoes, as mentioned previously. The conventional keel is a tapered one, measuring from $\frac{7}{8}$ to 1 inch wide where the keel is attached to the canoe bottom, and is the same in depth. It is on the median line of the canoe. Often a shoe keel is used in place of the tapered keel. The shoe keel is from $\frac{3}{8}$ to $\frac{1}{2}$ inch thick and from 2 to $2\frac{1}{4}$

inches wide. Large, heavy canoes, especially freight canoes, have from one to three bilge keels on each side of the main keel.

- *Canvas* of medium texture (for example, No. 8 or No. 10) is commonly used. On very large canoes, No. 6 is common, and No. 4 is used in exceptional cases. On very lightweight canoes that must have careful handling, finer canvas up to No. 15 is used.
- *Filler* is a mixture of products whose exact nature is not usually specified. Some fillers are mostly white lead. Some more recently developed are plastics.
- *Glass cloth* can be used in place of canvas for more durability.

Wood, Double-Plank Construction

In a double-plank construction canoe, the inside planks run crosswise from gunwale to gunwale, taking the place of ribs. The outside planks are narrow and run lengthwise. Between these two layers of planking is a waterproof cloth lining made of high-grade, closely woven muslin, treated with a waterproof marine glue. The two layers of planking are held together with over 7,000 copper nails, driven from the outside and clinched (bent over and flattened) on the inside. The canoe has both inside and outside stems, a keel, seats, or thwarts, and decks. The gunwales, of one-piece construction, are attached outside the hull, thus making a flush finish on the inside from deck to deck. All the bent parts of the canoe are formed by steaming selected pieces on special forms and holding them in place until they dry, after which they are released, to fit perfectly in their respective places in the canoe.

Molded Plywood Hulls

With the introduction of modern waterproof plastic resin glues, it became practical to mold watercraft hulls of plywood. Such craft are light and strong. In fact, the great strength of the molded plywood makes ribs unnecessary, thus eliminating much weight.

The molded mahogany plywood canoe is made as follows:
1. The form is covered with a layer of cellophane to prevent the canoe from sticking to the form.
2. Inside stems are fitted into recesses on the form.
3. The 1/16-inch-thick strips of mahogany veneer are coated on both sides with the plastic resin adhesive, except for those strips to be used as face veneer on the inside and the outside

of the canoe. These are coated on only one side. All are laid aside to dry for a day.

4. The first layer of veneer is then stapled to the form, with the strips laid all the way across at a 45-degree angle to the keel line. When the layer is completely on, all the staples are removed except those beyond the trim line at each gunwale.

5. The remaining three layers of veneer are similarly applied, each at right angles to the preceding one, with the strips arranged so that they overlap the seams beneath.

6. The bonding process of getting the four layers of veneer permanently glued to each other and molded into the shape of the form is done by placing the whole thing into an autoclave after first wrapping it in canvas and inserting it in a rubber vacuum bag. The door of the autoclave is bolted shut, and the air is withdrawn from the rubber bag through a special vacuum line. Steam is turned on to produce the heat and pressure needed. For 45 minutes the temperature is kept at 270°F. During this time, the resin melts and flows into all openings and pores, then hardens and sets, producing a permanently waterproof one-piece hull.

7. Then the form is withdrawn from the autoclave, the rubber bag and canvas cover are removed, and the hull is lifted and pried free of the form.

8. The remaining steps are the obvious ones of trimming, sanding, finishing, and putting in gunwales, breast hooks, and thwarts.

Molded plywood canoes are especially popular in Europe. Some excellent ones are used in the United States for flatwater canoe racing.

All-Wood Canoe of Rib-and-Plank Construction

The all-wood canoe is quite rare now in the United States. It was manufactured continually since its development in the 1870's. Builders now call it a canoe of longitudinal strip construction. Its ribs are of hardwood, ⅝ inch half round, spaced 2 inches apart, center to center. Its planking is of selected cedar not over 2 inches wide and ⁵⁄₁₆ inch thick. The planking is of shiplap cut; that is, a portion of each plank's width is cut away at each edge but on opposite sides, so that it will make an overlapping but flush joint with planks similarly cut. The joints are given a coat of a special waterproof gum compound, and the

planking is pulled together under pressure and nailed to the
ribs by large-headed copper nails, clinched on the inside of the
ribs. Brass bolts and screws are also used, namely in attaching
the reinforcing parts, such as thwarts, decks, outside stems, and
keel. Lightweight floorboards are screwed to the ribs on the inside so that the paddler's weight will be borne by the ribs, not
by the planking.

Canoes of this type were also made for canoe racing in the
United States until recently.

Aluminum

An aluminum canoe is formed in two longitudinal halves,
riveted together. A leading manufacturer makes such canoes as
described below.

The process starts with a rectangular sheet of aluminum alloy
several feet longer than the length of the finished canoe. The
ends of this sheet are clamped in hydraulically operated jaws,
which stretch the sheet longitudinally over a solid die. The
machine is capable of exerting pressure up to 140,000 pounds
during this operation. The formed "half canoe" is then removed
from the die and placed in a large press, where it is drilled and
trimmed to shape. It is then baked in an oven for 8 hours at a
temperature of 360° to temper and toughen it. Gunwales,
thwarts, seats, decks, and other reinforcing parts are also made
on special dies, which will eliminate most hand-forming. All
parts are cleaned and given a protective coating before assembly.
If a canoe is to be painted (for use in salt water), all parts go
through additional preparations, including having a coat of
corrosion-inhibiting zinc chromate primer. Some manufacturers
anodize all parts rather than paint them. Anodized aluminum is
highly corrosion resistant but more expensive than painted
aluminum.

When the two halves are prepared, they and the reinforcing
parts are put together with about 2,000 rivets. Each rivet goes
through from two to four thicknesses of aluminum. The seams
are made permanently watertight with neoprene (synthetic rubber) tape and a special compound. The canoe is then tested
under pressure for leaks. Finally, a flotation material called
styrofoam is installed in each end of the canoe and held in place
by bulkheads. The styrofoam is permanent and should not have
to be replaced unless attacked by petroleum products. Insects
have been known to infest styrofoam and cause its deterioration
in their search for nesting places. Early canoe models, however,

did not have the styrofoam material. Instead, they depended upon the watertightness of the buoyancy chambers. Canoes of this type should be tested for buoyancy in the swamped condition or should have their air compartments filled with styrofoam to assure permanent buoyancy. Some specific details of the aluminum canoe are as follows:

• Standard models have hulls made of aluminum alloy .051 inch thick, and the lightweight models are .032 inch thick.
• The manufacturer recommends the standard models for camps, liveries, and general use where rough handling may prevail and the lightweight models for experienced canoeists and those who have a great deal of portaging to do.
• Square-ended (transomed) canoes are manufactured for use with outboard motors.

Plastics

The term "plastic" is used to identify any boat made primarily of resins, fiberglass, nylon, polypropylene, or a variety of other plastic boatbuilding materials. The boats made from one or more of the "plastics" are rapidly becoming more and more plentiful. This increase in manufacture is primarily due to comparative ease of construction (as compared to construction of wood or aluminum boats), the strength and resiliency of the final product, and the reduced cost of construction.

Many large manufacturers are turning out excellent canoes. But these companies are not the only ones building boats— scores of individuals have turned to designing and building boats in garages, basements, and rented storefronts. In fact, al-

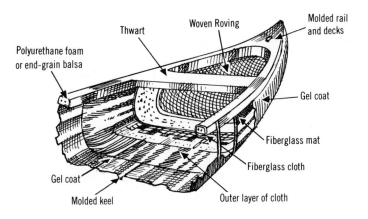

Thwart
Woven Roving
Molded rail and decks
Polyurethane foam or end-grain balsa
Gel coat
Fiberglass mat
Fiberglass cloth
Gel coat
Molded keel
Outer layer of cloth

most any person with a knack for working with his hands can build his own boat. He should, however, not rely on the brief descriptions presented here but should make the acquaintance of an experienced builder and learn firsthand before starting his own boat. At the very least, he should read a complete guide on the subject.

The methods of construction being used today are many. Whether the boat is homemade or factory built, this text will only outline some of the more commonly used techniques of construction and some of the materials used.

Prior to the building of any plastic boat, a mold must first be made, borrowed, or rented. The mold is used as the basis for the boat and therefore is the boatbuilder's number-one tool. Once the mold is properly prepared, various methods and materials can be employed to construct the boat.

The most common construction technique is hand lay-up. The cloth to be used is placed in layers into the mold and thoroughly soaked with resin. The elimination of problems is important. Working out all of the air bubbles and getting just the right amount of resin into the cloth are the main difficulties. When done properly, the hand lay-up takes a long time and is tedious. Provision *must* be made for elimination and venting of the toxic vapors throughout production time.

The spray-up method is used in mass production. The preparation of the mold is the same as in the hand lay-up system. The big difference is the application of the resin and glass. Often the glass is in the form of roving (twisted cord of glass fibers), fed into a "cut gun," which cuts the cord off in short lengths and sprays it along with resin into the mold. The final product is somewhat heavier and weaker than boats made with the hand lay-up procedure. The only advantage is in the spraying of the resin in premixed quantities. This spraying saves time.

Vacuum forming is an expensive and complex method of forming hulls. It takes special apparatus and materials. The materials are usually sheets of plastic or of plastic-foam sandwich, which become pliable when heated. When placed over the mold, the sheet is pulled into the mold and allowed to cool, forming a hull.

Other methods are those that, through pressure, squeeze out excess resin and air bubbles. These systems are not for the novice boatbuilder. Two of the more successful methods are vacuum bagging and pressure molding. Even these have their inherent problems.

In an effort to produce the ultimate boat, manufacturers, boatbuilders, and amateur experimenters have researched the subject thoroughly. They agree that a strong, durable, inexpensive boat is what they are looking for. It must be rigid yet soft enough not to shatter on impact. And, above all, it must be extremely lightweight while possessing all the above qualities.

The average paddler really does not need an ultralight boat. Therefore, a boatbuilder has some leeway in the materials available for constructing his boat. The "plastics" used are usually in resin form, using a cloth material as a reinforcement. In general, boats compounded from only one type of cloth tend to exaggerate the faults of that material. A composite lay-up, in which one material compensates for the weakness of another, emphasizes the strengths of both types. These composite cloths are used as the reinforcing fiber in polyester or epoxy composite canoes. Some cloths being sold are woven from fibers of glass, nylon, polypropylene, and aramid (the strongest and most durable—also the most expensive).

The resins used are commonly of two types, epoxy and polyester. Most manufacturers are using polyester resins because of their availability and nominal cost. Epoxy resins, being somewhat stronger than polyester, are in short supply and are more expensive. Epoxy also is toxic, and special precautions must be observed when using it.

Other plastics are being used with much success by large manufacturers but require special techniques in the formation of boats. One material, acrylonitrile-butadiene-styrene (ABS), is a laminate of substrate and core with an additional tough, cross-

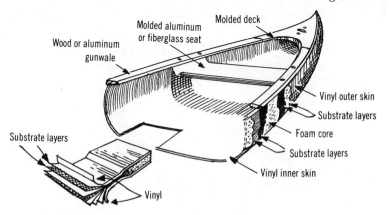

linked vinyl skin. ABS is in the form of large sheets, which are heat-molded as mentioned earlier. The advantage of this and other "space-age plastics" is their high impact resistance, light weight, and durability.

The prospective canoe buyer will find that the more involved the procedure of construction, the more a craft will cost. Also, a factor to consider is the availability of construction materials. Lack of supply will drive the cost up.

Just about any design of canoe can be molded from plastics. The only craft not made from plastics are those used in top-level flatwater competition. These, as mentioned earlier, are wood.

Open canoes are molded and outfitted with hardwood, vinyl, or aluminum (in thwarts, gunwales, and decking) for strength. They are usually constructed with built-in flotation chambers in each end.

Decked canoes of the closed-boat variety are molded in two halves, hull and deck (with cockpit), and then joined at the sides.

A variety of seat arrangements can be built into decked canoes. The most common seat is made of wood or aluminum. It can be installed at a slant for leaning against, as a thwart, or flat for sitting on. The latter installation reduces the weight on the paddler's knees. Other arrangements include a molded seat hung from the cockpit coaming. Another type is a closed-cell foam pedestal, which the paddler kneels astride. Flotation in decked boats is achieved by adding similar foam blocks or flotation bags.

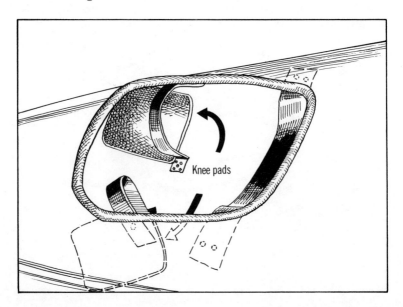

Knee pads

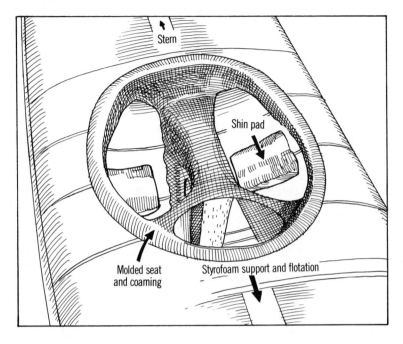

Stern

Shin pad

Molded seat
and coaming

Styrofoam support and flotation

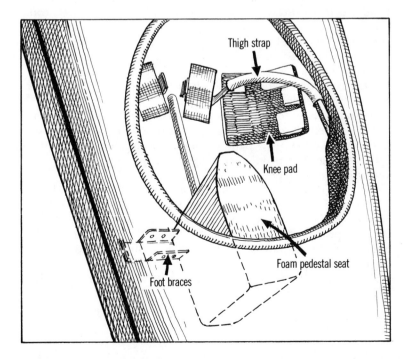

Thigh strap

Knee pad

Foam pedestal seat

Foot braces

3

PADDLES, ROPE, AND OTHER EQUIPMENT

PADDLES

As you gain experience as a canoeist, you will understand the importance of choosing your paddle carefully. The paddle is your most important asset, since it is the one tool upon which you depend continuously while afloat.

Prior to selecting a paddle, you should become familiar with its parts and their names. The following diagram will help you to learn the proper names for the various parts of both single- and double-bladed paddles.

Paddle Selection

As a beginning canoeist, you can get away with using just about any inexpensive paddle. Until you become more proficient in stroking and in maneuvering the canoe, the less expensive paddle will do nicely. However, it should be of a length conducive to effective paddling—long enough so that the grip will reach your eye level while the tip is resting on the ground.

Another simple method of selecting a paddle is to have it long enough so that you can curl one hand around the grip while curling the other hand around the tip of the blade with your arms fully extended.

As you become an experienced canoeist, you should use a more exacting method of selecting an appropriately sized paddle. Dimensions other than paddle length are dependent upon the intended use, the paddler's strength and physical stature, and the type of craft to be used.

The length of the blade should be such that the blade has a good "grip" on the water but should not be so long that it scrapes the bottom of a rather shallow river nor so wide that it inhibits proper use. A long blade does not need to be a wide blade and should not be so long that it hinders recovery following a stroke.

There have been paddles produced with very short, very wide blades for use in shallow water. The following illustrations

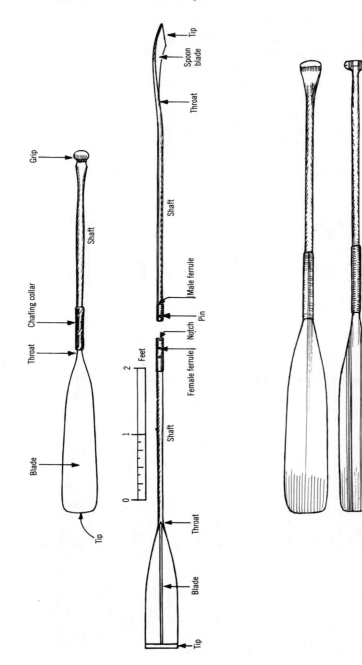

should give you a good idea of the various designs being used. The extra-wide paddles shown are used by strong or competitive canoeists; they give the additional surface area of blade needed for the powerful stroking used by competitors.

With the paddle blade fully buried in the water at the mid-point of a stroke, the shaft should be long enough so that the grip is at the paddler's forehead. A shorter shaft will lack power and may result in failure to immerse the entire blade. A longer shaft will cause the upper arm to work unnecessarily high and may result in pushing the paddle too deeply into the water.

This method of selection allows not only for the paddler's

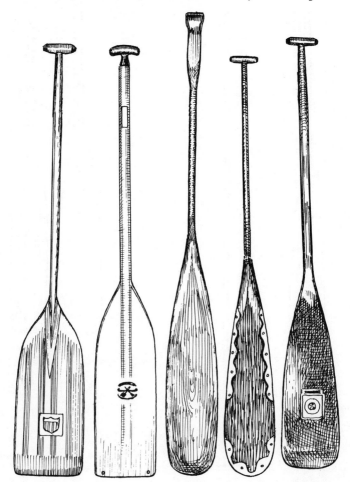

size but also for the type of boat, the height of the thwart, and other factors.

In another quick method used in selecting a paddle for shaft length, the paddle is supported by the hands (one on the grip, the other on the shaft), and with the shaft resting lightly on top of the paddler's head. The angles formed by the bent elbows should be 90°. The distance from the hand on the shaft to the throat of the paddle should approximate the amount of free-board of the paddler's canoe. This length of shaft is usually padded or wrapped to prevent it from being chafed or damaged by the canoe and to protect the canoe.

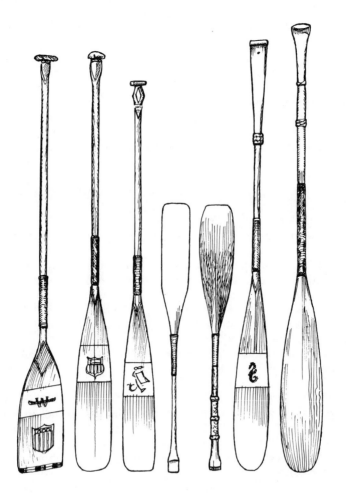

Materials

Materials used in making paddles vary from wood to aluminum and fiberglass. These materials are often used in combination as well as alone to produce strong, lightweight paddles.

Soft- and Hard-Wood Paddles

Many woods are used in the manufacture of paddles, with spruce, ash, and maple being the most common. Paddles made from spruce are light for their size; but, being made from a soft wood, these paddles should not be used in shallow water or where rocks or stumps are apt to be hit. One-piece spruce paddles are relatively delicate because they are more easily split or broken than any other paddle. The only advantage is one of manufacturing simplicity and small cost.

Spruce is used in making three- or five-piece laminated paddles, more commonly used in canoe racing. Although more expensive than unlaminated paddles, they are superior to paddles made from one piece of wood. Laminated paddles are less likely to split and almost never break in the shaft or at the throat. This is because the center piece, running from tip to grip, has straight-edge grain throughout its length, facing in the direction of the flat surfaces of the blade, where pressure is applied. The side pieces have the flat grain facing on the surfaces of the blade to resist splitting at the tip and edges of the blade. There should be no knots anywhere in the paddle, particularly in the shaft. When paddles are made of several pieces, they are made by hand, with considerable care being given to the features mentioned.

Paddles of one-piece construction are often mass-produced; consequently, you should examine such paddles before buying them, to make sure they have no knots. Other soft woods (fir, cedar, basswood) are sometimes used. Paddles of great beauty and extreme lightness can be made from cedar, but they require unusually careful handling.

Hardwood paddles are commonly made of ash or maple, and occasionally of other hardwoods. They are heavier than softwood paddles and consequently are usually not preferred when softwood paddles are available for use. The added weight may be partially reduced by thinning down the blade, and, in many cases, the shaft as well. Because they are made of hardwood, they resist splitting and breaking, even with hard or careless use. This does not mean that they resist outright abuse. Hardwood paddles warp rather easily, especially if left lying in the sun. On long trips, cruising, or any trip where shallows, gravel bottoms, rocks, and fast water are to be encountered, hardwood paddles could be taken along for intermittent use so that the softwood paddle may thus be protected from otherwise almost inevitable damage. Inexpensive hardwood paddles are mostly of one-piece construction, in view of the fact that their natural strength makes special construction unnecessary. Paddles laminated of both hardwood and softwood are made primarily for strength and light weight and are probably preferred over the one-piece paddles previously mentioned.

Fiberglass and Aluminum Paddles

A paddle made of fiberglass alone would have more faults than merits. A solid fiberglass shaft would be rather heavy, and a hollow shaft could be affected by heat, possibly warping excessively when left in the sun.

A compromise between aluminum and glass seems to result in one of the better designs of paddles, including wood laminates. Paddles of this construction have maximum strength as well as minimum weight. Also, they are highly resistant to hard use. The usual choice is a tempered aluminum shaft (either round or oval), covered with plastic or epoxy, joined to a molded and reinforced plastic-fiberglass blade.

Most manufacturers of quality paddles describe their paddles as epoxy-fiberglass blades with a fiberglass-covered shaft. Some have aluminum molded into the tip and abrasion-resistant Dynel fabric on the blade and throat to retard wear. The makers usually do not use polyester resin, claiming epoxy results in a much tougher and more rigid blade that will not delaminate.

Paddle Grips

A variety of good grip styles are available on most popular paddles. Remember that the grip is what relays the angle of the blade face to the paddler. The grip should be reasonably flat across the top and should permit the hand to hold on securely. The preceding illustrations show some of the more popular styles.

Double-Bladed Paddles

Although not commonly utilized with canoes, double-bladed paddles can prove useful in flatwater cruising. These paddles differ from those used with kayaks in that they must be approximately 9½ feet in length—7 feet being common for kayaks. Types used for canoe cruising generally have a ferrule joint in the middle of the shaft, allowing the paddle to be broken down for easy storage. More detail regarding double-bladed paddles is in chapter 15.

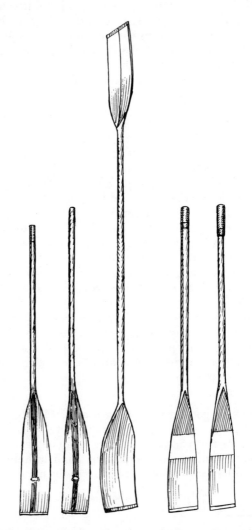

Paddle Care and Repair

Properly used and cared for, a well-selected paddle will last for many years. Few cheap paddles feel just right to the inexperienced canoeist, and some balancing is usually necessary. Most are found to be too heavy in the blade for proper balance. These can be improved by thinning the blade, although some are already too thin and will split. You should work for a paddle that, when held and used properly, does not give an awareness of weight in the blade. The paddle may also be fitted with a collar around the shaft, immediately above the throat, to protect it from chafing on contact with the gunwale or hull. This collar is usually plastic tape or some other easily applied substance.

Wood paddles should be kept well varnished, especially the tip and edges of the blade, with a good grade of marine spar coating. Because surface coatings scrape off after extensive use, many paddlers soak the bare wood of the paddle tip in linseed oil. If the tip were allowed to wear, moisture absorption would soon add excess weight, and general discoloration would set in. The blade may be painted before varnishing, if color is desired, or enamel may be used instead of varnish.

Usually it is not necessary to revarnish the entire paddle, at least not for several years, if good quality varnish was originally used. Some canoeists prefer not to varnish the grip, instead working it down to fit the hand and sanding it smooth. The absorption of moisture and oil from the hand by the bare wood will in turn prevent softening of the skin and will lessen the danger of blisters. Also, there is better control of the blade with a less slippery grip. To some canoeists, these factors seem trivial, and they interchangeably use paddles with the grip either varnished or not varnished.

Some specific guides for the care of paddles are given below.

- Store wood paddles in the shade outdoors, or in a ventilated place indoors. When possible, hang them up by the grip.
- Do not lay a paddle down where it might be stepped on during launching or landing operations.
- Avoid using the paddle as a pole in shallow water, or for fending off. (This does not refer to an old hardwood paddle purposely used for poling, nor does it mean that the paddle ought not to be used to fend off in an emergency situation.) As much as possible, use the paddle only to carry out the purpose for which it was made.
- Do not lean a paddle against a tree or other support in a manner that would allow it to be easily blown or knocked down.
- Learn to recognize poor grain in the shaft of a paddle; and to avoid breaking the paddle, apply power smoothly and steadily, rather than too suddenly. Breaking a paddle while paddling

is an experience every canoeist ultimately has. However, a skilled paddler can avoid breaking a paddle except under the most extreme conditions.

How To Make a Paddle

Making a wood paddle by homemade methods is a tedious labor of love, although a creative experience. It is easier to buy a paddle. If, however, you are handy with tools or if you would find pleasure and recreation in making a paddle, there is ample reason to believe that you can make a satisfactory one if you do not hurry. Buy the stock all cut out and planed to measurements modified for a paddle of suitable size for you or the person it is being made for. The paddle shown in these illustrations is a hardwood paddle: the wood is ash. If you make a softwood paddle (probably of spruce), as you are likely to do, it may be wise to increase the front-to-back measurement of the shaft by ⅛ inch.

Glue the pieces together with a good waterproof glue. Be very careful to arrange the pieces for gluing so that the shaft piece has the edge grain (the narrow, straight lines of wood fiber) facing to the front and rear. The wing pieces will fall into position without chance of error because of the difference between their width and thickness. You should have specified that these pieces be cut so that the flat grain (the wide, often curving, line of wood fiber) is on the wide surface. You may improve the appearance of the blade and in some cases increase its strength if you arrange the two wing pieces so that the directions of the flat-grain patterns of the wing pieces are symmetrical and so that the patterns are, when possible, curved toward each other.

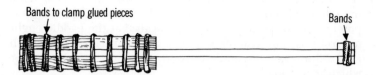

Bands to clamp glued pieces

Bands

When you have applied the glue to the proper surfaces, use C-clamps to hold them in place until the glue is dry. If you do not have appropriate clamps, use bands of rubber, cut from a discarded tire tube. When B and C are in place, glue on the two small pieces, D and E. It is a good idea, before starting, to take the sharpness off the outside edges of the pieces B and C, using a plane or coarse sandpaper. Thus you will not cut the rubber bands while forcing them into position.

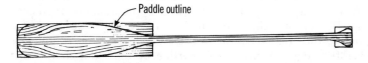

Paddle outline

When the glue is dry, take off the clamps or rubber bands and trace in dark pencil the pattern of a favorite paddle on both sides. Your job will be more accurate if you make a cardboard pattern from your favorite paddle and trace around the pattern onto the new paddle. When the lines have been traced on both sides, a convex-bottom plane is good for getting the desired concavity at the throat area.

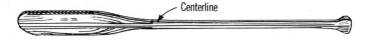

Centerline

The next step is to draw center lines down the front, back, and sides of the shaft and grip and around the edges of the blade, as a guide for the remaining work. Then, using a draw knife, jack plane, block plane, wood rasp, and coarse and fine sandpaper, work the paddle down to a final shape similar to that of your favorite paddle, incorporating whatever refinements you might wish, such as an improved grip or a thinner blade.

A fiberglass tip on the blade of a paddle will add no appreciable weight, since it will enable the blade to be made thinner for the same strength. The fact that it protects the blade from absorption of water through the tip may eventually mean less weight.

In applying a fiberglass tip for either a new or old paddle, feather-edge the tip and sides, where you want the fiberglass, to a thickness of approximately $\frac{1}{8}$ inch, and round off all edges. Cut the glass cloth, *diagonally,* a little over twice the width you want on each side of the blade and approximately 15 inches long. Do not stretch it lengthwise. Apply the mixed resin or epoxy to the area you want to glass, making sure to completely cover the edges. Apply the centerline of the cloth to the tip, allowing the ends to come along the edge of the blade toward the throat. As these ends are pulled toward the throat, you will

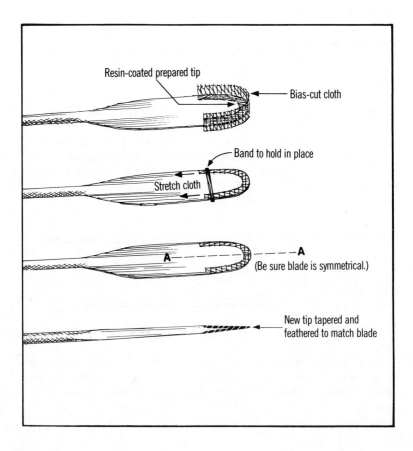

find that since the cloth tends to lie down on each side of the blade, it can be formed around small-radius corners between tip and sides with no wrinkles or puckers. Rubber bands around the cloth ends and blade will hold the cloth in place until the resin cures. Apply a coat of the resin, mixed as above, on top of the cloth, and allow it to cure. When the resin is dry, cut off excess fiberglass and sand the adhering cloth to a feather edge. Make sure to use a block behind the sandpaper to prevent a ridge at the edge of the glass.

A Word of Warning

Be careful with hand and power tools. If you have not used a draw knife before, you will almost certainly cut yourself unless you are careful at all times. A woodworker's vise and a workbench will make your work easier and safer. Make sure that all power tools are properly grounded.

THWARTS

Many stock-model canoes are provided with seats for the paddlers to sit on, and the thwarts are located in relation to the seats rather than for efficient paddling. Most canoe manufacturers will omit the seats and locate the thwarts where the buyer wishes them. Likewise, a canoe owner may take the seats out of his canoe as he wishes and relocate the thwarts where he wants them to be. As indicated elsewhere many times in this book, the Red Cross Small Craft program stresses the advisability of learning to paddle from positions that keep one or both knees in contact with the bottom of the canoe. This not only increases the stability and safety of the craft but also improves paddling efficiency by enabling the paddler to effectively use the power of his trunk and thighs in conjunction with his arms and shoulders. Another advantage resulting from the ability to use any one of a number of types of paddling positions is the freedom with which the paddler can shift himself from place to place in the canoe in order to use the forces of wind or current to his advantage. Proper location of thwarts aids him greatly, and removal of the seats gives more room in the canoe.

The illustrations show an effective rule of thumb for obtaining the most efficient configuration for thwart placement in two ranges of canoe lengths. One rule of thumb applies to canoes from 15 to 17 feet and would also be suitable for canoes less than a = approximately 14″   b = distance from midship thwart to foredeck   c = space from stern thwart to stern deck (will vary)   d = distance from end of canoe to innermost portion of deck

NOTE. The proportions shown will allow for appropriate paddling positions of tandem paddlers (marked *) and permit a great variety of positions for the solo paddler.

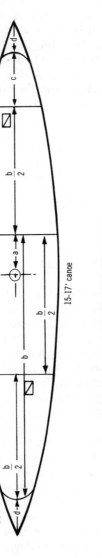

15-17′ canoe

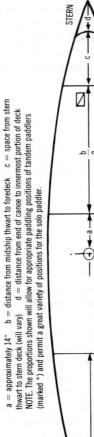

18-20′ canoe

15 feet; the other applies to canoes from 18 to 20 feet. Larger canoes require special planning.

The thwarts may be of the type ordinarily used in canoes, held by one bolt at each end, or they may be of the straight-edge type, 3 or more inches wide and held more securely to the gunwales with two bolts at each end. The bolts should be of brass, stainless steel, or other corrosion-resistant metal and should have large washers between the bolt nut and the underside of the thwart. The nuts should be tightened firmly and kept that way to lessen the danger of having the gunwales break at a bolt hole. Holes left in the gunwales of wood canoes should be plugged and sealed. The plug may be set in water-resistant glue. Later, the area should be varnished.

An additional thought that you should consider prior to changing the location of existing thwarts is how much the canoe is to be portaged. If you expect to do a great deal of portaging, a thwart should be centered for balance rather than offset 14 inches aft of amidships. However, if you are going to paddle the canoe solo quite often, the midship thwart should be offset the 14 inches mentioned. A clamp-on, movable thwart might be useful for frequent solo paddling.

PFD's—"LIFEJACKETS"

According to the law established by the Federal Boat Safety Act of 1971, specific safety equipment is required on all recreational boats. Among this equipment are personal flotation devices (PFD's). These devices fall into five categories that are approved by the U.S. Coast Guard: Type I, Type II, Type III, Type IV, and Type V. All personal flotation devices that are presently acceptable on recreational boats fall into one of the first four type designations. Section 175.15 (personal flotation devices required) of the law states:

No person may use a canoe or kayak unless at least one PFD of the following types is on board for each person:

(1) Type I PFD
(2) Type II PFD
(3) Type III PFD
(4) Type IV PFD

Descriptions of the four types of devices are as follows:

Type I—an approved device designed to turn an *unconscious* person in the water from a face-down position to a vertical or slightly backward position and to have more than 20 pounds of buoyancy. This device is recommended for offshore cruising and is acceptable for all sizes of boats. Example: a typical life preserver.

Type II—an approved device designed to turn an *unconscious* person in the water from a face-down position to a vertical or slightly backward position and to have at least 15.5 pounds of buoyancy. It is recommended for close, inshore cruising and is acceptable for all sizes of boats. Example: a typical buoyancy vest.

Type III—an approved device designed to keep a *conscious* person in a vertical or slightly backward position and to have at least 15.5 pounds of buoyancy. Although having the same buoyancy as Type II, the Type III has a lesser turning ability to allow for a comfortable design that does not hinder a person's movement in activities such as water skiing. This device is recommended for in-water sports, or on boats used on lakes, on bodies of confined water, and close inshore on larger bodies of water. It is acceptable for all sizes of boats. Example: a special-purpose device.

Type IV—an approved device designed to be *thrown to a person in the water and not worn*. It is designed to have at least 16.5 pounds of buoyancy. It is acceptable for boats less than 16 feet and canoes and kayaks and as a throwable device for boats 16 feet and over in length. Example: buoyant cushion or ring buoy.

You must take into consideration the type of boating activity
in which you will be involved and its location in order to appropriately select a PFD for your use. The Type I preserver is
much too bulky for paddling, and the Type IV throwables are
not designed to be worn. Although approved for use in canoes
or kayaks, these two types should be avoided whenever other
types are available.

The Type II vest is produced in a variety of sizes and is undoubtedly the least expensive device available. Its only apparent
drawback is the discomfort in wearing it over a prolonged period.
This device is recommended to be worn by weak swimmers or
nonswimmers at all times while in a canoe or kayak, and by all
canoeists whenever rough water is encountered. (Rough water
should be expected on any river.) WARNING: This device is
not designed as a kneeling pad and must not be used as such.
Kneeling on it will ultimately result in damage to the interior
of the vest, rendering it useless as a lifesaving device.

The Type III special-purpose devices are more to the liking
of boating enthusiasts. They were created to accommodate the
needs of persons engaged in water sports with a minimum of
restriction to the wearers, emphasizing comfort and mobility.
They are available in a variety of sizes. All the recommendations
and precautions as presented for the Type II should be observed
for the Type III as well.

The U.S. Coast Guard is quick to point out that *all* PFD's
for sale in stores must be in serviceable condition, legibly marked
with the approval number. On boats, they must be of an appropriate size for the persons who intend to wear them or are
wearing them.

The common term for PFD among paddlers is *lifejacket*. In
this book, therefore, the term *lifejacket* is used, but its reference
is restricted to the recommended equipment mentioned above,
i.e., Type II and Type III devices.

Further information on lifejackets will be found in the following sections dealing with canoe accessories.

CANOE ACCESSORIES FOR LAKE PADDLING

Knee Pads

Knee pads are recommended for comfort. In addition, pads
are a possible deterrent of irritation to the tissues surrounding
the knee areas.

You can easily obtain a variety of knee pads for paddling. Generally, two pads are necessary for each paddler, since the paddler's knees are spread wide while paddling. (Lifejackets or cushions are not to be used as kneeling pads.) Most people buy the strap-on type that hardware stores supply for gardeners and roofers. The two-strap pads are preferred.

Some canoeists would rather glue pads into the canoe. Perhaps the best pads for this purpose would be of closed-cell neoprene (from $\frac{3}{16}$ to $\frac{5}{16}$ inch thick), or closed-cell foam. Both of these materials are nonabsorbent. A very cheap type (since such pads do get lost) is a segment of inner tube with sawdust sealed in, or cork-filled canvas bags. Old tennis shoes can be used also.

Foot Braces

Foot braces, appropriately placed, can aid you in gaining a firmer base for efficient paddling. These braces could be permanently installed in such a way that various individuals of different body builds can use the same canoe.

Lines

Both the bow and the stern of the canoe should be rigged with lines. These lines should be attached with a bowline to towing shackles that are properly placed, usually on the outside stem and near the waterline. For wood canoes, the lines usually pass through holes in the breast plates and are secured by means of a stopper knot (figure-of-eight) to prevent them from pulling through. In any case, the lines should be of good quality and from $\frac{1}{4}$ to $\frac{3}{8}$ inch in diameter. Lines of smaller diameter would be difficult to handle. The lines should be long enough (approximately 15 feet) to be used in a variety of situations such as cartopping, tying up, towing another canoe, and rescuing. With one end of each line spliced to the canoe, the rest of the line should be coiled loosely in the canoe (never tied down), so that it will stream out in an upset. The coils should be placed in such a way that you will not get your feet tangled in them. One of the finest lines available for end lines is a brightly colored plastic line that floats. It is strong, and the $\frac{3}{8}$ inch diameter is easy to handle. Being made of polypropylene, it has the additional advantage of not deteriorating during long periods of storage.

Carrying Yokes

Since some carrying yokes are recommended only for the experienced canoeist, their use is not discussed in great detail in this book. There is a hazard in using carrying yokes improperly or in their use by inexperienced persons. The hazard has to do with neck injuries resulting from improperly balancing the canoe or from not lowering it correctly from the shoulders.

The small or weak person must be very careful not to wedge his head between the padded yokes while attempting to remove and lower the canoe. It is best for such an individual to use a centered and well-padded thwart for portaging or a shaped and padded yoke. In this way, if the canoeist should lose his footing, his balance, or his control of the canoe while it is being carried, he may avoid being seriously injured by the falling canoe.

Clothing

The range of clothing suitable for canoeing extends from bathing suits to mittens. Selection should be dictated by comfort, safety, and durability rather than by fashion. Clothing must keep you either warm or cool, or perhaps dry, and it must withstand water and mud and hard wear.

Woolen long-johns head the list for safety. They should be worn for canoeing from October to May, when the water is cold. The wool right next to your skin keeps you warm even when it is wet. It is a matter of survival when you spill into cold water.

Fancy long-johns can be bought at outdoor shops, or tough, scratchy ones can be obtained at an army surplus store.

The skindiver's wet suit is far warmer than long-johns and is recommended for those expecting to do much paddling in cold weather or on cold water.

Foul-weather gear can be a blessing. It should be light and loose fitting enough to permit full range of motion. Rain suits are good. Raincoats should be avoided, because water can dribble through the front. Ponchos are good only when you want to be blown downwind.

You should wear shoes at all times. The footwear selected should be appropriate for the intended activity and for weather conditions.

Lifejackets

As mentioned earlier in this chapter, lifejackets are a must, especially if you have limited swimming ability. Belt preservers of any kind are *inadequate,* since their buoyancy acts at your middle instead of at your chest. They can make handling yourself in the water more difficult, and a belt preserver will not support the head of a stunned or unconscious person out of the water.

Every person should try his lifejacket in a controlled setting prior to using it in actual practice. He should fall or jump into the water with it on and also try putting it on while in the water. All boaters must remember that lifejackets are *lifesaving* equipment and are not to be knelt upon or sat upon.

Miscellaneous Equipment

Bailers, sponges, extra paddles, extra clothing (in watertight containers), and many other items make up a list of miscellaneous equipment to be taken in a canoe on flatwater. The duration of the activity will determine, in most cases, what should or must be included.

CANOE ACCESSORIES FOR WHITEWATER

In addition to everything mentioned in the previous discussions, you should take into account the following important equipment when setting out on a river in either an open traditional canoe or a closed canoe or kayak.

Open Traditional Canoes

Thigh Straps

Thigh straps are very important when you are canoeing in rough water or on rivers. They give you a firm hold on the canoe, allowing you complete control while your hands are properly busy with the paddle. Using such straps, you will experience fewer spills, and when you do spill, you will fall free of the straps. However, straps should be used cautiously in combination with seats, since some canoe seats are installed much too

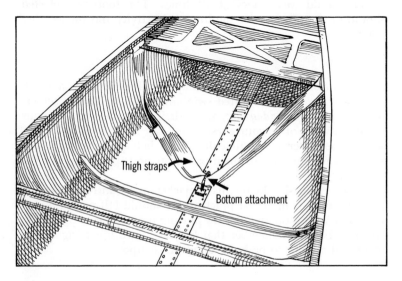

low. Once you use the straps, you will be amazed at the confidence they give, and you will never want to enter the rapids again without them.

Knee Pads and Foot Braces (*See illustration, page 73.*)

When used in conjunction with thigh straps, kneeling pads should be glued in place. Since the strap-on type of pad can catch on the thigh strap, most paddlers prefer permanently placed padding in the canoe. Foot braces are helpful.

Spray Decks

Spray decks or splash covers are a necessity when a canoeist expects to encounter rough water. The rubberized nylon covering the open canoe prevents most of the water that splashes over the

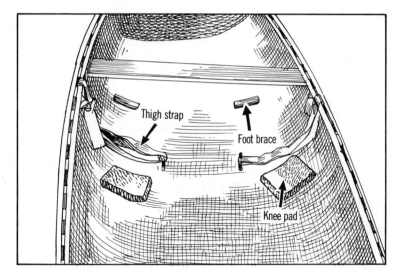

Thigh strap

Foot brace

Knee pad

canoe from entering. As illustrated, the cover can run from bow
to stern and can be wrapped and fastened over the gunwales. The
only opening would be where the paddler is positioned. There
have been decks and covers made from plywood, aluminum, and
fiberglass also. A properly fitted fiberglass deck seems to work
best.

Extra Flotation

Extra flotation permits a canoe to float higher when swamped. The advantage is one of safety and preservation. A canoe floating high is less likely to strike an underwater obstacle and be pinned against it.

Extra flotation for an open canoe should take the form of styrofoam (or other such substance equally as light and buoyant) and could be fastened into any available opening of the craft.

Clothing

Gloves of the wool or neoprene variety are needed in cold weather or cold water. Special designs permit a good grip on the paddle.

Shoes

Shoes are a must in closed boats to protect your feet from the inherent hazards of the boat itself as well as the problems mentioned previously. Shoes are also a must for river paddling, whether in open or closed boats. They protect the feet from slivers of glass (found in many fiberglass boats), the ever-present broken glass on river bottoms, and sharp rocks. Moccasin-type shoes or sandals are not recommended; they are too easily lost. In summer, you should use sneakers with several holes in them to let the water out.

In cooler weather you will want to wear wet-suit socks inside oversized sneakers. They are warmer than regular socks, are less likely to catch in knee straps and under seats or foot braces, and are better for swimming when the necessity arises.

Lifejackets

For rapids, you need as much flotation as possible. You need both flotation *and* padding on your back. When you are on your back (as you should be) in frothy water, flotation on your front is of little value. The padding provided by flotation on your back protects against injury that would result from striking your back against rocks, etc.

The lifejacket that you wear should be streamlined for low drag while you are swimming. It should give you freedom to paddle, and you should be able to climb into your canoe from the water while wearing it. Simply, the lifejacket should have a good fit.

Anyone who has known the relief of popping effortlessly to the surface after having been flipped into the rapids (and this means every experienced paddler) has quickly gained a lively appreciation of his lifejacket. Elementary safety demands the use of a lifejacket when paddling on rivers because, with few exceptions, the lack of a lifejacket has marked many fatalities in whitewater canoeing. A vest preserver, with a buoyant filling, is recommended. It should be cut high under the arms or have a crotch strap to keep it in place. No outer clothing should be worn over the lifejacket, since the clothing may snag a rock, stump, etc., trapping a paddler who has been capsized.

End Lines

The bow and stern lines should be 15 feet in length and at least ⅜ inch in diameter and should be made of a good quality floatable material. They should be attached and stowed (never tied), as indicated in the section on flatwater canoeing. A line attached to any river craft should never have knots or floats on the free ends because these may cause the line to become snagged on trees or rocks or around a paddler.

Spare Paddles

Spare paddles should be secured to the canoe in such a way as to allow for quick access in an emergency situation, such as a broken or lost paddle in a rough stretch of rapids.

Extras

Sponges and bailers are a necessity in rough water, although

a canoe can be easily dumped in shallow water. A bailer elimi-
nates the need to stop.

A 50-foot length of ⅜ inch line should be carried by at least
one canoe (the leading canoe, preferably) in a group of canoes.
It is a necessity when rescuing personnel or equipment.

A portage yoke or padded thwart should be used for portaging
if river touring or camping is being undertaken. Such equipment
is usually not necessary for river running.

Closed Canoes and Kayaks

Knee pads, thigh straps, and foot braces are just as important
in closed canoes as they are in open canoes. Kayaks, however.
use only foot braces and a tight-fitting seat.

Flotation Bags

Flotation bags are heavy, air-filled, watertight plastic bags designed to fit the hull form of the boat. Their purpose is to float
a swamped decked canoe or kayak. Many paddlers use dual-
purpose bags that are easily opened, in which they store extra
clothing, food, etc., thus keeping the items dry and still providing the flotation needed. Extra flotation can be obtained by
the use of closed-cell foam cut to fit between the hull and deck,
eliminating the need for flotation bags.

Spray Skirts

As shown in the illustration, the spray skirt attaches to a
coaming around the cockpit and has an elastic band sewn into

the upper part to keep the skirt tight around the paddler's torso. Spray skirts of this design are usually made of a rubberized fabric. Spray skirts made of neoprene (the same material used in making wet suits) usually are cut to fit the individual snugly enough to prevent water from entering the boat.

Both of the spray skirts mentioned above are used with closed boats and aid in making the craft reasonably watertight, thus enabling the paddler to undertake very rough water—commensurate with his ability, of course. Spray skirts will either stay on the boat or on the paddler if the two become separated. The paddler should be able to readily release the elastic around the coaming as a safety measure.

Helmet

Helmets are a necessity for those using whitewater boats in rivers. They protect the paddler from receiving a disabling blow on the head. Such a blow could be sustained after an upset in swift river currents. Helmets are available in a variety of designs.

Specialized Clothing

Wet Suit

A wet suit (neoprene rubber, nylon lined) is a much-desired item for rough rivers in early spring. When Eskimo rolling is the order of the day, long-johns just will not do. Unfortunately, wet suits are expensive. They also tend to get overly warm.

Paddle Jacket

A warm, plastic-coated nylon pullover, known as a paddle jacket, is a must when water is cold. When worn over a good sweater, it can replace a wet suit in moderately cold conditions and is much more comfortable. When worn over a lightweight shirt, it can take the sting out of a cold wave on warmer days.

Lifejackets

As discussed earlier in this chapter, special lifejackets can be used with closed boats. However, you must remember that a lifejacket is recommended to be *worn,* regardless of design, while in a closed boat on a river. No person should ever attempt paddling on a river without a lifejacket *on.* The Type II and Type III jackets and designs specifically for closed boats are highly recommended.

Lines and End Loops

Decked canoes and kayaks should have grab loops on *both* ends, large enough to easily pass a hand through, made of at least 1/4-inch-diameter rope of a good quality. A stern line from 6 to 8 feet long, secured to the rear deck with an elastic loop, is helpful for rescue purposes. A bow line should never be used by a paddler capable of Eskimo rolling, since it is likely to entangle his paddle.

EQUIPMENT FOR ROWING AN OPEN CANOE

A canoe makes an excellent rowing craft when equipped with detachable outriggers and sliding-seat rowing equipment. Rigging a canoe in this manner is a measure of economy, since it permits one craft to perform the function of two interchangeably. The canoe has more maneuverability and some of the carrying capacity of the typical rowboat and some of the speed of a racing shell.

The drawings show a sliding-seat unit that can be readily placed in a wooden canoe. Outriggers can be easily attached to

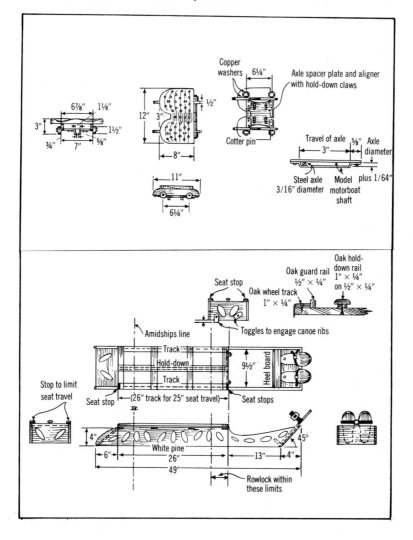

the gunwale without the use of bolts, screws, or other permanent fastenings. A pair of well-balanced, light oars can be made from a pair of larger ones.

The seat frame, a rectangular affair 49 inches long, 9½ inches wide, and 4 inches high, can be made from the planking of a light packing case. If you wish to keep the outfit really light, cut the lightening holes indicated. Any of the modern plastic resin glues can be used for excellent assembly, although screws

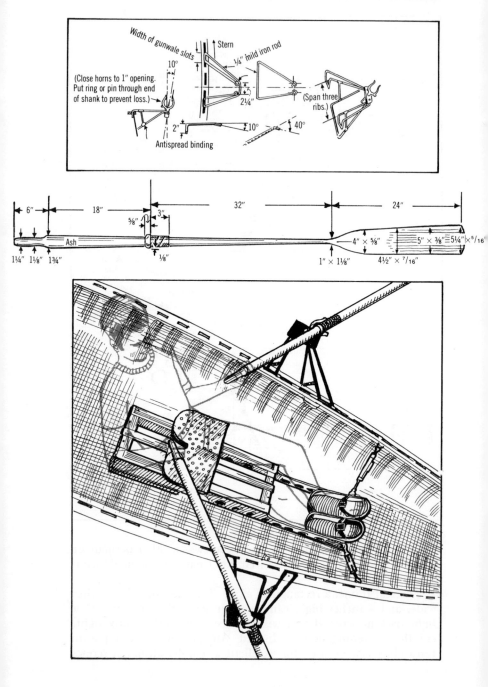

Width of gunwale slots

Stern

¼″ mild iron rod

10°

(Close horns to 1″ opening.
Put ring or pin through end
of shank to prevent loss.)

2¼″

(Span three
ribs.)

2″

10°

40°

Antispread binding

6″   18″   ⅝″ 3″   32″   24″

Ash

⅛″

4″ × ⅝″   5″ × ⅜″ ⸗ 5¼″ ⸗× ⁵/₁₆

1¼″ 1⅛″ 1¾″

1″ × 1⅛″   4½″ × ⁷/₁₆″

may be used if desired. Foot plates and toe straps (usually called boots) and the tracks may be purchased from the manufacturers of racing shells or obtained secondhand from some large rowing clubs that have old shells that eventually must be broken up. (The equipment in the shell is usually saved.) Additional hints can be obtained from the diagrams.

OUTBOARD MOTOR USE

Due to the growing popularity of propelling canoes with outboard motors, a section on safe operation is appropriate in this text. This discussion is concerned only with potential safety hazards involved while a person is engaged in motoring a canoe. For the basics of operating an outboard motor, the American Red Cross recommends that individuals enroll in a Basic Outboard Boating course prior to any activity involving outboard motors.

Small gasoline motors used in canoes should not exceed 5 horsepower, and 3 horsepower is recommended. These motors should have the minimum controls of neutral (gears not engaged) and forward; reverse is desirable. Various makes of motors incorporate a broad scope of features, such as a built-in gas tank in some and a separate gas tank with hose connections in others. The latter is normally a feature of larger motors.

A potentially dangerous part of outboard operation is the highly volatile gasoline. Keep the motor, the gas can, and the oil away from open flame. Leave cigarettes, pipes, cigars, and matches behind when you handle gasoline. Do the refueling only in a well-ventilated area and out of the canoe.

There are two accepted methods of attaching an outboard

motor to a canoe. The first is to have a special canoe of square-end design. This type of canoe is built for small motors and is perhaps safer than one with a side bracket because it keeps the center of gravity of the added weight centered over the keel line. Anyone who expects to do a great deal of canoe motoring should consider having a square-end canoe. These canoes also paddle surprisingly well.

The second method of mounting a motor is by the use of a side bracket. This method allows any conventional canoe to be adapted for use with a motor. The bracket should be *securely* mounted to the gunwale of the canoe with the actual motor mount as close as possible to the canoe, thus reducing the capsizing tendency of the outboard weight. The swinging of the motor should not be interfered with by the hull.

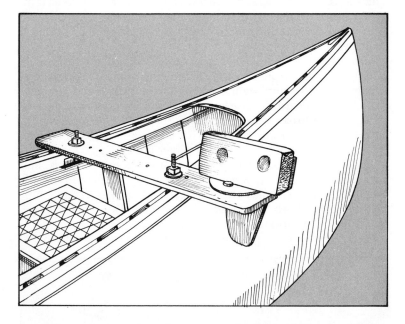

The actual mounting of the motor should be done from a dock or a pier or in shallow water. If you have a square-ended canoe, due to the narrow beam of the craft, you can bring the square end close enough to permit easy mounting of the motor. With a side bracket installed for operation on the port side, that side of the canoe should be against the dock or pier while you are mounting the motor. If you are using a separate gas tank, place it amidships or slightly forward of amidships for proper trim.

There are some hazards that can be avoided if the motorized canoe is handled properly. Proper procedure is as follows: You should start the motor in neutral and then shift, at slow idle, to forward. Once the canoe is underway, you should *gradually* increase its speed until the canoe reaches the desired cruising speed. Make turns, *at any speed,* cautiously and gradually, keeping in mind the narrow beam of the canoe. Failure to heed any of the above instructions could result in falls overboard, falls within the canoe, or a capsize. Because the motorized canoe has become a motorboat, it is required to be operated under all regulations governing motorboats, including rules of right of way and minimum equipment requirements.

ROPES AND SIMPLE KNOTS

There is probably no boat afloat that does not use rope somehow or somewhere. Canoes are no different. Rope is useful in numerous instances. Cartopping, portaging, launching, lining, tracking, rescuing, and many other activities would be very difficult without rope. Therefore, it is necessary to learn enough about rope to adequately get by and to make safer any method of tying or securing that is needed.

Varieties and Uses of Ropes

Rope is made of a variety of materials and in a multitude of sizes. This has its good and bad points. The different materials used vary in strength. The newer synthetic ropes are smaller and lighter than natural fiber ropes of the same strength, offering an obvious advantage. However, a smaller-diameter rope may be too small for comfortable or even safe handling by canoeists in stress situations.

The cost of rope varies with its material, size, and tensile strength. This cost plays an important role in the selection of rope to be used by canoeists. Many persons try to get by on a less expensive rope when a good quality one is needed.

Although not in great detail, the following information covers general care to be given to any rope or line used.

- When they are not in use, keep ropes and lines coiled neatly in dry, cool places and out of direct sunlight.
- Keep ropes and lines as clean as possible. They can be damaged from within by grit and dirt that has found its way into the braid or weave. When tension is applied, the grit inside will cut fibers, thus weakening the rope or line.

- Replace damaged or worn ropes and lines. If ropes or lines are needed in an emergency and they are not in good condition, the problem at hand could be made much worse.
- Avoid stepping on any rope or line, since stepping on it damages it and shortens its useful life.
- Make sure that all rope used is finished off on the ends so that it will be prevented from fraying or unlaying. Synthetic rope can be melted to produce a smooth, neat, secure end that is no larger than the rest of the rope. Twisted natural-fiber ropes should be whipped and dipped in a lasting coating to protect the whipping. Whipping can be accomplished by using flax or cotton twine. The twine should be treated with a mixture of beeswax and resin to strengthen and waterproof it. (A waterproof friction or adhesive tape can be used as a temporary whipping for any line.)

Specific uses for different types of rope for canoeing activities are recommended below.

- Polypropylene or polyethylene, from ⅜ to ½ inch in diameter —Polypropylene or polyethylene is recommended for use as a rescue rope due to its light weight, elasticity, and floatability. Any rope used for rescue purposes should not be used for any other purpose, since its strength should be preserved for life-saving.
- Cotton—When wet, cotton rope becomes stiff, and a knot or hitch is almost impossible to untie. This quality makes cotton rope ideal for end loops on closed boats and for lashings anywhere.
- Manila—As with any other plant fiber rope, manila gains in strength when wet and, at the same time, shrinks. This feature promotes its use for tie-down purposes, either on car racks or storage racks.
  NOTE. Only the finest grade of plant fiber rope should be used, since this grade is the strongest, most reliable, and longest lasting. However, one drawback of manila rope is its susceptibility to rot when it is left in moist places.
- Nylon—Nylon's use is universal in canoeing. It will outlast most other rope and is very elastic and strong but does not float. It can be used for anchor line, mooring rope, rescue line, and end lines—also for tying down if care is taken with regard to its elasticity.
- Dacron—Dacron has good strength and is not as elastic as nylon. Its uses are the same as for nylon.

Knots, Bends, and Hitches

The safety of your equipment and yourself depends on your knowledge of the use of ropes and lines. This knowledge includes the proper application of a few simple knots, bends, and hitches. These will fit your needs in nearly every canoeing situation.

Knots

Knots are generally used in binding objects together or in forming a temporary loop.

• The *square knot* (or reef knot) is probably the most widely known of all knots. Its only use around canoes, however, is for lashing items to the canoe or for tying gear together.

• The *bowline* is perhaps the most useful and reliable knot that can be used around canoes. It is used to put a loop into the end of a rope or line, and such a loop can be used in a multitude of ways.

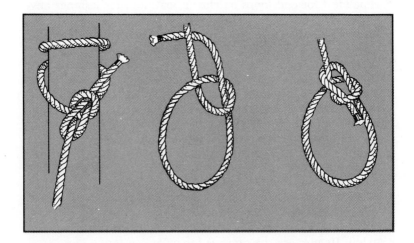

Bends

- The *sheet bend* is the best method to be used in tying two ropes together. It is trustworthy and easily understood and can be used with confidence. An additional turn can be taken to make a *double sheet bend,* which is even more secure and can be untied under tension.

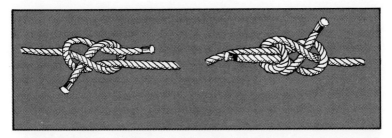

- The *Englishman's bend,* or *fisherman's knot,* is another bend used to tie two ropes together. It is made by tying two overhand knots back-to-back with their ends pointing in opposite directions.

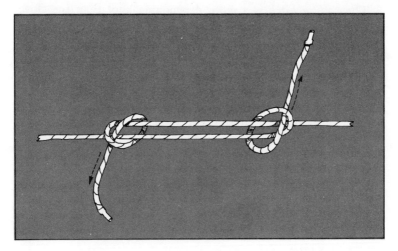

Hitches

- The *clove hitch* is a simple tie that can be used in various circumstances. It is the quickest to tie and the easiest to remember.

- The *rolling hitch* is a more dependable knot than the clove hitch and is more often used when attaching a line to a smooth surface or to a larger rope. The pull can be parallel with the item tied to or perpendicular to it.

Stopper Knot

- The figure-eight knot makes the best stopper to keep the end of a line or rope from running through a hole in a canoe deck.

It can also be used at the end of a throw rope. The figure-eight knot is far superior to the commonly used overhand knot because the figure-eight is easily untied and will not jam.

4

CANOE TRANSPORTATION

CARRYING AND LIFTING

The inexperienced person may regard a canoe as awkward and difficult to carry. Actually, the contrary is true if effective methods are employed and canoes of suitable size are used. The effectiveness of the method chosen to carry the canoe depends on the weight of the canoe, the number of people to do the job, and good direction from *one* leader.

Do not push or drag a canoe; such action can cause damage. It is better to carry the canoe. There are several methods of carrying that you can use, depending on the number of people available, the weight of the canoe, and other factors. You should always apply the principles of proper lifting for safety. Lift the bulk of any object using the muscles of your legs rather than your back. Squatting to pick up a heavy weight is preferable to bending over. It tends to keep your back straight and your spine upright.

Keep back straight

Lift with legs

Two-Man Carry

Having one person at each end is a typical way to carry a canoe. Hand and arm placement should allow maximum comfort and should provide security against dropping the canoe.

Two-Man Carry, Alternate Method (See illustration, top of page 92.)

It is easy for two persons to carry a canoe on their shoulders. The canoe is lifted to the overhead position and carried in such a manner that the stern thwart rests across the shoulders of the person at the rear, and the bow deck rests on one shoulder of the person in front.

Carry Amidships (See illustration, bottom of page 92.)

Before launching the canoe, it is desirable for two persons to shift from the end-carrying positions to positions opposite each other amidships. The transfer is best done by setting the canoe down on the ground or dock. Frequently this carry is used as a method for making fairly short carries when there are no obstructions, such as trees or narrow passages.

Four-Man Carry

It is often advisable for several persons to carry a canoe; for example, when the carriers are small or the canoe is large and heavy. Carrying a heavy canoe without sufficient help is discouraging to the canoeist and should be avoided.

When there are rocks, stumps, or other forms of rough terrain on a portage, the canoe may be carried bottom-up in order to protect it from damage.

On long carries, it may be advisable for the four-man carry to be made on the shoulders. The carry is easier this way, and obstructions are more easily avoided.

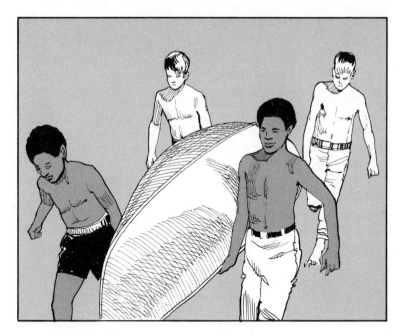

Three-Man Carry

The three-man carry is a good compromise when one person is larger and stronger than the other two. If the smaller two are relatively very small, they should carry near the end of the canoe; the nearer they approach the size and strength of the larger person, the farther they should be from the end, thus assuming a larger portion of the total weight.

An alternate method is to carry the canoe on the shoulders, as shown (see illustration, page 94).

Chain Carry

In the chain carry, the carrier (or carriers) between canoes has two ends to lift and carry. This person should consequently be stronger than the persons carrying only one canoe.

When each canoe has two carriers, they should both be on the same side of the canoe.

One-Man Carries

One-man carries should be attempted only by physically mature individuals, with lightweight canoes. Experienced canoeists, however, could undertake these lifts with heavier canoes.

One-Man Carry on Hip

The easiest way for one person to carry a canoe a short distance is to grasp it by the near gunwale with both hands at a place of balance amidships. The canoe is thus lifted and rested against the carrier's hip during the carry.

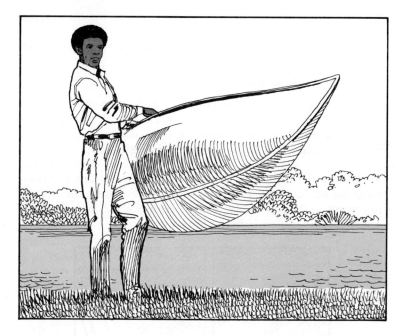

One-Man Single-Shoulder Carry

In this and all one-man carries, you must guard against wind

and make allowances for it. If the wind is strong, one-man carries are inadvisable.

One-Man Overhead-Shoulder Carry

This carry, used on portages, is probably the most efficient of all one-man carries for relatively short distances. With one end of the canoe still on the ground, lift the canoe to a rest position on your thigh. Then lift it to shoulder height and turn it over as you lift it above your head. Move backward until you can lower the canoe onto your shoulder. With a little minor adjustment for balance and with your hands holding onto the inwales or resting on them as shown, you are ready for the carry. Padding across your shoulders is helpful on long carries.

Amidships Lift for Straight-Arm Overhead Carry

Carrying a canoe overhead with your arms straight is useful for placing a canoe on a high rack or on top of a car or for carrying a canoe a short distance when other types of one-man carries would be awkward because of obstructions.

To start the lift for the straight-arm overhead carry, grasp the near gunwale amidships with both hands, a shoulder width apart, and lift the canoe a little off the ground.

Make minor adjustments of hand positions if necessary to get the canoe in balance. Roll the canoe sharply onto your thighs,

flipping the far gunwale upward and catching it with one hand. (If the midships thwart is missing, do not use this method, since it may damage the canoe unless the canoe is otherwise well constructed.) Then, change the grip on the near gunwale so that your thumb is on the inside.

Swing the canoe up overhead, aiding with a lift of one knee if necessary. The canoe will then be in the position shown in the illustration.

Lock your elbows and keep your arms vertical to take some strain off your arm muscles.

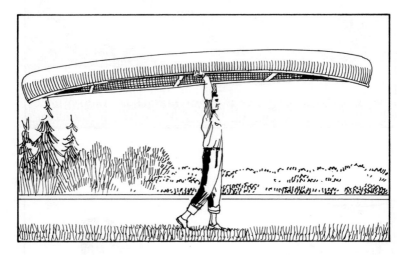

Modified Overhead Carries

Lowering one gunwale to shoulder level is a restful modification of the straight-arm overhead carry and is used to avoid overhead obstructions. Lowering the canoe still more so that it rests in the crook of the arm is a modification having the same advantages and more.

Decked-Boat Carrying

Due to their light weight, solo closed boats can be carried rather easily by simply resting the upper side of the cockpit on one shoulder. That arm would be inside the cockpit and that hand would securely hold the boat.

This same principle is used by two people carrying a two-man decked boat.

Two Persons Lifting a Canoe on and off a Car

Canoeing activity today very often involves the use of an automobile for transportation to and from the water. Cartop

carriers (car roof racks) are almost standard equipment for canoeists. Lifting the canoe on and off is made easier and more efficient if the two lifters proceed carefully, to avoid the risk of dropping the canoe. Lifters should make sure to place their hands carefully prior to lifting the canoe onto or off the racks. Dropping the canoe is almost always caused by incorrect placement of hands, thus causing a twisting and binding of the arms and back while lowering the canoe.

Cartop Carrying

There are two important factors to consider before securing a canoe to a cartop carrier: the reliability of the carrier and the reliability of the ropes and tie-downs.

There are many varieties of cartop carriers, ranging in design from the type with suction cups on the roof (least desirable) to those that lock onto the car's rain troughs (gutters). Some have features that permit the carrying of more than one boat, and some are equipped with cradles for closed boats as well as open boats. The carriers are usually secured with straps and hooks, turnbuckles and hooks, or clamps that attach directly onto the rain trough. One thing is necessary, however: there must be some trustworthy way of securing the racks to the automobile.

There are many commercial carrying rigs on sale in hardware stores, department stores, sportsmen's outfitters supply stores, and other places. Nearly all such carriers are adequate. It is not intended here to recommend a specific way to carry and tie on a canoe but rather to show satisfactory examples.

Securing the Canoe to the Car

The tie-down material must be of sufficient quality and strength to withstand the abuse of securing a canoe. When tying the canoe to the carriers and to the car, use straps or use nylon rope of at least $\frac{1}{4}$ inch in diameter. In general, rope seems superior to the straps supplied with some brands of carriers, because of its adjustability.

The canoe should be tied to *both* carriers and should also be tied to the car from both the canoe's bow and stern.

Many people successfully use *heavy* shock cord with hooks to secure the canoe to the roof racks but are quick to point out the necessity of using rope at the bow and stern. The shock cord method is quick and efficient. Rope can also be used with equal efficiency, but you should make sure to use the appropriate knots. (See the section in chapter 3 on ropes and simple knots.)

From the bow and stern, the lines securing the canoe to the car should form a V-shaped bridle, to be tied to each side of the car's bumpers. When tying the ropes to the bumper, be careful not to tie around any sharp edges. If you must tie around sharp edges, make sure to pad the rope. When possible, you might install small eyebolts through the bumpers. These not only protect the rope but also facilitate tying. It is virtually impossible to tie to the bumpers of some modern cars without such eyebolts, and you should consequently plan ahead. A single line tied to the center of the bumper may allow the canoe to slide off the racks to be dragged alongside the car if the canoe or a carrier comes loose from the car. These bow and stern lines should not merely be slipped through the bow and stern loops or fittings but should be tied securely to prevent the line from slipping.

If the same canoe is to be carried repeatedly, cradles or stops may be bolted to the racks. These make the canoe easy to position and eliminate most of the shaking at higher, open-road speeds.

Carriers and ropes should be checked for security and tightness at every opportunity. Ropes tied tightly the night before often will be found tied loosely in the morning and will need retying.

One thought that has plagued many drivers is "What if a rope should break or the rack should come loose while the car is on the road? Are the remaining ropes secure and strong enough to hold everything in place until a safe stop can be made?" Knowing your equipment and knowing how to tie ropes properly should put your mind at ease.

Cartopping Closed Boats

Closed boats of light construction cannot be tied as tightly as the more solid open canoes. The light deck is easily crushed if the boat is tied down upside down. The usually stiffer hull is less subject to damage if the boat is tied right side up. Tying it this way, however, can result in distortion of the hull, which would adversely affect performance. This distortion problem can be minimized if a contoured and padded cradle is attached

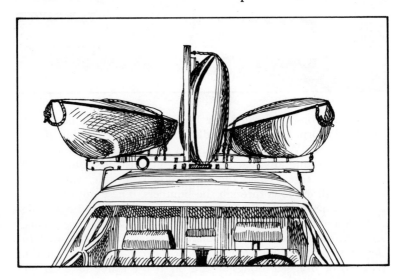

to the racks, but the cradle also makes the racks usable only for certain boats, thus creating a disadvantage if other boats are ever to be carried, as on club or group trips. Generally, the best way to carry several closed boats on a car is to stack them on their edges on prepared racks. In any case, the basic principle of tying the boats *securely* to the racks *and* to the car should be carefully observed.

One-Man Placement of a Canoe on a Car

Placing a canoe on a cartop carrier is easy from the straight-arm overhead carry position. Stand close to the car, midway between the two carriers. Lean toward the car until you can rest the back of your forearm on the car roof. This position will give you the leverage you need to lower the canoe the remaining distance to the racks and to slide it into its proper position. If the racks are not covered with soft material, sliding the canoe into place will scrape the varnish off the gunwales of nonmetal canoes. To prevent such damage, lift the gunwale off one rack and set it over a few inches and then do the same at the other rack, repeating this alternate procedure until the canoe is in place. You can do this without changing the position of your hands on the near gun-

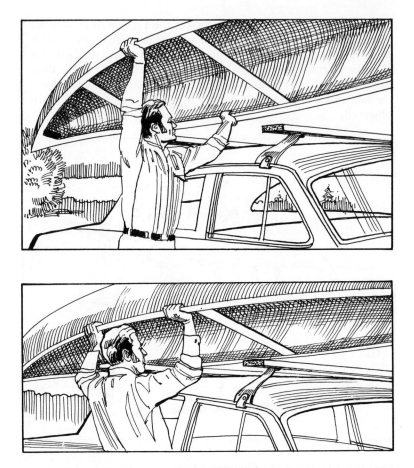

wale. NOTE. Paddles and other gear must be secured in the
canoe before the canoe is put onto the car.

LAUNCHING

Putting the canoe into the water and taking it out again should
be done carefully and smoothly and without damage to the canoe.
Ordinarily, the canoe should not be pushed, pulled, or slid into
or out of the water over beach, bank, or dock. When you are
launching, it is best to let the canoe right down onto the water
from a lift position. It should be lifted with the same care when
being taken out of the water.

Two-Man Launching

If two canoeists are launching the boat, it should be launched hand over hand, end first, onto the water. When the canoe is entirely clear of the bank, let it down on the water full length and guide it to a position parallel to the bank. To lift the canoe out, reverse the steps. If you are launching at a shallow beach, launch the canoe at right angles to the beach and hold it with its end just touching the bottom at the water's edge.

Tandem Cross-Corner Launching

When two dock sections are at right angles to each other, it is often convenient and easy for two persons to launch the canoe across the corner and likewise to lift the canoe out across the corner.

One-Man Launching, End First

From a simple lift position, one man can feed the canoe end first onto the water. When the whole canoe is clear of the dock or bank, let it down onto the water and guide it around to a parallel position alongside. To lift the canoe out, reverse the steps.

Parallel Launching

An experienced canoeist frequently employs the parallel method of launching. This method is especially practical with a lightweight canoe. Allow the canoe to slide down over your knees onto the water, with the ends of your shoes preventing it from scraping against the dock. Two canoeists may use the same method with greater ease.

Boarding

The best way to acquire agility and balance while boarding any craft is to slow down the boarding process so that it becomes a series of deliberate, controlled movements. When mastered, these movements may be blended gradually to achieve the desired smoothness.

Stand or kneel on one knee near the edge of the dock or bank, facing the bow of the canoe. Place your outer foot in the canoe, directly over the keel. Transfer your weight from the dock or bank directly *downward* onto the foot in the canoe. At the same time, grasp both gunwales with your hands, being careful not to pinch your fingers between the boat and the dock. Remove your foot from the dock and place it beside your other foot in the bottom of the canoe. You are then aboard and may take your position for paddling. For debarking, get up from your paddling position and reverse the procedure for boarding.

When two people board a canoe from a dock or bank, the bowman usually boards first because the bow position is a little closer to midships than the stern position, and the canoe will consequently remain in better trim. Sometimes, however, when the canoeists are large or heavy and the canoe is not measurably large, it may be better to have the sternman board first, but not at the stern position. He boards just aft of the midship thwart,

kneels on both knees, and holds onto both gunwales. Then the bowman boards and takes his normal position. Boarding in this way helps to keep the canoe on an even trim during the procedure.

When two people board a canoe at a beach or shallow-water shore, one man adjusts the canoe so that its end is just barely touching bottom at the water's edge and braces the canoe between his knees with his hands. The other steps around him into the canoe, keeping his weight low, and moves down the centerline, holding onto the gunwales, to his position at the far end. The man on shore then moves the canoe out about a foot farther away from shore, steps in, and, using the crouching procedure, moves to or beyond amidships until the canoe is afloat and free of the beach. The first man in then paddles the canoe out from the beach and the other moves to his own paddling position.

When boarding a canoe at a beach or wherever the water is shallow or when there is a current, you can often place the canoe parallel to the beach rather than at right angles to it. Move it out into water of several inches depth and step in, using the same principle of boarding that applies to boarding from a dock or bank—stepping into the center, grasping both gunwales, and keeping your weight low.

For boarding one canoe from another, follow the procedure used for boarding from a dock (see chapter 5 for illustrations). You can board a decked canoe in much the same manner as an open canoe, except that it must be placed parallel to the shore or dock so that you can step directly into the cockpit. More care must be given to balance, since the boat is less stable than an open canoe.

Boarding a kayak is a special skill and therefore is discussed in Chapter 15, "Kayaks and Rafts."

When you launch a canoe into fast water, you should launch it and point it upstream and preferably in an eddy. This procedure enables you to peel off and proceed downstream in a forward direction. (See chapter 10 for directions on peeling off.)

5

CANOE TRIM AND PADDLER POSITIONS

Canoes, because they are lightweight, shallow-draft craft, are sensitive to weight distribution and the effects of wind and waves. The paddlers' positions affect fore-and-aft trim as well as side-to-side (athwartship) trim and greatly influence canoe handling. An improperly trimmed canoe is difficult and dangerous to handle.

Safety must be foremost in a canoeist's mind. Therefore, an understanding of weight distribution and its effects on stability prepares the paddler for determining the best positions for paddling under varied conditions. With this knowledge and the paddling skill developed in the various positions, the paddler becomes an integral part of the canoe and is better able to make it respond accurately to his strokes.

WEIGHT DISTRIBUTION AND STABILITY

Stability is the first and foremost condition for safe boating, especially with long, narrow boats such as canoes. Canoes in reality are floats. The stability of the float depends primarily on its shape and the position of its center of gravity (CG). The more expansive the float over the water and the lower the center of gravity, the more stable the float becomes.

Stability in this instance is a function of the *righting moment,* which is composed of two equal forces. These two forces are opposed to each other in two directions:
1. Downward—the weight of the float, acting through its center of gravity. (CG is the same as the center of mass.)
2. Upward—buoyant lift (hydrostatic pressure on the surface of the float), acting through the center of buoyancy (CB).

An empty canoe resting quietly on the water has the two centers, the center of gravity (CG) and the center of buoyancy (CB), in the same vertical plane. The canoe is evenly trimmed fore and aft and athwartship.

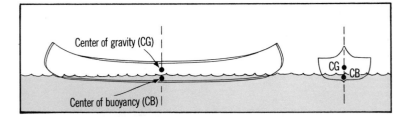

If weight is added to the canoe in the form of a heavy pack, the CB reacts so as to stay in the same vertical plane as the center of gravity. The following illustration shows the pack placed into an end of the canoe and off center. The resultant changes in the CG and CB are noted.

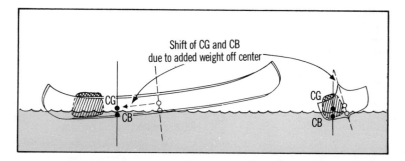

In the above illustration, undesirable conditions of stability result because the effective length of the canoe is shortened and the effective width is narrowed, leaving the same canoe on a smaller base. If the pack were centered fore and aft and athwartship, a more desirable condition of trim would result, thus maintaining maximum stability with the CG and CB much the same as they were in the first illustration.

The preceding discussion on weight distribution and stability shows the CG and CB within the hull of the canoe. The center of buoyancy will always fall within the hull of any boat or canoe. However, the center of gravity can be fixed outside of the canoe, depending on the weight and size of the objects loaded into the canoe. For instance, a person standing in the canoe raises the CG of the total unit above the gunwales. If the CG, in this raised position, is moved beyond the edges of the canoe, a capsize or a fall overboard will result, due to the twisting force created by the condition described and known as overcoming the righting moment.

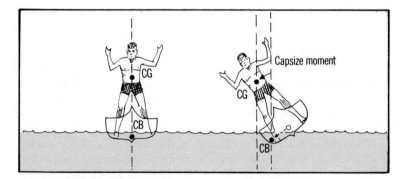

A sudden change in trim caused by some outside force, such as wave action or collision, will result in a twisting force that can be corrected by the automatic shifting of the center of buoyancy. This will be true only if the center of gravity remains in its original position with respect to the hull. The twisting force in this case is the righting moment.

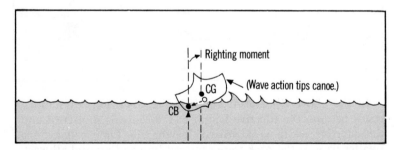

The underwater hull forms of round-bottom boats do not change appreciably when such craft are heeled (tipped to one side). This fact accounts for their relative instability unless ballast, inside or outside, in keel form, is added. Of course, canoes do not have built-in ballasted keels, and therefore the paddlers' weight must be used as the stabilizing force. This stability is accomplished by concentrating the weight very low in the canoe.

The art of paddling can therefore be best developed and learned from the kneeling position. This position offers the increased stability desired and allows the paddler to most effectively use the muscles of his thighs and trunk in conjunction with those of his arms and shoulders. Paddling positions other than kneeling can be advantageous to the experienced canoeist.

These positions should not be attempted, however, until the beginner or novice canoeist has developed a feel for the canoe and has become competent in the basic paddling stroke from the kneeling position. It is good to have a kneeling pad to make kneeling more comfortable and to prevent possible irritation to the tissues surrounding the knee areas.

ONE-MAN (SOLO) POSITIONS

There are several suitable positions for one-man paddling. These involve forms of kneeling and sitting and locations in the canoe.

Cruising Position

The cruising position is that of kneeling on both knees on the bottom of the canoe while at the same time leaning or sitting on a thwart or on the forward part of a seat.

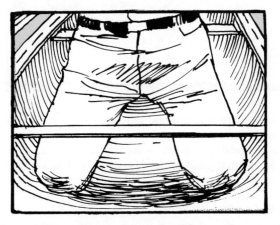

For solo paddling, this position should be taken as near to amidships as thwart placement will permit, except that ordinarily a midship thwart is not used unless it is offset (see chapter 3, section on thwarts). The most efficient all-round paddling position involves the use of a midship thwart that has been especially offset about 14 inches aft of amidships.

A comfortable modification of the cruising position on both knees is to straddle a bedroll or similar gear. Doing this permits adjusting your location in the canoe with less regard to the location of thwarts. This position has been found good for

children who are not big enough to sit on a thwart and at the same time kneel on the bottom.

When a midship thwart is located at the exact center of a canoe, the normal position for the paddler is at a quarter thwart, not at the stern thwart.

One-Knee Cruising Position

The one-knee cruising position is often called the relief position because it is frequently alternated with the normal cruising position. You lean back on the thwart, allowing the thwart to support the bulk of your weight, while kneeling on one knee and extending the other leg forward. Brace your forward foot against the edge of a canoe rib or in some other manner. Always kneel on the knee that is on the paddling side.

An alternate relief position is to kneel in a full upright position away from the thwart. This position has the advantage of being possible anywhere in the canoe but is very unstable and

should not be used by the novice until he has acquired the ability to keep the canoe in balance while paddling.

High Kneeling or Racing Position

The high kneeling or racing position is used in the organized sport of flatwater canoe racing. It is sometimes used, in open canoes, by experienced canoeists for covering distance in the shortest time with the least effort. It requires a great deal of practice and conditioning.

There are a number of important factors to consider in learning this position. If you are going to paddle on the left (port) side, as illustrated, kneel on the pad with your left knee at or near the bilge on that side. Your thigh and trunk should be erect above your knee. The line from your knee through the hip and shoulder is not vertical but usually slants forward about 10 degrees. Extend your left leg, below the knee, diagonally aft across the canoe, with the bottom surfaces of your toes, or the bottom of the toe of your soft-soled shoe, gripping the bottom of the canoe between two ribs near the keel line. Extend your right

leg forward, with a comfortable bend at the knee. Place your right foot firmly on the ribs of the canoe near the keel line, and point your toes diagonally forward to the left, not straight ahead. This firm triangular base, consisting of the left knee, left toes, and right foot, promotes smoother paddling by lessening undesirable body motion. The pressure exerted by the heel and/or toe of your right foot will vary, with emphasis on one or the other, to control and stabilize this paddling position.

A brace for each foot and a knee pad may be preferable and should be permanently placed in the canoe if you use this position frequently. This brace insures you a stable and firm "fit" in the canoe for greater control and stability.

Sitting Position

Most canoes are constructed with seats installed. The seats add strength to the canoe and offer a relief paddling position. Seats do, however, when you paddle from them, raise the center of gravity. Therefore, a seat should be located as far below the gunwale as is practical and should not trap your feet if you are kneeling. Seated, you have less control over the craft; in a kneeling position, you have greater control, generated through your knees, thighs, trunk, shoulders, and arms. The seated position, therefore, should be used only as a relief position in calm water. You should never attempt a passage in rough water or rapids in a seated position.

Avoid solo paddling from a bow or stern seat, unless a pas-

(Knee braced.)

senger or duffel is carried, because no satisfactory condition of trim could be achieved from such a position. When conditions permit, if you are in a sitting position you should firmly brace one knee under the inside portion of the gunwale and keep it firmly against the hull. You can then exert pressure on the hull by drawing the foot toward you and bracing it against the bottom of the canoe. This position gives you a reasonably firm hold on the gunwale and provides you with maximum control for this position. At no time should you bring your knees close together.

Standing Position

Although not recommended for novices, the standing position for paddling is useful and reasonably efficient under some circumstances. It is a good relief position on long cruises over smooth water and may be used for looking ahead when approaching shallow, rapid water.

When you are standing, your feet should be positioned to afford maximum security for you, thus preventing you from losing your balance. One of the best positions is with your feet apart (about shoulder width) and separated fore and aft. Your knees should be flexed slightly to absorb any unexpected vertical movement. Your body should face diagonally forward rather than straight ahead.

TANDEM POSITIONS

When two people paddle together in a canoe, they are spoken of as a tandem crew, or as paddling in tandem. The positions and principles of kneeling and sitting are the same as those for

solo paddling, but the locations of the paddlers are different.

The typical and conventional tandem cruising position is that in which the sternman is located at the stern thwart and the bowman at the bow thwart.

A less common but excellent position, especially for rough water, is the so-called heavy-weather position. In this position, the paddlers turn the canoe around, using the stern as the bow, so that they can position themselves closer together by having the bowman use the midship thwart and the sternman use the bow thwart. This arrangement requires the "offset" midship

thwart (see chapter 3, section on thwarts). With both paddlers near the middle of the canoe in a kneeling position, the ends of the canoe rise more easily when encountering waves, so that less water will be shipped when paddling in rough water. At no time should canoeists sit on the seats when paddling in rough water or whitewater.

The heavy-weather positioning of a tandem crew is also excellent when an experienced canoeist wishes to teach an inexperienced adult or child how to paddle. It places the instructor and the student close together, and such an arrangement is good from the standpoint of safety and for coaching. It also provides for good trim of the craft.

In modern closed downriver racing canoes, the paddling positions approximate the positions defined for heavy-weather

paddling in open canoes, while in a C-2 slalom or cruising canoe (see chapter 2), the cockpit locations approximate the conventional cruising positions. However, the C-2 canoe should be custom outfitted for balance. Most C-2's can be bought partially finished with respect to placement of cockpits. The cockpit holes, in this case, are cut small so that they can be enlarged fore and aft to properly place paddlers for trim. If this is not possible, a stern-heavy canoe is better than a bow-heavy canoe under most conditions. In the C-1 closed boat, trim is fixed by adjusting the location of the cockpit.

In tandem, the high kneeling (racing) position is fundamentally the same as for solo paddling. The necessary added factor is for each canoeist to position himself in the canoe with consideration for his partner. Since the two paddlers will counterbalance each other, each may kneel close to the side of the canoe. The difference in weights will determine how close to the side each may kneel and still maintain even trim of the craft from side to side. It is customary for the two to kneel closer together in the canoe when using this position. Past experience of racing crews has indicated the superior efficiency of the high kneeling position as described above. However, this position is highly unstable for the novice, and instability is compounded in tandem. It should only be used by experienced paddlers under optimum conditions.

The position of both tandem paddlers should also be such that the canoe trims even fore and aft. This trim can be achieved by the making of slight adjustments after the approximate positions have been taken. It is easily determined how the trim is by the

feel of the craft under way at a little more than moderate speed. If it is too heavy in the bow, the canoe will steer with some difficulty and will plow through the water, pushing out a bow wave. If the craft is too heavy astern, the bow will rise noticeably more than it should when speed is attained, and there will be an actual feel of the stern dragging too deeply in the water.

POSITIONS WITH PASSENGER

A typical passenger-paddler combination is that of the fisherman and his paddler. When the fisherman is trolling, he should sit in the bottom of the canoe, using the forward thwart for a backrest, with a cushion under him and another at his back if he wishes. His paddler should have both knees on the canoe bottom. Since this arrangement is stable, there is little danger of capsizing during the excitement of catching a fish. When the fisherman is casting, it is customary and safer for him to face forward and take a kneeling position. In quiet-water areas, he may at times sit on the seat or thwart for greater comfort. If he catches a fish, he should drop back to a kneeling position for greater stability.

When fishing is not involved, the passenger should always sit in the bottom. Usually, the passenger should use the bow thwart for a backrest, adding cushions if desired. The paddler should be located at the stern thwart.

A way to arrange the positions of paddler and passenger when there is a great difference between their weights is to have the paddler use the stern end as the bow, thus being enabled to kneel on the midship side of the bow thwart, with the passenger sitting forward of the offset midship thwart. This arrangement keeps the canoe in reasonably good trim fore and aft in spite of the significant difference in weights.

When the weight difference is not very great, the paddler may use the bow thwart and have the passenger sit facing him at the midship side of the offset thwart. Reasonably good trim results.

Generally, the overall principle is to arrange paddler and passenger (or duffel) so that the canoe trims well fore and aft and athwartship. These positions and the placement of added weight should be determined at shore. Accidental falls and capsizing are apt to result when unnecessary movement is undertaken.

THREE IN A CANOE

The placing of the occupants when there are three people in a canoe follows the principle of maintaining good trim of the canoe. If the third person is a passenger, he should sit in the bottom near amidships.

Under some conditions, such as when the wind makes paddling difficult and there is a long way to go, it may be wise for all three to paddle. The bowman and the man in the center both paddle on the same side, the sternman on the opposite side. The canoe may be trimmed well and paddled efficiently in this way.

It is not advisable to have three persons in a canoe when the craft will encounter high winds, fast-moving water, or rapids.

EXCHANGING POSITIONS IN A CANOE

Exchanging positions in a canoe while afloat in calm water is not hazardous if correct procedures are used. Exchange of positions is often desirable in an instructional program to give paddling experience to canoeists in both positions and to provide relief. When possible, exchange of positions is best accomplished at shore.

If conditions warrant it, the exchanging may be done afloat, as follows: (1) The bowman stows his paddle in the bow, or places it amidships if it is a favorite paddle and he wishes to use it when he has changed to the stern position. The sternman keeps his paddle in the water for control and stability. (2) The bowman places his hands on the gunwales and rises to a crouching position, feet close together over the keel, and then steps backward over the bow thwart to take a seated position in the bottom amidships, with hands on the gunwales. The seated position should be slightly toward one side to leave room for the sternman to step around the seated man. The bowman should also be prepared to drop one hand off the gunwale when the sternman steps by him. When the bowman has reached the midship position, the sternman stows his paddle or relays it to the bowman for storage if it is to be used at the bow. (3) The sternman places both hands on the gunwales, rises to a crouching position, and walks forward on the median line of the canoe, keeping his hands on the gunwales at all times. When he reaches the seated bowman, he steps around him (or straddles him) and continues on to the bow position. At the bow, he takes the correct kneeling position, picks up his paddle, and gets the paddle promptly back into the water for control and stability. (4) When this has been accomplished, the person sitting in the bottom rises to a crouching position and steps backward, while keeping contact with the gunwales, to take a new position at the stern. When his paddle is manned, the exchange is complete.

TRANSFERRING PASSENGERS FROM ONE CANOE
TO ANOTHER

Before transferring from one canoe to another, the paddler
who is to transfer moves to the midship position in his canoe as
described earlier in this chapter. Once in position and ready for
transfer, he rises to a crouching position, keeping his weight low
on the centerline and his hands on the gunwales. (The gunwales
of the two canoes should be held firmly together during the
transfer.) He places one foot into the canoe to be boarded,
along the centerline, and transfers his weight *downward* on that
foot, moving both hands to the gunwales of the newly boarded

canoe. The last step is for the paddler to bring his other foot aboard and take up his paddling position. Moving into the second canoe is much the same procedure described under "Boarding" in chapter 4. Every effort should be made to avoid catching hands and fingers between the two canoes while they are being held together.

SPECIAL CONSIDERATIONS WHEN WIND IS BLOWING

Paddling on quiet, smooth water is restful, peaceful, and charming in a way all its own, but it is confining, because such water can be found only in certain places or at certain times. If a person does much canoeing, he will have to encounter the force of the wind and cope with it from time to time. It can be hard work, but there is satisfaction in store for paddlers who use the force of the wind to their advantage and experience success rather than disappointment.

When you are paddling solo and the wind is blowing hard enough to make paddling difficult with the canoe trimmed in the normal manner, the trim of the canoe will have to be changed so that the wind will help keep the canoe on course. How the trim is changed will depend on the direction from which the wind is blowing and the course desired.

When paddling into the wind, you should have the canoe trimmed heavier at the bow. In other words, the end that is pointing into the wind should be deeper in the water than the other end. The light end, as a result, will be blown downwind, and thus the canoe will be kept on a straight course. The normal cruising position, kneeling on both knees or on one knee, is adequate when paddling downwind. Usually, the high-kneeling position will be better when the canoe is going into the wind, due to the position's greater efficiency.

When paddling downwind, have the canoe heavy at the stern.

When paddling across the wind, locate yourself in the canoe so that it trims in such a way that as the wind blows, the lighter end (the bow) turns toward your paddling side. If you do this, you will not have to apply a steering correction; in other words, the wind will be helping you keep the canoe on a straight course. For example, if you are paddling across the wind and on the lee side (downwind side), which is usually the best thing to do, you should move farther aft, thus trimming the canoe so that it is light in the bow.

If, on the other hand, you are paddling on the windward side (the side the wind is coming from) of the canoe when going

across the wind, you should move forward of amidships, thus trimming the canoe so that the stern is light.

The foregoing facts about trimming the craft in a wind are not merely theoretic advantages. They are so functional that they make reasonably comfortable paddling possible in wind conditions that are ordinarily regarded as prohibitive. You will discover, however, that as your skill develops you will be able to cope with moderate wind conditions while you are at the normal solo paddling position amidships, regardless of the canoe's heading.

Tandem crew members encountering strong wind should move to positions closer together and hence nearer the midship portion of the canoe (for the reasons given in the discussion on tandem paddling in heavy weather) and perhaps use the high-kneeling position. Since a tandem crew does not have the same problem of steering that a solo paddler has, their prime concern is lightening the ends of the craft.

It is true that the principles of using the wind to help steer would apply in tandem as well as solo paddling, but the advantage gained in using the wind might be overcome by the risk of shipping (taking on) water.

If the canoe is shipping water when heading directly into the waves, set a course at a slight angle to them. At the same time, try to keep the gunwale on the windward side a little higher than the other gunwale. You can tack up to windward in this manner —and downwind also, although the latter is more difficult in most severe conditions. If conditions get very bad, it is best to sit in the bottom and concentrate on keeping the canoe from swamping until the storm blows over or until the canoe has been blown in to shore or within reaching distance of a location protected from the wind, such as the lee of an island or projecting land. If the canoe swamps, follow the rescue measures indicated in chapter 7. These methods work even in severe circumstances.

6

PADDLING STROKES AND TECHNIQUES

STROKES

Handling a canoe with precision and safety is more quickly learned if the art of paddling is broken down into specific elements called strokes. After these strokes are learned, they may be combined and blended or altered as desired (or required) for smooth and skillful paddling.

All of the strokes mentioned in this chapter incorporate one or more of the following components: forward, backward, right, and left. These are the four basic directions in which a person can make a canoe move. Combinations of basic strokes can cause the canoe to move diagonally forward or backward or can make it turn.

Ideally, you should apply strokes on only one side of the canoe (usually your stronger, better side) and should apply leverage in an efficient manner. Also, it is important to strive to accomplish one basic theory in paddling: to place the paddle and move the canoe toward it. In reality, the paddle will slip slightly through the water as the canoe reacts to the power applied to the paddle, but still you should envision the paddle as the base for canoe movement.

The first seven strokes discussed are essential to the development of a flatwater paddler. Of course, all of the strokes mentioned should be known by any person considering himself to be an all-around canoeist, and most certainly by anyone attempting to paddle on rivers.

Forward, or Power, Stroke

The forward stroke is used to move the canoe ahead *without turning*. It is regarded as the foundation stroke upon which all others are built and is therefore explained in greater detail than the others. In short, the forward stroke is made close to the side of the canoe and parallel to the keel, with the shaft of the paddle moving in a vertical or near-vertical plane. The side of the pad-

dle that pulls on the water is called the power face of the blade. The opposite side of the blade is the back face.

One hand grasps the grip of the paddle and the other hand grasps the shaft several inches above the blade or throat. With the paddle held vertically, the blade should be in the water with the throat just at the water surface. The lower forearm is parallel to the gunwale and just above it. The upper hand (grip hand) "punches out" at about eye level. Thus the desired paddle length is dependent on the paddling position used, as well as the build of the person using the paddle, as described in chapter 3.

For some experienced paddlers, the position of the lower hand on the shaft is where the fingers lie when the grip is placed well up into the armpit and the arm is allowed to lie straight along the shaft. To begin the stroke, extend the lower arm forward full length in a firm but not strained position. The upper arm is bent at the elbow so that the fist is beside the head, near eye level, and the elbow is at shoulder height or lower, as desired. This is the starting position of the stroke. The trunk of the body leans slightly forward and rotates about the spine to provide somewhat greater reach as the blade bites the water. The lower arm pulls directly backward, parallel to the keel, and the upper arm drives forward in front of the head. If the elbow of the upper arm is not at approximately shoulder height initially, it must be raised as the stroke begins in order to get the maximum thrusting power from that arm and the muscles of the back and shoulder. The upper arm is expected to do fully as much work as the lower arm; and for a long time, until the muscles involved are built up, the paddler will think it is doing more work. The movement of the upper arm must be directed so that the arm will not only exert steady power but also will permit paddling close to the side of the boat but parallel to the keel. Its drive is therefore diagonally forward, ending when the arm is fully extended with the grip hand out over the water. The lower arm pulls backward until the hand is at or near the hip or thigh. The effective power interval of the stroke is from the forward position to a little beyond the vertical position of the blade. This is the reason for stopping the stroke when the bottom hand is at the hip. There is no need to be precise about the stopping point, however, since it comes naturally to most persons. Carrying the stroke farther aft is unnatural, but sometimes it is deliberately done with the belief that it improves the stroke.

It must be remembered that in paddling, the paddle is not pulled through the water; rather, the paddle bites the water as it is inserted into it—almost as if the water were solid—and the canoe is moved to the place where the paddle grips the water. It can be seen, then, that if the power is exerted when the blade is much beyond the vertical, the canoe will be drawn into the water, producing a drag and causing unnecessary movement, or bobbing, of the craft.

At the end of the stroke, both arms are relaxed completely, with the upper arm dropping down as if into the canoe. This action, aided by the water forces acting on the paddle, causes the blade to rise promptly to the surface, although most paddlers

control the paddle to the surface. The recovery is made by feathering the blade in a wide sweep above the surface of the water to the starting position. The blade is not exactly flat during the recovery; its leading edge is elevated slightly, so that if the blade hits the tip of a wave it will be deflected up instead of burying into the water. Furthermore, the recovery should be made close to the water and relatively quickly, with as much relaxation of arm muscles as possible. All this is essential to smooth, graceful, sustained paddling.

No appreciable body motion is necessary with the bent-upper-arm method of paddling described above. Only a slight flexion, extension, and rotation of trunk and shoulders accompanies the arm action. In paddling, elimination of unnecessary body motion contributes to the desired grace, smoothness, and efficiency. However, in actual practice, many paddlers lean forward for the catch and put their body into the stroke, while others use shoulder rotation during the stroke.

Simple Back Stroke

The simple back stroke utilizes the back face of the blade and is used to stop headway and to make the canoe move backward. Sometimes it is referred to as "holding." The movements involved are generally the reverse of those used in the forward stroke, and the back face of the blade is then used to apply force. The back stroke starts where the forward stroke ends. The bot-

tom arm pushes down and forward while the upper arm pulls up and back. In addition, at the beginning of the stroke, the body leans somewhat backward and at the end, somewhat forward. Thus, some of the power for this stroke is derived from a pull with the strong abdominal muscles, not from the arms and shoulders alone. The recovery is from forward to aft, with the blade feathered. If there is much headway on the canoe, the back stroke will initially be merely a *holding* stroke. It will not be practical to follow through completely until the canoe has stopped. Once stopped, the canoe will make way astern with repeated back strokes.

The illustration shows how a solo paddler applies a back stroke for going astern. The curved path of movement for the stroke, as shown at right, is to keep the canoe pointed straight and to have it hold its course as it stops or moves astern. This will be better understood after reading the sections on the "J" stroke in this chapter.

At the start of the back stroke, the blade is held in the water squarely as power is applied. As skill is acquired, however, you will learn to modify the stroke by changing the pitch of the blade a desired degree in order to check sideward movement as the canoe is brought to a stop by "holding" (stopping the forward movement) or as it is moved astern by repeated back strokes.

An alternate method of holding when the canoe is moving relatively slowly is to slice the paddle into the water slightly forward of your position in the canoe. Then hold the paddle firmly in the vertical position with the flat surface of the blade against the direction of motion. The shaft of the paddle may be held firmly against the gunwale of the canoe to increase the effectiveness of this holding method.

Draw Stroke

The primary purpose of the draw stroke is to turn the canoe or to move it sideward. The mechanics of the stroke are fundamentally the same as those of the forward stroke, except that the draw stroke starts abeam rather than ahead and moves toward the canoe rather than parallel to it. It is especially important for you to grasp the shaft firmly with your lower hand, maintaining your forearm at an angle near 90 degrees to the shaft throughout the stroke. To move the canoe sideward, start the draw stroke directly abeam of your position in the canoe. The blade enters the water parallel to the keel and is drawn directly in toward the paddler. Since most novice paddlers let the canoe override the paddle, the stroke should end and the recovery start about 6 or 8 inches from the side of the canoe.

To turn the canoe, you should first understand that all strokes used in turning it should have their major components along the circumference of a "turning circle" centered at the center of gravity of the loaded canoe and can be of any radius. By applying force with the paddle along this circle, you can use the most efficient method of turning.

Tandem paddlers may easily apply the draw on a circle that has a circumference passing through both bow and stern paddlers' shoulders. Note that the blade angle would not be parallel to the keel at the beginning of the stroke but will be parallel at the end.

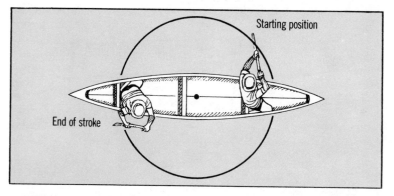

The solo paddler will find the draw more difficult. Since he is kneeling at the center of the turning circle, he must reach forward (or back) to do an effective draw. For maximum efficiency, the paddle must follow an arc of the turning circle, and the blade must be perpendicular to the arc of motion. This technique is very similar to the paddle movement in the sweep strokes but it is usually more difficult to master.

The most efficient recovery of the paddle, once a draw stroke has been completed and when repeated draws are needed, is to quickly rotate the paddle 90 degrees so that the power face of the paddle is astern. Slice it through the water away from the boat, rotate it again, and repeat the draw.

Since the draw can be performed in any direction, it should be realized that when the paddler reaches back within the stern to the amidship quadrant, the power face of the blade will be ahead rather than astern. Therefore, for the bow or side draws, the power face is astern, while for the stern draw, the power face is ahead.

An alternate (although slower) method can be used for the recovery, if the paddle can be brought out of the water. Once completing the draw, you drop your upper arm toward the bow and in front of you. This action slices the blade smoothly to the surface, where it is recovered as in the forward stroke. Relax both arms momentarily and feather the blade, keeping it close to the surface while you reach for the next stroke.

The draw stroke may be modified to a diagonal draw of any desired degree. You may wish to move the canoe slightly ahead or astern while moving it sideward. In these cases you would start the draw stroke from forward or aft of the true lateral position. The stroke should, however, normally finish at your hip, as does the regular draw stroke. In moving the canoe diagonally sideward in this manner, reach toward your objective with your paddle. This is a good general rule for determining the starting point of a diagonal draw. The same principle is involved if you are attempting to move the canoe sideward with the draw stroke when there is a headwind causing movement that, although sideward, is also diagonally to the rear. You can correct the condition by using a diagonal draw, which starts forward of the starting position of the regular stroke. If the wind is blowing from astern, you would make similar adjustments in the opposite direction.

If the wind is from abeam (directly from one side), and one end of the canoe swings while you are moving it sideward with the draw stroke, you can correct the condition by starting the draw directly abeam as usual but finishing it forward or aft of your position as necessary, in accordance with whichever end is swinging.

Cross Draw

No switching of hand positions is necessary with the cross draw. You lift the paddle across the boat to the offside while your body and arms are twisted fully to that side as shown in the illustration. The power face of the blade is what pulls against the water. The hand on the shaft is palm down, while the palm of the grip hand faces forward.

The action of the cross draw is similar to that of the draw, with recovery over the water. Also, it is more powerful than a pushaway on the normal paddling side and has the added factor of putting the paddler in a better position to brace if necessary.

Pushaway

The pushaway stroke uses the back face of the blade and is the opposite of the draw stroke in the same way that the back stroke is the opposite of the forward stroke. Its purpose is to move the canoe sideward in the direction opposite the paddler's side. You start the stroke with the paddle blade near or somewhat under the side of the canoe and with your upper arm over the water. You exert the push, directly abeam, with your lower arm, while you pull your upper arm in toward you.

The lower-arm action is more powerful if you start it with your elbow close to your hip, and with your wrist and forearm lined up straight behind the heel of your hand. You make the recovery by turning the blade 90 degrees at the end of the stroke and slicing it back through the water to the starting position. An alternate method of recovery is made over the water. When you perform the recovery in this manner, you should slice the blade into position from the direction of the stern rather than drop it vertically into position.

As in the case of the draw stroke, you may modify the pushaway stroke to a diagonal pushaway by pushing out in a direction, or angle, forward or aft of abeam. This modification may be necessary at times because of conditions of wind or current or when it is desirable to move the canoe ahead or astern while at the same time moving it sideward.

As shown, the draw and the pushaway may be used by tandem paddlers to move the canoe directly to the side.

Sweep Strokes

Forward sweep strokes, as the name implies, are wide sweeps of the paddle, using the power face of the blade, to swing the canoe for pivot turns or partial turns, to maneuver among obstacles, to follow along the bends of streams or rivers, to make sudden changes of direction in paddling, to aid in holding a straight course in crosswinds, and for general incorporation with other strokes as may be necessary for precise control of the canoe. Reverse sweeps, using the back face of the blade, are the opposite of forward sweeps but have many of the same functions.

Solo Sweep

A solo sweep covers an arc of about 180 degrees, from approximately directly ahead to directly astern. It is used by *one man* paddling from a position at or near amidships. You may use the whole full sweep or any portion of it, according to how much you wish to turn the canoe. When efficiently done, the stroke has a path of movement that is a true arc of the turning circle (described under "Draw Stroke") , beginning near the bow and ending near the stern. The basic arm movements are the same as those used in the forward stroke, except that the upper arm pushes out from near the waist rather than from near the shoulder, and the lower arm swings wide over the water in a broad sweep away from the side of the canoe. The first half of the sweep, from directly ahead to broad abeam, pushes or swings the bow of the canoe in the direction opposite the paddling side. The second half, from broad abeam to astern, draws or swings the stern to the paddling side.

It is important to maintain a firm grip on the paddle shaft and keep the lower forearm at an angle of nearly 90 degrees to the shaft. The early part of the stroke is done mostly with lower-arm pull and body rotation. Upper-arm push comes into play midway through the stroke. If the canoe has no forward movement at the outset, it can be turned completely with several of these strokes without being moved out of its general location on the water; in other words, it will do a pivot turn. In actual practice, this pivot turn may be aided if you slack off on power application during the midpoint of the stroke and emphasize the first third and the last third of the arc, because the middle third will have a slight tendency to move the canoe forward or astern as well as to swing it. Recovery of this stroke is the same as recovery of the forward stroke, with stress on relaxation of the arms and on keeping the blade feathered and close to the water, except that

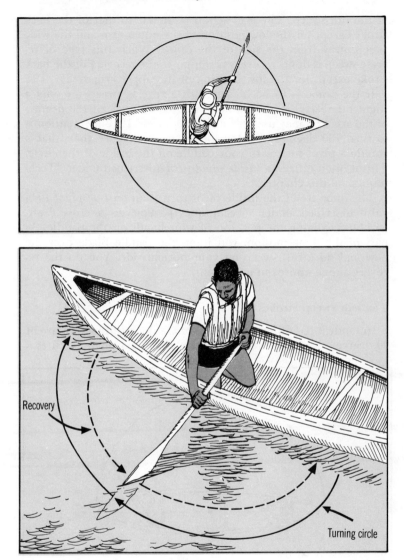

the hand on the paddle grip remains at waist level rather than being returned to shoulder level.

Reverse Solo Sweep

The reverse sweep may be carried out by starting astern and ending ahead for a full 180-degree arc and is the direct opposite of the full sweep. The arm action is similar to that of the back stroke except for the low position of the upper arm and the wide sweep away from the side of the canoe. When this type of reverse sweep is done, recovery is similar to the recovery of the back stroke except for the low position of the upper arm.

If the canoe is to be turned with a reverse sweep for only a slight number of degrees, you do not need to use all 180 degrees of the arc. You may use only about 90 or less. If your intention is to turn 180 degrees—or, for special reasons, more than that— you do a pivot turn with your paddle on the inside of the circle. This is often called an *inside pivot turn* (described under "Techniques" in this chapter).

The opposite of the inside pivot turn is an *outside pivot turn* (also described under "Techniques"). You do a cross draw, without changing the position of your hands on the paddle. As part of the same motion, you jump the paddle blade over the bow and do a full sweep on your normal side. You do the recovery as one unbroken movement.

Tandem Sweep Strokes

In tandem paddling, sweep strokes are done through an arc of 90 degrees or less on the turning circle. The bowman executes a

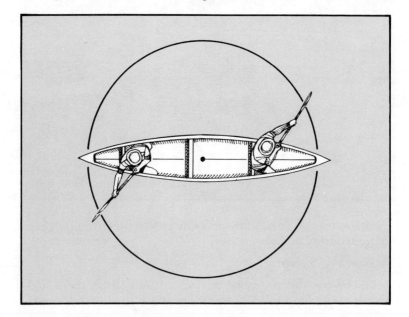

forward sweep stroke from directly ahead to directly abeam of his position. He does a reverse sweep from directly abeam of his position to directly ahead.

Since the bowman is located forward of the pivotal point of the canoe, any sweep or reverse sweep paddling done outside the quadrant indicated in the above illustration will tend to neutralize the stroke by working in the wrong direction. For example, if the bow paddler carries his sweep stroke much beyond the point shown in the figure, it will be directed in toward the canoe, thus tending to pull the bow back toward the paddling side.

The sternman's sweep starts abeam of his own position and goes 90 degrees to astern, pulling the stern over to his paddling side. Any sweep starting forward of this will have the negative effect described in relation to the bow sweep strokes, above. The reverse sweep for the sternman starts astern and goes 90 degrees to abeam of the paddler.

The pushaway (described earlier) for the sternman is really only the beginning of a reverse sweep. The full arc is not completed, since the purpose of the pushaway is to move the boat sideward rather than to turn it.

The recovery for sweep strokes is low, with flat or feathered blade.

In tandem paddling, the bowman often uses a sweep of 45 degrees or less as needed to swing the bow slightly or to help keep the canoe on course in a crosswind. This sweep of small degree is usually done at the forward part of the bowman's 90-degree quadrant. Sometimes, however, the bowman should not use a sweep in a crosswind, but should resort to "paddling wide." This is merely doing the forward stroke out about a foot or more away from the side of the canoe. Usually, there is just a shade of the sweep stroke at the very beginning. There is more forward propulsion to this method of holding the canoe on course than to a regular sweep stroke. When the canoe is under way on a straight course, the sternman also should resist a crosswind by paddling wide. When necessary, he can add a sweep of small degree at the very end of the stroke.

When sharper turns are done, the bowman and sternman coordinate sweep strokes and reverse sweep strokes, each using the full arc of 90 degrees.

J Stroke

The J stroke is used to keep the canoe on a straight course. It is used almost continuously in solo paddling, when going straight ahead, and by the sternman of a crew whenever needed.

J Stroke in Solo Paddling

Since it is impossible to paddle directly under the keel of a canoe, a paddling stroke tends to throw the canoe off course in the direction opposite the paddling side under normal conditions of little or no wind or current. It is therefore necessary to do something to offset this condition and keep the canoe on a straight course. Most beginners solve the problem by paddling first on one side and then on the other or by trailing the paddle astern at the end of each stroke, using it as a rudder. Both of these practices are inefficient. The steering stroke, called the J stroke, is used by experienced canoeists. Doubtless it has been so named because in its unrefined form it actually forms a J when done on the left side of the canoe. Not all skilled paddlers do the J stroke alike in detail; therefore, an effort is made here to acknowledge shades of variation.

In general, the J stroke may be regarded as a modified forward stroke. In solo paddling, the stroke usually starts slightly away from the side of the canoe and proceeds as a diagonal draw of slight degree, thus holding the bow over toward the paddling side. The emphasis on this diagonal draw depends on the conditions of wind or current; sometimes none will be needed. After the diagonal draw, the stroke is the same as the forward stroke during the forward pulling portion, except that an effort is made to paddle as much under the side of the canoe as is possible. A little more than halfway through the stroke, the power face of the blade is turned gradually outward to a final blade angle of about 45 degrees. This is done by flexing both wrists and rotating the thumb of the grip hand away from the body or downward. Some paddlers start to turn the blade a little before the halfway point of the stroke, others at the halfway point, and some a little more than halfway. Pulling the paddle through the water with

the blade at an angle in this manner forces the stern of the canoe to move away from the paddling side, thus helping the initial diagonal draw to hold the canoe on a straight course. Toward the end of the stroke, the shaft of the paddle slides along the gunwale (outwale portion) for about 10 inches to take the strain of steering off the muscles of the lower arm. When you are first learning the J stroke, it may be necessary to use a prying action against the gunwale at the very end of the stroke, thus actually doing a *J* on the left side or a reflected *J* on the right side (see illustration, top of page 155). As skill comes, however, this prying action may gradually lessen and may finally be eliminated if desired. It must be mentioned, though, that some very excellent paddlers do use prying action of a refined nature when doing the stroke. Rather than turning the power face of the blade outward about halfway through and continuing to pull straight back, they wait longer before turning the blade and then turn it more quickly, though smoothly, just before touching the gunwale with the shaft. When the shaft touches the gunwale, the back face of the blade is directed diagonally to the rear at about the same degree as the initial diagonal draw at the start of the stroke.

Pry occurs here

At the end of the stroke, the upper arm is lowered as the blade is lifted quickly out of the water. Recovery is made close to the surface of the water, with the blade nearly flat and the leading edge elevated slightly.

J Stroke in Tandem Paddling

In tandem paddling, the sternman uses the J stroke as often as necessary to keep the canoe on course. Because he is aft of the pivotal point (center) of the canoe, he does not employ the diagonal draw at the start of his stroke but, as in the forward stroke, he makes his catch close to the side of the canoe and exerts pressure directly aft, parallel to the canoe. From halfway through the stroke to its completion, however, it is done the same as in solo paddling with the same possibilities of variation. The recovery likewise is the same relaxed movement described for the forward stroke, sweep strokes, and solo J stroke. Similarly, the blade is kept flat and close to the water during the recovery, with its leading edge elevated slightly. Since the canoe is narrow at the sternman's position, he usually does not need to touch the gunwale when doing the J stroke, because his stroke comes closer to the keel line (under the centerline of the canoe) than in solo paddling and hence is more effective, with a minimum of steering movement. Also, when the sternman is in the normal cruising position on both knees or on one knee, his hip is close against the gunwale at this location, and he can use pressure against his hip rather than the gunwale when extra steering pressure is needed.

Stern Rudder

The stern rudder is the elementary method of steering a canoe on a straight course. To do it, merely trail the paddle astern at the end of a stroke, with the power face of the blade toward the boat, and by applying the necessary pressure with the back face of the blade out away from the stern, keep the canoe on course. It is inefficient (causes slowing of forward momentum) as a normal method of steering and is hence used only in special situations. For example, it is good to use in a shallow, weedy place, where the normal J stroke would result in getting weeds twisted around the paddle blade. It is also good in shallow, rocky places, where the twisting action of the J stroke might result in a split paddle blade if the blade should catch between two rocks. Effectively, the stern rudder is just a small reverse sweep.

Stationary Strokes

This section will include the following strokes applied in a stationary manner: the draw, pushaway, and cross draw. These stationary strokes work only if the boat has good forward speed through the water. The term *stationary* refers to what the paddler does with the paddle, not the motion of the canoe. The stroke's ultimate effect on the canoe is either a draw or a pushaway.

The *stationary draw* is used in solo paddling to move a canoe sideward toward the paddling side while underway without changing its heading. Sideslipping a canoe in this way is particularly advantageous when an obstruction such as a rock, log, or stump is seen too late for you to alter the canoe's course and steer around it. To do the stroke, hold the paddle, blade in water, vertically about 2 feet away from the canoe and somewhat aft of your paddling position. Turn the forward edge of the blade outward, away from the canoe about 30 degrees, and hold

Blade angle

Resultant canoe movement

it there firmly. Hold both arms, rigidly in place, of course, so that the paddle acts as a rudder, moving the canoe diagonally sideward. This means that your lower arm must exert pressure toward the canoe while your upper arm exerts pressure away from the canoe. The exact location in which to hold the paddle depends on the desired direction of movement. When the paddle is in the right position, the canoe will move sideward without changing heading. Corrections are easy to make; if the bow moves over faster than the stern, move the paddle a little farther aft until the canoe moves sideward evenly. Rotating your trunk a little more toward the paddling side is an easy way to do this. If the stern is moving over faster than the bow, make a correction by moving the paddle forward a bit.

A stationary *cross draw* is also possible. Considerable trunk rotation is necessary in order to get the paddle into the water far enough aft to assure that the canoe will move sideward

squarely. The cruising position on both knees gives the most
flexibility in this respect.

In tandem paddling, either the bowman or the sternman may
use the stationary draw to move his end of the canoe diagonally
sideward while the canoe is underway. For example, in the illustration on page 160, the sternman does a stationary draw in
coordination with the bowman's stationary cross draw to move
the canoe diagonally sideward. Obviously, the stationary draw's
effect quickly declines as forward movement slows. If additional
sideward movement is needed, the followup strokes to use are the
draw, pushaway, and sculling strokes.

The *stationary pushaway* is the opposite of the stationary draw.
It moves the canoe diagonally sideward in the direction opposite
the paddling side when the canoe has from moderate to considerable headway. When a solo paddler sights an obstruction
directly ahead and so close that he cannot safely pass it by
altering his course and steering around it, he can sideslip past
it by using the stationary pushaway. Other obstructions sighted
farther ahead may influence his decision to use it, since the
stationary draw would be normally selected because of its greater
adaptability and ease of execution. There are, of course, other
maneuvering positions in which a paddler might wish to use

the stationary pushaway—for example, to move diagonally in
alongside a pier.

To perform the stationary pushaway, "cut in" the blade to a
vertical position in the water, close to the side of the canoe, as
for the beginning of the regular pushaway stroke. Angle the
forward edge of the blade about 45 degrees toward the canoe.
Hold the shaft firmly against the gunwale and brace both arms
rigidly. Considerable effort is normally required to keep the
paddle from being pushed back. The paddle in this position
acts as a side rudder to move the canoe diagonally sideward in
the direction opposite the paddling side. You must brace your-

self well when doing this stroke, or you may fall overboard or lose the paddle. If the stern moves over faster than the bow, slide the shaft a few inches forward along the gunwale until the condition is corrected.

In tandem paddling, the stationary pushaway instead of the cross draw may be used by the bowman. The sternman may use it instead of the stern rudder. It may also be used in coordination with the stationary draw. The fact that the stationary draw and stationary cross draw are normally used by the bow paddler indicates that the need for bow rudders has passed. A solo paddler may also use these strokes for the same purpose by reaching ahead of his position on either side of the canoe. Also, the shaft of the paddle at the lower hand can be braced against the gunwale to provide a firmer "grip."

It must be pointed out that the result of using any stationary stroke is loss of momentum and that these skills are limited in their application.

Sculling Draw and Pushaway

The sculling draw is an effective method of moving the canoe sideward toward the paddle and is used in the same situations that the *draw,* mentioned earlier, is used. The efficiency of the sculling draw stems from the fact that there is practically no negative phase or recovery interval. Also, it can be combined with a high brace to aid in controlling the canoe. To do the sculling draw, place the paddle blade in the water vertically, a comfortable distance from the canoe. Move it fore and aft in a path from 2 to 3 feet long, parallel to the canoe. Turn the leading edge away from the canoe at an angle of from 20 to 45 degrees to the path of the stroke. As the blade is pressed forward, its forward edge is turned away, producing a diagonal pressure from the power face of the blade that moves the canoe sideward in somewhat the same manner that a revolving propeller moves a ship ahead. At the end of the forward movement, turn the blade sharply so that the trailing edge is turned away. Then move the paddle toward the stern with the same effect, again using the power face to continue moving the canoe sideward.

If one end of the canoe starts to swing around when you are sculling in solo paddling, do the sculling a little more toward the other end of the canoe to correct the condition. If the wind is causing the canoe to move ahead while it is going sideward, increase the angle of the blade at the end of the forward movement, and the forward canoe movement will be checked. If the canoe is being blown backward while it is being sculled sideward, increase the angle of the blade on the backward movement to check this condition.

In tandem paddling, the sculling draw stroke is used by either the bowman or the sternman in place of the draw stroke and in place of sweep and reverse sweep combinations in pivot turns. It is also used in coordination with a sculling pushaway stroke to move the canoe sideward.

The sculling pushaway has the same function as the pushaway stroke: moving the canoe sideward in the direciton away from

the paddle. The position of the paddle in the water and the path of movement are the same as for the sculling stroke, with two exceptions: first, the path of movement is closer to the canoe; second, the leading edge of the blade, although at the same degree of angle, is turned toward the canoe rather than away from it, and the back face of the blade is used, rather than the power face. Modifications to meet or counteract the force of wind or current follow the same principles that are applied to these elements when the sculling stroke is done.

Pry

The pry can be applied by a solo paddler at the end of a power stroke or independently. When it is used independently, it's effects will be to quickly move the canoe sideward, as with the pushaway, or to turn the canoe.

If you are solo paddling and find it necessary to use the pry, slice the paddle into the water alongside the canoe and behind your paddling position. Keep the paddle close to the gunwale, at a desired location on the gunwale, and apply strong force with your arms, using the gunwale as the fulcrum, and then pry the back face of the blade outward. This pry has powerful leverage, and unless the shaft and gunwale are protected, they will become damaged if you use the pry with any regularity.

If you are solo paddling you can combine the pry with a power stroke by applying it at the end of the stroke, as described on page 154. Do this about the time that the power stroke begins to lose its effectiveness and therefore does not waste moves or energy. The power strokes referred to here are the forward stroke and the back stroke. In whitewater, a quick pry at the end of the forward stroke is preferred to the J stroke for steering.

The combination of forward strokes and pry when done properly does not drag against the gunwale; rather, the shaft touches the gunwale at a point as the blade rotates to slice through the water as the canoe continues to move forward. The prying action is executed cleanly, crisply, and quickly. With the blade properly feathered, there is virtually no braking action to forward momentum, only power and turn.

In tandem paddling, the pry is used at either the stern or the bow to move that end of the canoe over and is used at the stern for a forceful turn. It is preferred to the cross draw, especially for small changes of direction, since it can be applied more quickly and without removing the paddle from the water. The pry can be more effective when combined with a sweep for larger turns. In whitewater, the bow pry can bring about an extremely sharp turn when worked against a current. However, the cross draw gives a greater feeling of stability because it lends itself more readily to bracing.

Also it has been found that if the paddle should strike the river bottom or an obstruction while prying, it can capsize the canoe. Therefore, do not use a pry on the downstream side of the canoe in shallow water.

The stern paddler, when using the pry to turn the canoe, pries at the effective end of the forward stroke. As with the solo paddler, the sternman should not let the paddle go beyond his position before applying the pry.

Compound Back Stroke

The compound back stroke is a very powerful method of backing the canoe. It enables you to make better use of leverage and strength, and once learned, will be an excellent addition to your skills. This stroke can be described as a kind of back draw followed by a forward pushaway, parallel to the keel line. In order to initiate this stroke, rotate your shoulders to the paddling side, far enough to enable you to reach back alongside the canoe. In doing so, you must maintain your normal position from the waist down, thus keeping firm contact with the canoe and maximum control.

By using the power face of the blade and inserting it into the water as far back as possible, pull the paddle (in much the same manner as in the power draw) up alongside your paddling position. With the blade still vertical, rotate the blade so that

the stroke can be completed. Use the back face of the blade, by pushing the paddle forward. Add a corrective turn of the blade, back face away from the canoe, at the end of the stroke to keep the canoe on course.

At the end of the stroke, recover the paddle over the water, power face down and feathered. This action automatically puts the paddle in position as you twist your body and reach for the next stroke.

Low Brace

The paddle brace is the great contribution of kayaking to canoeing and is the most significant addition to canoeing skills to be made in many years. With this method, you can put full reliance on the paddle and can use it not only to steady the canoe but also to lean it into turns.

Additional benefits include correction of impending capsizes

and even the righting of the canoe from an upside-down position.

In the low brace, lay the paddle flat on the water with the palm of the grip hand up and the elbow of the throat hand above the paddle. Because of the leverage gained by reaching far out to the side, a quick push down on the paddle will cause the canoe to roll to the opposite side. This is a necessary skill to prevent capsizing.

In an extreme crisis, put your head and upper body into the water and bring the canoe around with your knees and hips. Bring your body back aboard only at the very end of the recovery, just as in the Eskimo roll (described in chapter 7).

As shown in the illustration below, the low brace can be used by the stern paddler to steady the canoe while the bow paddler initiates a turn.

High Brace

In some instances, a brace, a draw, and a canoe lean are all needed at the same time. When they are needed, the best method with which to apply all three is with a high brace. Use this method by reaching directly out from the canoe with the blade while keeping your upper arm straight to hold the grip of the paddle high. The result is a drawing action of the paddle. Because of the extreme reach of your lower arm, you can lean out over the water, banking the canoe.

The bracing action comes either from the angle of the paddle off the vertical or from the depth of the blade in the water. Too much angle will spoil the lean of the canoe, therefore your upper hand should be high and the blade should be buried in the water. If you suddenly need a righting moment, you should either pull harder or go into a low brace.

TECHNIQUES

With the canoe stationary in the water, it can be turned end-for-end by a solo paddler without forward or backing movement. Simply pivot it on its center of gravity until you reach the desired heading. You can make the canoe pivot with the bow either toward the paddling side (inside pivot turn), using a reverse sweep, or away from the paddling side (outside pivot turn) by the application of modified sweep strokes. The modification of the sweep strokes consists of reaching much farther out, away from your paddling position.

Inside Pivot Turn

Do the inside pivot turn as follows: From your paddling position amidships, reach as far aft on the paddling side as possible and, by using the back face of the blade, begin an extra-wide reverse sweep stroke. Push the paddle in a wide arc toward the bow. When the midpoint of the stroke is reached, turn the paddle so that the power face of the blade completes the arc. Of course, your hands remain in contact with the paddle and do not change their grip.

Forward Stroke

Reverse Sweep

Bow Draw

The wide pivot turn sweep will turn the canoe but will also cause some sternway. To prevent the canoe from traveling in a wide circle, use a forward stroke well under the canoe at the end of the bow draw. Subsequent reverse sweeps can be done following the forward stroke.

Outside Pivot Turn

The outside pivot turn is a smooth-flowing series of skills beginning with a wide cross draw to the bow and followed by a wide sweep. The power face of the blade is used throughout.

The recovery is the same as is used with the sweep, except that you must recover over the bow and twist the paddle to initiate the cross draw as close to abeam of the paddling position as possible.

APPLICATION OF STROKES TO RIVERS

Experienced paddlers will find a use for all of the foregoing strokes sooner or later on rivers. Some strokes are better than others in selected situations and, therefore, are stressed for river paddling. For instance, the back stroke is perhaps more important than the forward stroke when a canoeist is in fast water. The back stroke permits the canoeist to slow the boat long enough to select a proper course. It also aids in keeping the canoe from burying into high waves.

The braces are heavily relied upon in river paddling. They enable the paddler to stabilize the canoe when entering opposing currents, to lean the canoe, and to bank into turns.

The prys, draws, and pushaways are also used a great deal and often in combination with other strokes. The draw, having a righting moment, can be used to stabilize the canoe in an emergency. In contrast, the pry tends to have a capsize moment.

Sweeps are used primarily for maneuvering and have little practical use beyond that. Even the rudder-type skills have a use if the water is placid and the canoe is moving with respect to the water, as opposed to moving over the river's bottom.

To say just how or when a particular stroke should be used would be difficult. There are certain maneuvers that require a stroke or combinations of strokes, and these are described in chapter 10. Therefore, as you gain experience, you will be able to more intelligently put the strokes mentioned here into use. These skills, naturally, will come only with a complete understanding of the basics described and with practice of the strokes until they become second nature.

7

RESCUE TECHNIQUES

Self-rescue methods should be practiced until they are so well mastered that falling overboard, swamping, and capsizing cease to be emergencies and become mere incidents instead. These methods are, after all, nothing more than ways to handle a canoe and yourself in special situations. The fact that all of them can be used in novelty events indicates that, although requiring practice, they are not difficult but are actually fun. The swimming rescues taught in lifesaving courses are rarely necessary in canoeing; nevertheless, canoeists should be encouraged to take these courses.

PRELIMINARY PRACTICE

In order to practice the skill of boarding a canoe from deep water, you must first be familiar with getting into the water safely from the canoe. This skill may also be needed when you want to go swimming if the shoreline is not suitable for making a landing or if the bottom near shore is unsuitable for swimming activity. When you do swim, loop the bow painter around your shoulder after you are in the water so that you can tow the canoe while you are swimming.

Practice in Going Overboard

The first step in going overboard is to stand in the canoe with your feet together over the keel or centerline (clear of the thwart), grasping the gunwales. With your weight supported by your arms, vault over the side and separate your legs like a pair of scissors as they clear the side and start downward into the water. When you enter the water, close your widely separated legs with a vigorous scissors kick to check your momentum. Transfer the hand that was on the far gunwale to the near gunwale as your body passes over the gunwale. Slap the other hand and arm down on the surface of the water laterally and begin

sculling to help your legs check the downward rush of your body
into the water. Entry into the water has thus been made without
your losing contact with the canoe or submerging your head.
That is why vaulting overboard is preferred to diving overboard,
when contact with the canoe is lost. Diving from the canoe is
therefore discouraged as a general practice.

Practice in Hand-Paddling

If you lose your paddle overboard and do not have a spare, sit or kneel low on the bottom and use one hand and forearm as a paddle. In this manner, you will be able to maneuver the canoe slowly but surely into position to pick up the lost paddle, or to get back to shore if the paddle cannot be recovered. All of the forearm as well as the hand should be used to get added power. Proper positioning of your body to make maximum use of the wind is also important.

SELF-RESCUE

What To Do If You Fall Overboard

It is a general—and erroneous—belief that capsizing and swamping are the only common situations from which the inexperienced canoeist must rescue himself. The truth is that often the canoeist loses his balance and falls overboard without swamping or capsizing the canoe. This accident is rare among trained canoeists who paddle from kneeling positions but is more common among the untrained who sit on the seats with their knees elevated and not braced.

If you are canoeing solo and fall overboard, grasp the near gunwale with one hand as you go over the side. Do not allow your body weight to fall on the gunwale, since your weight could swamp or capsize the canoe. Your grasp should be firm enough to maintain contact with the canoe; otherwise, the canoe may be blown away. If you lose your grasp on the gunwale when falling overboard, come to the surface, then immediately swim to the canoe and hold onto it for restful support. If the canoe gets away from you and is being blown away faster than you can swim, swim to shore instead of trying to catch it. Swim slowly and rest frequently to conserve your strength. But if the shore is near and you have contact with the canoe, use the canoe for support while swimming with one arm and your legs, towing or pushing the canoe to shore, where you can get back aboard.

If you are not near shore when you fall overboard, you will have to reboard the canoe from deep water. The method used should be commensurate with your ability and strength. Perhaps the easiest way to reboard a dry canoe is to reach over the gunwale near amidships and place your hands in the near bilge.

Press down while kicking your feet to the surface behind you until you have pressed the canoe in under you. Keep your head low.

When your head is near or against the far side, roll over to a sitting position (see illustration, page 181).

From the sitting position it is a simple matter to swing your legs aboard and get back to an appropriate paddling position.

If you are paddling tandem and both you and your companion fall overboard, reboarding would be fundamentally the same except that one person could stabilize the canoe from the opposite side while the other climbed aboard (see illustration, page 182).

The latter person could then sit in the bottom and stabilize the canoe while the other boarded in the same manner as described for the solo paddler.

If the paddlers involved in a fall overboard are physically strong and agile, the following methods of reentering a canoe could prove to be more effective.

At a position where you can reach across the canoe, and yet as near to amidships as possible, grasp the far gunwale with one hand and the near gunwale with the other hand. Get your feet up near the surface of the water and keep them there with a strong kick. With your arms, pull the canoe in under you. Help your arms with a continuous, vigorous, strong kick. Exert pressure downward on the far gunwale by getting your elbow high on that side as soon as possible. Continue to draw the canoe in under you until you reach a position of balance. Then do a quarter turn or roll backward and sit in the canoe.

If the canoe is too wide for you to reach across as described above, it will be easier to board it with the aid of a thwart. To get aboard, grasp the thwart with one hand just beyond amidships (more than halfway across the canoe) and hold the near gunwale with your other hand. Kick vigorously and pull with both arms, pulling the canoe in under you until you feel that your weight is supported mostly on the thwart. With the strength of both arms and a vigorous kick, move farther into the canoe and do a quarter turn and sit on the bottom of the canoe.

Still another and very successful method (primarily for long or aluminum canoes) is to climb into the canoe at either end, using the deck for support. This action is initiated by getting to one end beside the canoe and kicking while getting your arms on top of the deck.

Kick again to get your hands down, your elbows up. Get your torso across the top of the deck, coming to a point of balance across the canoe. Then swing one leg aboard and carefully climb in. This is not an elegant or graceful maneuver but is effective for those with adequate strength and perhaps takes less skill than other, more complex methods.

As with all other skills found in this text, various self-rescue methods must be tried so that you can find the method best for *you*. Then you must practice the method to proficiency.

What To Do If the Boat Capsizes or Swamps

When a canoe capsizes, stay with it. Use its buoyancy for support. If you are near shore, push, tow, or paddle the canoe to shore. If you are a skilled swimmer, it is possible for you to learn how to empty the canoe with the shakeout technique (see "The

Shakeout" in this chapter), then you can board it, pick up nearby floating gear, and continue your trip. If you are away from shore and help is coming, just hold on gently but firmly to the canoe until help arrives or roll it upright and sit in it. The latter action will be more restful.

The above methods represent a variety of ways in which self-rescue may be carried out in the event of a canoe's capsizing. Remember, when you find yourself in the water, you should be *wearing* a lifejacket.

Swimming a Capsized Canoe to Shore

When a capsizing takes place relatively close to shore, the simplest method of self-rescue is to hold onto the canoe with one hand and swim it to shore with your other hand and your legs. Take your time; rest as often as necessary. It is important not to climb onto the canoe but to use it as a buoyant aid to help keep you at the surface. Keep your body in the water, with your head above the surface. When two canoeists capsize, they should hold onto the canoe from opposite sides.

Boarding and Hand-Paddling or Paddling a Swamped Canoe

When a canoe is capsized or swamped far from shore, the safest and least tiring procedure when help is not near is to get in it and hand-paddle or paddle it to shore. If it is capsized, bottom-up, take a position near amidships and grasp the keel, rolling the canoe slowly to the upright position. (The only canoe that would float bottom-up is a wooden canoe.) To board the canoe, place both hands inside on the bottom. Then raise your legs to the surface behind you. By kicking and pressing down gently with your hands, half drag and half swim your way over the near gunwale until your chin reaches the far gunwale. Keeping as much of your body in the water as possible, roll over on the back of your neck, spreading your arms along the gunwale and resting your legs in an extended position over the opposite gunwale. This produces an outrigger type of balance and checks any tendency of the canoe to roll. Gently sit down in the bottom and slowly pivot around to a position where both legs are under the midship thwart, with your thighs (just above the knees) pressing firmly up against the thwart near each gunwale. Your arms and hands may be extended sideways, and sculling may be done as necessary to maintain stability until you are adjusted to a comfortable position. You may then hand-paddle or paddle the canoe to shore.

If the water is rough and large waves are pounding the shore, get out of the canoe as you get to shallow water or near shore and hold onto the offshore end of the craft so that the canoe will be carried in ahead of you and not be thrown hard against you, possibly causing you to be injured by rocks, gravel, or other underwater hazards. It would be best to empty the canoe, if possible, prior to landing.

An important consideration in understanding self-rescue in these situations is that the human body and most canoes are buoyant. The human body is supported by the water to the extent that the average person can rest motionless on his back with his face clear of the water. A canoe, even though swamped, has only to support those parts of the body that need to be out of the water and not the entire weight of the person using the canoe for self-rescue. This is why it is possible for the canoe to support as many people as can comfortably get into it.

Emptying a Swamped Canoe in Deep Water

Splashing and Bailing

Another method of self-rescue is to empty the swamped canoe while in deep water. The simplest way to do this is to lie in the canoe with only your face above water, splashing the water out of the canoe by kicking or using your hands until the freeboard gradually increases enough to allow you to sit without submerging the gunwales. You may dispose of the remainder of the water by bailing with your cupped hands, shoe, hat, or other device.

The Shakeout

The shakeout is the quickest method of emptying a swamped canoe in deep water. It is essentially a swimming skill rather than a canoeing skill. It should be deemphasized until other skills are mastered, because it is rarely needed. Many modern canoes do not permit an effective shakeout technique, owing to the inside overlap of the gunwales.

With the canoe in the rightside-up position, move to one end and face the length of the canoe. Force your end of the canoe down into the water so that it is completely underwater but just under the surface. Give the canoe a vigorous thrust forward (an arm's length). This action should cause from one-third to one-half of the water to come out over the submerged end. Keep a firm grip on the end and raise it abruptly at the moment the water ceases to run out over the end; otherwise, much of it will be taken back in again. If the canoe is large and heavy, it may be necessary to stroke with one arm and your legs to accomplish the thrust. Use one or two more thrusts if necessary. Hold the end firmly until the surge created by the thrust has quieted.

Move to midships and grasp the gunwale on your side with both hands, a shoulder width apart, with thumbs on the outside. Then begin the shakeout. Lower the near gunwale close to the water, leaving an inch or less of freeboard. Thrust directly forward from your shoulders to start the water surging from side to side.

There is a dual thrust in "shaking out." One thrust is minor and is used to set up the wave motion of the water in the canoe; your arms must not fully extend for this thrust. Watch the wave, and as it hits the near gunwale, thrust vigorously in a *horizontal* direction, not downward. This is the major thrust.

Coordinate your leg kicks with your arm thrusts so that you do not hang onto the canoe. Do not pull the near gunwale underwater. The scissors kick is most effective, unless you happen to have an unusually strong breaststroke kick or eggbeater type of kick. Time your thrusts with the surge of the water toward you so that the water will come out over the gunwale rather than hit the freeboard and bounce back into the canoe. The near gunwale will rise 2 or 3 inches between thrusts. Your timing will be helped if you make sure that the far gunwale is always higher, so that there will be less depression of the near gunwale necessary before thrust. Constantly watch the surging water in order to establish the best timing.

It will be necessary to regulate your breathing so that exhalation takes place as the oncoming water clears the gunwale into your face. Timing, rather than strength, is the key factor in the whole operation. Many skilled persons can do the shakeout with one hand if the canoe is not too large. Your final thrusts will have to be more vigorous to get out the last bit of water and make a thorough job of it.

When the canoe has been emptied, board it as described earlier in this chapter. You can then pick up floating paddles and other gear, or resort to hand-paddling in the event that all paddles are adrift.

Although it is not necessary to know the shakeout skill, its use may eliminate long or harmful exposure to cold water (immersion hypothermia, discussed in chapter 8) if a capsizing occurs.

One additional method for tandem canoeists to use in emptying a swamped canoe in deep water is possible if the canoeists are skilled swimmers and are strong, and the canoe is light. This method is informally referred to as the "Capistrano flip." Two paddlers with practice can do this with most standard canoes.

The key to success in attempting the Capistrano flip is, once the canoe is capsized and swamped, to get as much air as possible trapped under the inverted hull. The procedure is as follows:

1. Get alongside the capsized canoe and put on your life-jackets. (The lifejackets will give you added buoyancy to help hold you at the surface during the thrust.)
2. Turn the canoe upside down over yourselves.
3. Trap air under the hull.
4. Lift one gunwale slightly to break the suction.
5. Give a strong kick and push up on the gunwales.
6. At the top of the thrust, push harder with one arm than the other, thus causing the canoe to be flipped over in midair, landing alongside you.

If the flip is done properly, the canoe will land almost empty and ready for reboarding.

Emptying a Canoe at Shore or Dock

Emptying a canoe at shore or dock may be difficult and may also damage the canoe unless you use suitable methods. Several methods are described and illustrated in this section. Situations that differ from these may be handled by adapting the principles given here to the specific situation.

At Shore or in Shallow Water

A canoe can be emptied in shallow water by two persons. The craft should first be lifted by its ends. If it is bottom-up, it should be rolled sideward as the lift begins. This action breaks the suction and makes the lift easier. If the canoe is in the swamped position initially, it should be rolled sideward before you begin the lift, so that it is lifted out of the water without your lifting any of the water. When it is empty, turn it right-side-up and set it down on the water or carry it ashore.

To empty the canoe in shallow water by yourself, move it parallel to shore in about 18 inches of water. Stand on the off-shore side and roll the inshore gunwale toward you, gently lifting the canoe out of the water.

Continue to lift, with one shoulder under the gunwale if necessary, until the canoe is entirely free of the water. Then rest the lower gunwale on one knee and set the canoe back on the water.

One person may also empty a canoe in shallow water by getting under it in water of about waist depth and lifting it clear of the water and then turning it over with a rolling motion, upright onto the water. This method is much the same as the "Capistrano flip," except, of course, that you are standing on the bottom in the former maneuver. This lifting and righting of the canoe should be accomplished using legs and shoulder and arm muscles and keeping the back straight, thus avoiding strain.

Another method of emptying a canoe alone at shore is to float the swamped canoe in to shore until one end touches bottom at

the water's edge. If the end in deep water is depressed a little, the other end will go farther up onto the beach. Grasp the deep-water end slowly and without any lift, roll the canoe over onto its side. Then lift the canoe out of the water without lifting any water, so that only the end of the canoe is touching the shore. When all the water is drained out, roll the canoe upright and set it down on the water.

At a Dock

If a canoe is to be emptied at a dock, the procedure may be carried out if you follow the principles of emptying the swamped canoe over another canoe, as discussed later in this chapter.

Another method is as follows: With the canoe in the right-side-up position, lift one end slowly and gently, permitting the water to run out. The canoe will slide out of the water without trapping and lifting any water inside. Bring the end in over the dock, at which point a partner can help. When the end is in over the dock not more than 3 or 4 feet, roll the canoe over (bottom up).

Continue hauling in until the canoe is out of the water and in a balanced position. The canoe can then be turned upright and carried away or carried in its present position to a place where it can be set down on the dock or on a rack; or it can be launched.

Another way to empty a canoe at a dock is to grasp the far gunwale near amidships as the swamped canoe lies alongside the dock and gently roll the canoe toward the dock. Then, standing up, lift the canoe just enough to let the end of the bow and the end of the stern overlap the edge of the dock. Resume rolling the canoe until it is out of the water and up on the dock. Continue the roll until the canoe rests upside down on one gunwale and its ends.

Aluminum canoes with buoyancy chambers in their ends may be easily emptied at a dock if you lift one end of the canoe and gradually roll it bottom up so that it is supported on the water by the buoyancy chamber in its other end. By keeping the near end high, you can roll the canoe upright without taking in any great amount of water.

Self-Rescue on a River

The rescue of yourself, others, *and* equipment is very important on rivers. The following information relating to rivers contains much detail on the rescue of equipment and describes
tactics related only to river situations. Some of this detail will
be briefly touched upon in Chapter 10, "River Canoeing," as a
reminder to perhaps reread this entire section.

For practice, roll the canoe over in a safe current. Self-rescue
methods should be practiced so that capsizing is relegated to the
category of incident rather than emergency.

Capsize Rescue

In whitewater, a few spills are inevitable. *All* canoeists should
be well practiced in rescuing themselves and others while paddling rivers. The first consideration if a capsize does occur is
that of the safety of people in the water. The canoe and equipment should receive attention only after the persons in the water
are taken care of.

The reasons for capsizes in rivers vary, but regardless of the
reason, proper methods must be used *quickly* to avoid serious
injury to the canoeists in the water and damage to the equipment.

Overboard paddlers must get to the *upstream end* of the
canoe and stow their paddles in order to have both hands free.
Going hand-over-hand along the gunwale or scrambling right
across the boat, they must get there fast! Failure to do this could
result in their being trapped against a rock by the canoe. The
forces on a canoe that is pinned on a rock by a 5 m.p.h. current
can total 2,100 pounds. The force of this weight is enough to

crush and render helpless an unfortunate paddler. Getting to
the upstream end of the canoe lessens the potential of being
trapped and is one of the most important safety rules in river
canoeing.

Once at the upstream end, you can kick to get the canoe parallel to the current. In this way, it is more likely to get through
the rocks safely. Then you can try to kick the upstream end into
an eddy, a sort of back ferry (see chapter 10). If you succeed,
you can salvage your own canoe.

Hold onto your canoe. The exceptions to this rule are rare.
With it properly downstream of you, the canoe is your biggest
and best life preserver, even though you are wearing a lifejacket.
You will not submerge as easily, you will be easier to spot, and
you will be a bigger target for a rope thrower. If you receive a
rope, snub it at the extreme upstream end of the canoe. Never
tie it. Hold onto the doubled rope so that you can let it slip
if this rescue attempt goes amiss. If you are unable to hold the
canoe, let it go and allow the rope to swing you to shore.

In bitterly cold water, you may have only a minute or so of strength left. Abandon all else and strike out for shore as fast as you can, to avoid a life-threatening situation.

Sometimes there is no choice about holding on. If you are thrown clear, or if the canoe pins in against an obstruction and you are swept clear, ride on your back, feet downstream and at the surface. Keep your hips and feet up, otherwise you may do somersaults and could hit underwater obstructions. Try to slow yourself down and get into an eddy, where you can wait for rescue or climb out. *Never* try to stand up in fast-moving current or in a chute unless the water is too shallow for swimming. Try to get into an eddy or slow-moving water *before* standing up. If you have a long swim to shore in swift current, remember that your swimming speed may be only a quarter or a tenth of the speed of the current. In this case, swim straight toward shore without trying to go diagonally downstream or upstream. Do not aim for any particular rock or tree because it will soon be upstream, and you must not waste energy swimming to it. If someone throws you a rope, you may be lucky enough to have it land across your body, so that you can grab it before it sinks. Be ready for a tremendous pull when the slack is gone. Just hold on; do not tie the rope, because you may have to let go. (Lifejackets should be form-fitting to permit ease in swimming, thus giving less drag.)

When you get ashore, you should put on dry clothes, especially in cold weather. Other canoeists can usually contribute sweaters and pants. If you must wear wet clothes, make sure to wring them out thoroughly before putting them back on. You can often get warm again by paddling. If you have only one set of dry clothes, save it for the end of the day unless there is a threat of hypothermia. (See "Hypothermia" in chapter 8.)

Eskimo Roll

The Eskimo roll is a method of self-rescue for paddlers using *decked boats*. Although the method is useful for righting an open boat, its main purpose is to effect a *complete* rescue of a decked boat, enabling the paddlers to continue on their way. Since an upset can occur at just about any time while on whitewater, every person using a canoe or a kayak should acquire this necessary skill.

The rolls described here relate directly to the canoe and use somewhat different techniques than those used for the kayak roll (see chapter 15).

Because of the differences in the center of gravity and the wider beam of the canoe as compared to the kayak, the canoe is a bit more difficult to roll. The Eskimo roll done with a canoe requires more effort and different techniques, as described below. It must be pointed out that the methods shown here are only two of a variety of ways in which to do a canoe roll, and the description and diagrams are included only to show the principles involved. To save time and energy, you should learn the roll under competent supervision and with a helper in the water who can assist you in rolling back up.

Of the two techniques described below, the push roll is probably easier to accomplish than the draw roll but is somewhat more complex, since it requires more paddle manipulation.

Neither the draw roll nor the push roll will be successful if the rhythm of the stroke is broken or the application of the necessary power is lost. In these instances, the boat will tend to settle back to its original upside-down position. If you do not lean far enough to *the side* at the end of the roll, the attempt will be unsuccessful. Bending toward the deck is one of the worst errors of novices. You should rotate about your spine so that when you bend, you bend toward the water. Your forehead should leave the water last.

There are other methods of accomplishing an Eskimo roll. Choose the one best suited to you and master it *before* venturing onto whitewater in a decked canoe.

The Push Roll

The push roll will enable you to get the best leverage and to more efficiently apply the power at your disposal. It also will give you the longest effective stroke and the lowest possible center of gravity after your body emerges from the water.

Note in the illustrations that initially the paddler is leaning far to his off-side and, later in the maneuver, that he is leaning radically to his paddling side. He accomplishes this change by quickly snapping his hips and legs (canoe attached) under his body while he uses his arms and shoulders to push his torso out of the water with the paddle.

Once the canoe is upside down, the paddler sweeps the paddle from the bow to abeam on his off-side. In so doing, he keeps the power face of the blade down and provides a sculling force to begin the righting moment.

This action will bring the paddler's body nearly to the surface. When the paddle reaches a point abeam of the paddler, he pulls it down slightly and quickly rotates it so that the back face is then down.

Then without breaking the rhythm of the stroke, he continues to push down (and slightly forward).

At the same time, he snaps his hips under him and leans radically toward his paddling side as his back and torso emerge from the water.

A final push should enable him to bring his shoulders and head from the water to a normal paddling position.

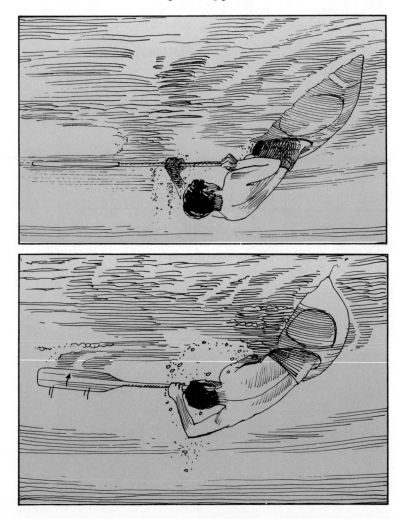

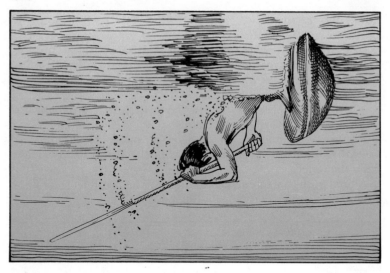

The Draw Roll

The following illustrations show that at its beginning the draw roll is similar to the push roll. The difference is that in the draw roll the paddle is not rotated but is kept in the initial position, using the power face of the blade throughout the stroke.

The roll is started with the paddler sweeping from the bow. After reaching a position directly abeam of his off-side, he vigorously pulls in a drawing motion with the paddle.

At the same time, he snaps his hips under him. Again, he must lean radically toward his paddling side.

He brings his shoulders and, finally, his head, out only after giving a last forceful thrust when the boat is nearly upright.

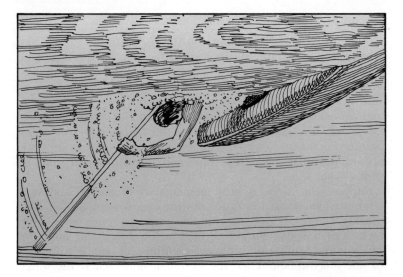

Noncapsize Rescue

When the canoe is stationary on the rocks and no capsize has taken place, the water rushes against it, rises up the side, and eventually pours in. It pours in most readily when the canoe is broadside but it will also pour in at the end when the canoe is in line with the current. You must quickly jump out *upstream* and hold the gunwale up so that water cannot come in. Lift the canoe off the rocks and hold it in the current by the stern painter so that it is parallel with the current, while you get back aboard (bowman first). It is important for you to wear shoes to protect your feet.

Suppose the canoe is held momentarily broadside against a large boulder. Lean the canoe downstream toward the boulder quickly, before the river flows in and traps the canoe against the rock. The bowman should perform a low brace and hold the canoe into a leaning position, even sculling his paddle from side to side downstream. Then the sternman must act. If the water is too deep or the current is too fast for him to jump out upstream, he might jump onto the rock. The bow would then be swept down, and the canoe would pivot and go past. If the sternman has the painter in his hand, he may pull the canoe back into the eddy behind the rock and get in. If the rock is awash and slippery, it is better for the sternman to throw his weight forward so that the current can push harder on the bow and pivot the canoe around the rock.

Sometimes the bow will slide up on a rock, and the canoe will stop and then swing stern-downstream. It may slide free by itself, or you can push it free with your paddle. Do not get rattled because you are running rapids backward. Both paddlers simply look over their shoulders. When you get to a good, big, safe eddy, get the canoe straightened out.

If you ship water and feel it sloshing about your knees, great care is needed so that you do not roll over. Brace, backpaddle, and get into an eddy for dumping. You have much better control of your destiny while upright and with your paddles in action. If the water finally fills the canoe completely, get out even though you could stay upright. Let the canoe ride high so that it is less likely to be pinned on rocks.

RESCUE OF OTHERS

Flatwater Situations

A canoe is not essentially a rescue craft. Except in the hands of a skilled canoeist, it is somewhat sensitive and unstable for general rescue purposes. A rowboat or motorboat is the proper craft for rescue in most flatwater situations. In some cases, however, a drowning person far from shore may be reached more quickly by a canoe manned by a skillful paddler. Of course, when a canoe is the only craft on hand in an emergency, the rescue should be undertaken by anyone sufficiently skilled to use it. As your skill in paddling and self-rescue develops, you should gradually develop your competence to help or rescue others. Experience has shown that the rescue methods mentioned here are efficient, adaptable, and not difficult to learn.

Tired-Swimmer Rescue

Keep your eyes on a swimmer who is too far from shore. If the person appears to be getting tired, paddle alongside and offer help. Rather than coming all the way in, head-on, and letting the tired swimmer hold onto the bow—where he will be out of your reach—turn broadside to the swimmer and extend your paddle. Then you will have the victim at the widest part of the canoe, where you can control both him and the canoe.

Note that in the illustrations the canoeist is relying heavily on the use of the paddle to stabilize the canoe. It may be wiser for most paddlers to sit down in the bottom of the canoe before making contact with the swimmer, so that they would be ready to brace against any unexpected attempt of an excited, tired swimmer to climb aboard before being told to do so. Placing a hand on the swimmer's shoulder will keep him from boarding before he is instructed to do so.

In many instances, you might only find it necessary to allow the tired swimmer to hold onto the gunwale for a brief period of rest and then to accompany him while he swims to shore. In some cases, it may be wise to give him a tow; that is, to paddle the canoe to shore while the swimmer holds onto the gunwale. This would be the best course when shore is reasonably close and also when the swimmer is too heavy to take aboard safely.

When the victim is very tired, far from shore, and not too heavy, you may allow him to climb aboard. He should climb in

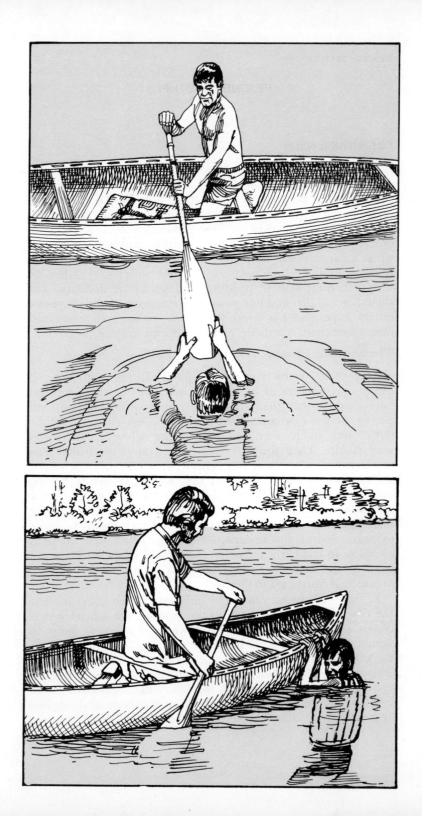

near amidships, where the canoe is widest. You may help with
one hand while stabilizing the canoe with the other. Once
aboard, the rescued person should sit in the bottom amidships
while being paddled to shore.

Helpless-Victim Rescue

A very tired swimmer who cannot help in his own rescue will
have to be lifted into the canoe—or, if he is too heavy for that,
he will have to be tied or held to the canoe while being towed
to shore. This method should be used also for unconscious but
breathing victims and for victims who have become asphyxiated.
If you are unusually skilled in canoeing, you may lift the victim
in over the gunwale if he is not too heavy. You should practice

this skill sufficiently so that when used in a real situation it will not result in swamping or capsizing the canoe. The first step is to place the victim's arms over the gunwale, and then you enter the boat. The next step is to grasp the victim by his arms, near the armpits, and lift his trunk in over the gunwale until, by jackknifing, you can let the victim down into the canoe. Lift the victim's legs in and position his body as comfortably as possible in the bottom. If he is merely very tired or is unconscious but breathing sufficiently, you should paddle him to shore, where further help will be available. A tandem crew could lift the victim into the canoe more easily than could one man. The principles for two people would be the same except that with one person lifting on each side, the job would be easier,

since the rescuers could work from kneeling rather than standing positions.

If the victim is too heavy to lift, you may lash his wrists together under a thwart and tow him to shore. Make sure his face is kept clear of the water at all times. A tandem crew would make the rescue simpler: one person could hold the victim's forearms in over the gunwale while the other paddled the canoe to shore and help.

Recovery of a Submerged Victim

In some instances it may be necessary for you to go overboard to recover a submerged victim. You should use a method that permits the canoe to remain under control, because if the canoe

blows away or is carried away by a current while you are
rescuing the submerged victim, both you and the victim will be
in danger. A tandem crew will not have trouble in this respect,
because one canoeist can dive overboard for the victim while the
other keeps the canoe under control nearby. If you are paddling
solo, make a loop at the eye of the bow painter and place it
around your ankle, making sure that the painter is not led under
a thwart. Or better still, if there is a long length of line in the
canoe, loop it around one of your shoulders and under the opposite armpit. With either of these rigs, you may then go overboard, recover the victim, bring him to the side of the canoe,
and administer mouth-to-mouth resuscitation if necessary. This

can be given either in the water or from the boat with little
loss of time. Once the victim is breathing on his own and you
are aboard, lift him into the canoe, if possible, or lash his wrists
under a thwart while towing him to shore as discussed above.

An alternate method of keeping the canoe from drifting in a
wind is to swamp the canoe prior to diving for the victim.
Mouth-to-mouth resuscitation of the victim can be given by
bringing him right into the swamped canoe with you, then
positioning him. NOTE. A canoe should never be deliberately
swamped in a river situation. If the shore is nearby, the canoe

could just as easily be beached prior to the attempt to recover a trapped or submerged victim.

Towing a Canoe

Towing a canoe is not a common practice, but once in a while towing may be helpful and wise. For example, a strong head-wind may make it impossible for children of camp age to make headway by paddling. If their ultimate objective is to windward and if overall program planning calls for them to arrive at a certain time, towing would be sensible.

The towing motorboat should be handled by a skilled operator who operates his craft safely. A towing shackle, or some other

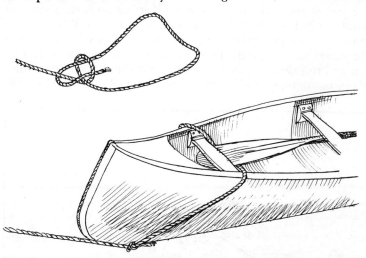

means to provide a pull from waterline level, should be used. A waterline-level tow will keep the canoe riding with its bow slightly higher than its stern, thus eliminating the possibility of its burying into a wave and being swamped, or running off course and being capsized. If more than one canoe is being towed, the canoes should be towed in single file, using the towing bridle on each canoe. The motorboat operator should proceed at moderate-to-slow speed, in accordance with how rough the water is. Towing speed should be no greater than paddling speed.

Canoe-Over-Canoe Rescue

If you see a canoe capsize, your first concern should be for the canoeists. Rescue of their canoe and equipment is secondary,

although nearly always the operation may be carried on as a
whole. First, call to the victims, directing them to remain with
their canoe and to hold onto it for support. Approach the capsized canoe quickly but calmly, coming alongside, parallel to it.
Either side will be satisfactory unless there is a strong tide or
current, in which case the downwind side or the upstream side is
best. Direct the victims, if there are two, to hold onto the ends
of your canoe, one at each end. Hold the capsized canoe alongside with your paddle blade.

When you are satisfied that the victims are safe and will remain in their places until they are given further instructions,
proceed to rescue their canoe. If the canoe is upside down, grasp
the keel of the overturned canoe, or if it has no keel, place your
hands on its bottom, and roll it slowly toward you. When the far
gunwale is within reach, grasp it with your other hand and roll
the canoe to the upright position. Take paddles and other gear
out and put them in the bottom of your canoe. Pull your canoe
ahead or astern, grasp the end of the swamped canoe, and lift the

end slowly up across your canoe, not more than 2 or 3 feet. Then
roll the canoe bottom-up and draw it across your canoe until it
is resting empty on the gunwales in a balanced position. Then
roll it rightside up and slide it back onto the water.

To get the crew back into their canoe, place both canoes side by side, holding their gunwales tightly together with the outwale of the rescued craft under that of the rescuing craft unless excessive tumblehome prevents. Have the victims climb aboard one at a time. The first one in may help you hold the two canoes together while the other climbs in. When both are aboard, return their paddles and other gear.

NOTE. If the canoe should capsize or swamp in a river, every effort should be directed toward getting the canoe to shore once the paddles are rescued. The canoe-over-canoe rescue should be resorted to only if the distance to shore is great, if the shoreline is inaccessible, or if the rescue must be made immediately. Also, this rescue method can be used, with some alterations, if both canoes are capsized.

River Situations

Almost everyone wants to be a hero and rescue someone, but few will learn or practice the skills in advance to be able to carry them out properly. This lack of preparation often results in a safety hazard to all concerned.

Rope-throw rescues are common where canoes or people are stopped by rocks and where rope throwers are posted in advance. The throwing line should be about 60 feet long. The use of ⅜-inch rope is recommended, not for the rope's strength but for its ease of handling. Manila is good, but polypropylene floats, is brighter in color, and does not rot—although it is more slippery for tying knots and for holding onto. Do not put ring buoys or even monkey fists on the end. They are too likely to be caught between rocks.

A manila line should be wetted, coiled in clockwise loops, and tied in two coils to a thwart at the start of the trip. You throw one coil and an end, and the second coil feeds off your other hand, with the remaining end being securely tied or held. Make sure the free end is facing forward on both coils. Underhand throws give better accuracy, but bushes sometimes make a side-arm throw necessary.

Aim is all-important. If your target moves with the current, you must throw slightly downstream of it. The rope should fall downstream of victims, because they will be looking downstream in most instances. However, it should be within arm's reach so that it can be grabbed before it sinks. The victims are less likely to miss the throw if they are floating on their backs with feet on the surface, or if they are at the upstream end of a canoe. If, however, they are on a rock, aim just upstream so that the current will take the rope to them.

When the swimmer takes hold of the rope and the river takes up the slack, there will be a tremendous pull. The rope, or the rescuer and the rope, will be dragged into the river unless a good belay is used. Put the rope around your hips at belt level and sit down quickly at a spot where you can brace your feet. Your left hand on the rope to the swimmer is used for feeling the action of the rope and your right hand is used for braking. The friction of the rope around your body will aid in holding the rope. (Necessary friction can also be gained by be-

laying the rope around a tree instead of your body.) If additional rope is needed, do not permit it to slide through your hand, since it may get away from you and cause a rope burn. Instead, feed it out carefully. This is the hip belay used by mountain climbers, and it is an essential skill.

When carrying out a river rescue, *go after people first* and do not worry about their canoe until you are sure they are safe. If they are being swept down the river, you might possibly chase them with another canoe. Perhaps you can take them aboard or push them into an eddy. Rescue with a closed boat is simply a matter of enabling the victim to grab the stern-end loop or toggle and to drape himself over the stern deck, and paddling him to shore. If the water is very cold, the rescue is not complete when you get victims ashore. They may be so weak from cold that they are completely helpless. You will have to put dry clothes on them and get them warmed up with a fire, with a warm non-alcoholic drink, or in any way you can devise. Hypothermia (see chapter 8) is an ever-present danger when canoeing in cold weather and/or cold water. When the people are safe, look after their canoe. Perhaps the most common type of canoe rescue (if the canoe has been separated from the paddlers) is to chase the victim's canoe down with another canoe, pick up the rescued canoe's painter, and tow the craft to a safe spot. Remember that the two boats must not be tied together. You must be able to release the tow line in case of impending danger.

Everyone should watch for paddles floating free. Once such paddles are gone, canoeists may not catch up to them again.

Canoes that have large flotation tanks at the ends can be emptied if there is a rock where a person can stand. Otherwise, get the canoe to shallow, standing-depth water and empty the water out toward shore or downstream.

If the river is wide and there are no frequent rapids in the area, a canoe-over-canoe rescue is practical (even in current and waves). The rescue canoe must be across the upstream end of the swamped canoe. The victims should go hand-over-hand to opposite ends of the rescue canoe so as not to get caught on the downstream side of it. The bowman of the rescue canoe keeps the craft perpendicular to the swamped canoe, braces it, and leans it down to help the sternman get the end of the upset canoe over his gunwale singlehanded. From here, the rescue is completed just as described earlier for the canoe-over-canoe rescue. When empty, the rescued canoe is pushed back downstream. The rescued canoeists return to their canoe hand-over-hand along the gunwale (they should not swim) and climb in. The rescuing canoeists check to see that the former victims have two paddles and then back the rescue canoe away to give them paddling room. Prior practice of this skill is a must to insure smooth performance in an emergency.

Salvage of canoes pinned in rocks is not uncommon. Once pinned there, the canoe is undergoing stresses and forces almost beyond belief. The quicker the canoe can be rescued, the less chance there is for irreparable damage.

The illustrations that follow show three different situations, the first of which is the least likely to cause much damage. In this illustration, the canoe can be easily rolled and lifted out of the water and away from the rock. The other two instances show increasing force holding the canoe against the rock. Remember that when fully submerged, a 15-foot canoe in a 5-m.p.h. current is withstanding 2,100 pounds of force. There is a way to use some of this great force to advantage when lifting or rolling by hand fails. It involves raising one end of the canoe while barrel-rolling the canoe upstream. This is probably the most effective use of a $\frac{1}{2}$-inch rescue line, because of the way it is placed. When in place and under tension, the line exerts pressure on the whole canoe so that the keel, gunwales, hull, and thwart share the strain of the pull.

Begin by attaching a line to a painter on the end of the canoe most likely to be the upstream end when freed, and secure it on shore. Next, use the rescue line to roll the canoe by attaching

219

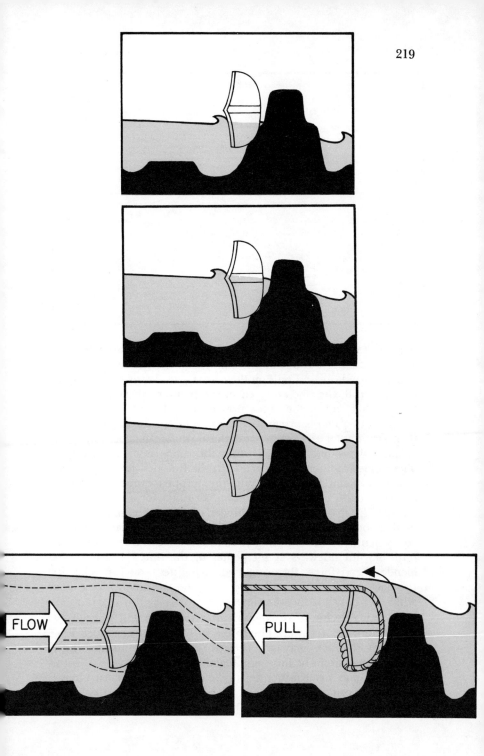

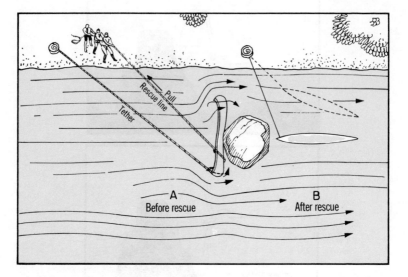

A
Before rescue

B
After rescue

the line to the thwart nearest to the rock after passing it over and around the bottom of the canoe as shown. Then get your manpower ashore and pull on the rescue line. As the canoe begins to barrel roll, the line attached to the painter can be hauled on to pull that end of the canoe upstream so that the force of the water on that end is progressively less. The upstream end should then rise out of the water, and the downstream end can then be pushed around the rock while the canoe is rolled upright. The canoe can then be rescued with the line tied to the painter.

You may not be able to pull the trapped canoe free. Some canoeing clubs carry a "come along" or other form of block and tackle. The snap rings, or carabiners, of the rock climber can be used as pulleys to gain a mechanical advantage. Lacking such equipment, you can try tying your line to a stout tree. When you push or pull sideways at the center of the line, there is a tremendous end force. By using two such lines, you can take up the slack on one while pulling sideways on the other. The canoe will move only a little each time.

You may decide to tie your painter to a tree and come back when the water is lower. The forces will then be very much less. However, the rocks may have chewed "mouse holes" in the canoe, or the canoe might be missing altogether.

Canoes may need minor repair before continuing. An aluminum canoe can often be pushed back into shape by putting it on a grassy spot and having several people stand on it. If there are tears in the skin or pulled rivets, waterproof duct tape, from your "maintenance" kit, will stop the leaks and last out your trip. A fiberglass canoe can be patched temporarily with 2- or 3-inch duct tape. On long trips you should also carry glass cloth, resin, and catalyst.

Rescues are very common. You will learn a lot about them as you gain experience in whitewater canoeing. They can be a daily occurrence and can be part of the fun—when *all* canoeists know how to carry out appropriate rescues and practice proper techniques.

8

ARTIFICIAL RESPIRATION AND FIRST AID

Because the Red Cross helps to prevent injury and loss of life by teaching people the skills necessary for their greater enjoyment of water activities, this chapter is included in this book. It is intended only as a reference or review of those procedures that might be necessary in the event of injury or sudden illness. Since canoeists frequently paddle in areas far from immediate medical attention, it should be the concern of all canoeists to be able to care for themselves and others. Therefore, it is recommended that a Red Cross first aid course be taken, under the competent supervision of a first aid instructor.

ARTIFICIAL RESPIRATION

Because of the environment, canoeists may encounter life-threatening situations that involve stoppage of breathing. The dangers of prolonged submersion, electrical shock, and carbon monoxide poisoning are of special concern to the canoeist.

Weak swimmers and nonswimmers should wear a lifesaving device at all times when on or about the water, and precautions should be taken to prevent anyone from falling overboard.

Extreme care must be exercised around boats in handling electrical tools or appliances that are operated by current from shore-based powerlines. Even low-voltage systems can produce a fatal shock when directly grounded to the water. This is primarily a hazard around boat liveries and camps. Also, there is a danger of being struck by lightning. Such an occurrence could cause cessation of breathing and other injuries.

Cases of carbon monoxide poisoning have occurred in an open motorboat, outboard-powered canoes, and auxiliary sailboats while under power and moving downwind. With boat speed and wind speed approximately the same, exhaust fumes may be drawn up and over the transom and into the after section of the boat.

When heaters, other than the electric and catalytic type, are used to warm up enclosed areas, they should be equipped with fans to carry the smoke and fumes out of the area where they are being used. The area should be kept ventilated at all times in order to replenish the oxygen supply.

Charcoal cookers and heaters without flues are especially hazardous in enclosed areas. Since little smoke or flame is noted, the tasteless and odorless but deadly carbon monoxide can quickly change a small, poorly ventilated area into a gas chamber.

Victims of injury or sudden illnesses, such as heart failure, who stop breathing or have difficulty in breathing need immediate help. They may turn blue (or cherry red in the case of gas poisoning) and quickly lose consciousness. Because of its simplicity and effectiveness, the mouth-to-mouth method of resuscitation is recommended for all cases requiring artificial respiration. Such respiration can be given immediately after rescue—even in water of standing depth or if adequate support is used—and does not depend upon special equipment for its application. If the directions given below are carefully followed, the lungs of a nonbreathing victim can be, in most cases, adequately ventilated.

1. Clear the mouth of any obvious foreign matter.
2. Tilt the head back so that the chin is pointing upward. This maneuver should provide for an open airway by moving the tongue away from the back of the throat. (If additional clearance is needed later, it may be necessary to pull or push the jaw upward into a jutting-out position.)

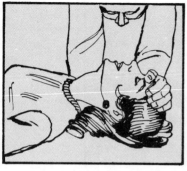 

3. Open your mouth widely and place it tightly over the mouth of the victim. Pinch the victim's nostrils shut and blow into his mouth. If the airway is clear, only a moderate resistance to the blowing effort will be felt, and the victim's chest will visibly expand.

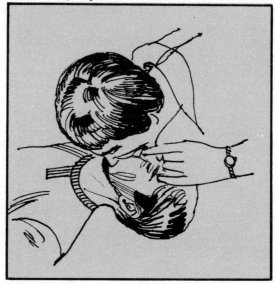

4. Remove your mouth and allow the air to escape. Repeat the blowing effort.

For an adult, blow vigorously at the rate of about 12 breaths per minute. For a child, take relatively shallow breaths 20 times a minute. For an infant or small child, place your mouth over the mouth and nose and give shallow puffs of air about 20 times a minute.

If resistance to the blowing effort is experienced, recheck the head position and hold the jaw forward.

If the airway should remain blocked, quickly turn the victim onto his side and administer several sharp blows between the shoulder blades in the hope of dislodging foreign matter. Clear the mouth while the victim is still on his side. Infants and small children should be suspended head downward when an attempt is made to clear the airway.

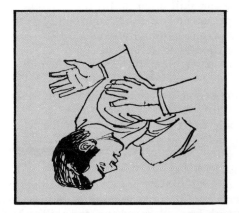

Keep the victim lying down during and after treatment and avoid chilling or overheating of his body. Most successfully treated cases of prolonged submersion respond in a matter of minutes, but stoppage of breathing caused by electric shock, drugs, and gas poisoning may require ventilation of the lungs for a matter of hours. Medical attention in all instances should be sought as soon as possible.

EMERGENCY FIRST AID

Proper knowledge and skill in first aid are particularly necessary for those individuals who are responsible for the safety of others who are in their party. The application of first aid knowledge and skill often means the difference between temporary and permanent disability and the difference between rapid recovery and long hospitalization.

First aid training is of value in—

• Teaching prevention and care in accidental injury or sudden illness.
• Training people to care for those caught in natural disaster or other catastrophe.
• Equipping individuals to deal with the whole situation, the person, and the injury.
• Helping the first-aider to distinguish between what to do and what not to do.

The limitation of time in case of an accident or sudden illness may be so critical in terms of minutes, or even seconds, that only a person with first aid knowledge and skills who is on hand has any opportunity to prevent a fatal outcome. The first aid trained individual may encounter a variety of problem situations. The first-aider's decisions and actions will vary according to the circumstances that produced the accident or sudden illness and according to the number of persons involved, the immediate environment, the availability of medical assistance, emergency dressings and equipment, and help from others. The first-aider will need to adapt what he or she has learned to the situation at hand, or to improvise. Sometimes, prompt action is needed to save a life. At other times, there is no need for haste, and efforts will be directed toward preventing further injury, obtaining assistance, and reassuring the victim, who may be emotionally upset and apprehensive as well as in pain.

General Directions for Giving First Aid

In case of serious injury or sudden illness, while help is being summoned, the first-aider should give immediate attention to the following first aid priorities:

- Effect a prompt rescue.
- Make sure that the victim has an open airway and give mouth-to-mouth or mouth-to-nose artificial respiration, if necessary.
- Control severe bleeding.
- Give first aid for poisoning or ingestion of harmful chemicals.

Once emergency measures have been taken to insure the victim's safety, carry out the following procedures:

- Do *not* move a victim unless it is necessary for safety reasons.
- Keep the victim in the position best suited to his condition or injuries; do not let the victim get up or walk about.
- Protect the victim from unnecessary manipulation and disturbance.
- Avoid or overcome chilling by using blankets or covers, if available.

If exposure to cold or dampness is likely, place blankets or additional clothing over and under the victim.

- Determine the injuries or cause of sudden illness. After immediate problems are under control—
  1. Find out exactly what happened. Information may be obtained from the victim or from persons who were present and saw the accident, or in the case of sudden illness, saw the individual collapse.
  2. Look for an emergency medical identification, such as a card or a bracelet, which may provide a clue to the victim's condition.
  3. If the victim is unconscious and has *no* sign of external injury, and if the above methods fail to provide identity, try to obtain proper identification either from papers carried in the victim's billfold or purse or from bystanders, so that relatives may be notified. (It is advisable to have a witness when searching for identification.)
- Examine the victim methodically but be guided by the kind of accident or sudden illness and the needs of the situation. Have a reason for what you do. In general, proceed as follows:
  1. Loosen constricting clothing but do not pull on the victim's belt, in case spinal injuries are present.
  2. Open or remove clothing if necessary to expose a body part in order to make a more accurate check for injuries. Clothing may be cut away or ripped at the seams, but utmost

caution must be used, or added injury may result. Do not expose the victim unduly without protective cover, and use discretion if clothing must be removed.

3. Note the victim's general appearance, including skin discoloration, and check all symptoms that may give a clue to the injury or sudden illness. In the case of a victim with dark skin, change in skin color may be difficult to note. It may then be necessary to depend upon change in the color of the mucous membrane, or inner surface of the lips, mouth, and eyelids.

4. Check the victim's pulse. If you cannot feel it at the wrist, check for a pulse of the carotid artery at the side of the neck.

5. Check to see if the victim is awake, stuporous, or unconscious. Does the person respond to questions?

6. If the victim is unconscious, look for evidence of head injury. In a conscious person, look for paralysis of one side of the face or body. See if the victim shows evidence of a recent convulsion. (The tongue may be bitten, producing a laceration.)

7. Check the front of the victim's neck to determine whether he is a laryngectomee. A laryngectomee is a person whose larynx has been partially removed by surgery. Most laryngectomees carry a card or other identification stating that they cannot breathe through the nose or mouth. Do not block the stoma (air inlet) of a laryngectomee when carrying out other first aid, since blockage could cause death from asphyxiation.

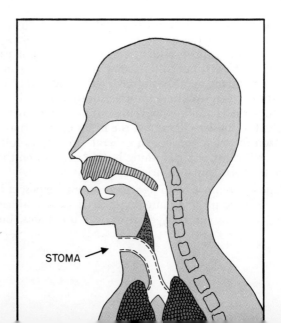

STOMA

8. If poisoning is suspected, check for stains or burns about the victim's mouth and a source of poisoning nearby, such as contaminated food, plants, and chemicals.

- Carry out the indicated first aid:

1. Apply emergency dressings, bandages, and splints, as indicated.

2. Do not move the victim unless it is absolutely necessary.

3. Plan action according to the nature of the accident or sudden illness, the needs of the situation, and the availability of human and material resources.

4. Utilize proper first aid measures and specific techniques that, under the circumstances, appear to be reasonably necessary.

5. Remain in charge until the victim can be turned over to qualified persons (for example, a physician, an ambulance crew, a rescue squad, or a police officer), or until the victim can take care of himself or can be placed in care of relatives.

6. Do not attempt to make a diagnosis of any sort or to discuss a victim's condition with bystanders or reporters.

7. Above all, as a first aid worker, know the limits of your capabilities and make every effort to avoid further injury to the victim in your attempt to provide the best possible emergency first aid care.

First Aid for Severe Bleeding

When blood is spurting or gushing from a wound, it must be controlled immediately, or death will result within a few minutes.

Direct Pressure and Elevation

Direct pressure by hand over a dressing is the preferred method for the control of severe bleeding. In an emergency, in the absence of compresses, the bare hand or fingers may be used, but only until a compress can be applied.

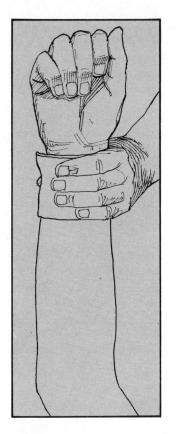 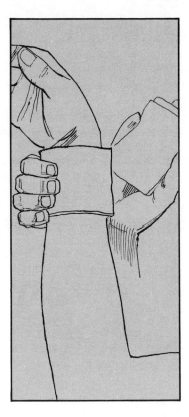

On most parts of the body, a pressure bandage can be placed to hold pads of cloth over a severely bleeding open wound and free the hands of the first-aider for other emergency action.

Also elevate (raise the affected part to a level higher than the heart) if there are no fractures or if additional pain or harm will not be inflicted.

If blood soaks through the entire pad without clotting, do not remove the pad but add additional layers. Do not disturb blood clots after they have formed within the cloth.

If direct pressure does not control the bleeding, apply pressure at the appropriate pressure point while maintaining pressure over the wound as well as continuing elevation. A pressure bandage can be applied over thicknesses of dressings to maintain constant pressure once bleeding is controlled.

If the bleeding is from a wound in the arm, apply pressure

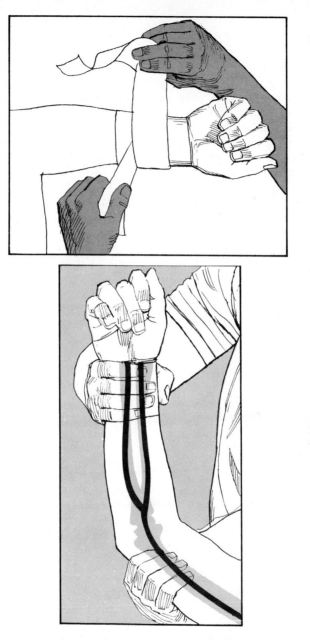

to the brachial artery. This pressure point is located on the inside of the arm, in the groove between the biceps and triceps,
about midway between the armpit and the elbow. Apply pressure by grasping the middle of the victim's upper arm, with

your thumb on the outside of the arm and your fingers on the inside. Press or pull your fingers toward your thumb, using the flat inside surface of your fingers, not your fingertips.

If the bleeding is from a wound in the leg, apply pressure to the femoral artery, pressing it against the pelvic bone. This pressure point is located on the front of the thigh, just below the middle of the crease of the groin where the artery crosses over the pelvic bone on its way to the leg.

Apply pressure by placing the heel of your hand directly over the spot described above. Lean forward with your arm straightened to apply the pressure (see illustration, top of page 233).

It is important when using the pressure points (brachial or femoral arteries) that you maintain pressure over the wound as well as elevation (see illustration, bottom of page 233).

Tourniquet

If the above methods do not control severe bleeding and the victim is in danger of bleeding to death, the tourniquet may be used as a *last resort* to save.life.

The tourniquet should be used only for the severe life-threatening hemorrhage that cannot be controlled by other means. This method is used only on the arm or leg. Once a tourniquet is applied, care by a physician is imperative.

To apply the tourniquet—

1. Place the tourniquet just above the wound but not touching the wound edges. If the wound is in a joint area or just below, place the tourniquet directly above the joint.
2. Wrap the tourniquet band tightly twice around the limb and tie a half knot.
3. Place a short, strong stick (or similar object) on the half knot and tie a full knot.
4. Twist the stick until bleeding is stopped.
5. Secure the stick in place.
6. Attach a note to the victim giving the location of the tourniquet and the time that it was applied.
7. *Once the serious decision to apply the tourniquet has been made, the tourniquet should not be loosened except on the advice of a physician.*
8. Treat for shock and get medical attention for the victim immediately.

Do not cover a tourniquet.

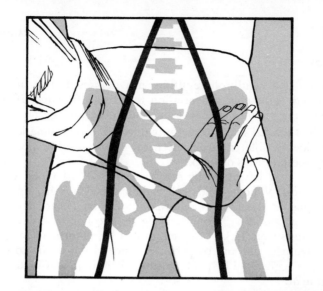

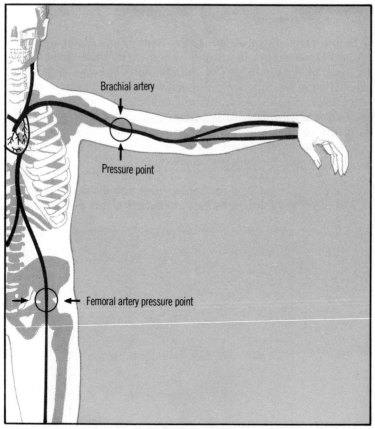

Brachial artery

Pressure point

Femoral artery pressure point

Shock

Shock is a condition resulting in a depressed state of many vital body functions, a depression that could threaten life even though the victim's injuries would not otherwise be fatal.

Injury-related shock, commonly referred to as traumatic shock, is decidedly different from electrical shock, insulin shock, and other special forms of shock.

Shock may be caused by severe injuries of all types: hemorrhage; loss of body fluids other than blood (as in prolonged vomiting or dysentery or burns); infection; heart attack or stroke; or poisoning by chemicals, gases, alcohol, or drugs. Shock also results from lack of oxygen, caused by abnormal changes in body temperature and by poor resistance of the victim to stress. Shock is aggravated by pain, by rough handling, and by delay in treatment.

Signs and Symptoms

In the early stages of shock, the body compensates for a decreased blood flow to the tissues by constricting the blood vessels in the skin, in the organs of the abdominal cavity, and in the skeletal muscles. The following signs may develop as a result:

- The skin is pale (or bluish) and cold to the touch. In the case of victims with dark skin, it may be necessary to rely primarily on the color of the mucous membranes on the inside of the mouth or under the eyelids, or on the color of the nail beds.
- The skin may be moist and clammy.
- The victim is weak.
- The pulse is usually quite rapid (over 100 beats per minute) and often too faint to be felt at the wrist, but perceptible in

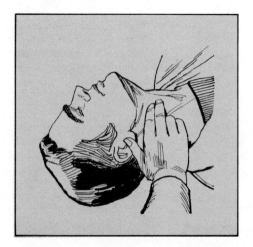

the carotid artery at the side of the neck. It can also be felt at the femoral artery in the groin.

- The rate of breathing is usually increased; it may be shallow, possibly deep and irregular.
- If there has been injury to the chest or abdomen, breathing will almost certainly be shallow, because of the pain involved in breathing deeply.
- A victim in shock from hemorrhage may be restless and anxious (early signs of oxygen lack), thrashing about, and complaining of severe thirst.
- The victim may vomit or retch from nausea.

If the victim's condition deteriorates, the following additional signs may be noted:

- The vicitim may become apathetic and relatively unresponsive.
- The victim's eyes may be sunken, with a vacant expression, and the pupils may be widely dilated.

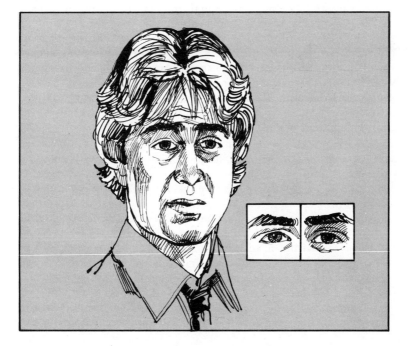

- Some of the blood vessels in the skin may be dilated, producing a mottled appearance, which indicates that the victim's blood pressure has fallen to a very low level.
- If untreated, the victim eventually loses consciousness, the body temperature falls, and the person may die.

Objectives of First Aid Care

Objectives of first aid care are to improve circulation of the blood, to insure an adequate supply of oxygen, and to maintain normal body temperature.

First Aid Procedures

Give urgently necessary first aid immediately to eliminate the causes of shock, such as stoppage of breathing, hemorrhaging, or severe pain.

Steps for preventing shock and for giving first aid are as follows:

1. Keep the victim lying down.
2. Cover the victim *only* enough to prevent loss of body heat.
3. Get medical help as soon as possible.

The body position for a victim must be based on the injuries. Generally, the most satisfactory position for the injured person will be that of lying down to improve the circulation of blood.

If injuries of the neck or lower spine are suspected, *do not* move the victim until he is properly prepared for transportation, unless it is necessary to protect him from further injury or to provide urgent first aid care.

A victim with severe wounds of the lower part of the face and jaw, or who is unconscious, should be placed on his side to allow drainage of fluids and to avoid blockage of the airway by vomitus and blood. Extreme care must be taken to insure an open airway and to prevent asphyxia. When there is no danger of aspiration of fluids, a victim who is having difficulty in breathing may be placed on his back with his head and shoulders raised.

A person with a head injury may be kept flat or propped up, but his head must not be lower than the rest of his body.

If you are in doubt concerning the proper position of the victim based on injuries sustained, keep him lying flat.

A victim in shock may improve if his feet (or the foot of the stretcher or bed) are raised from 8 to 12 inches. If a victim has

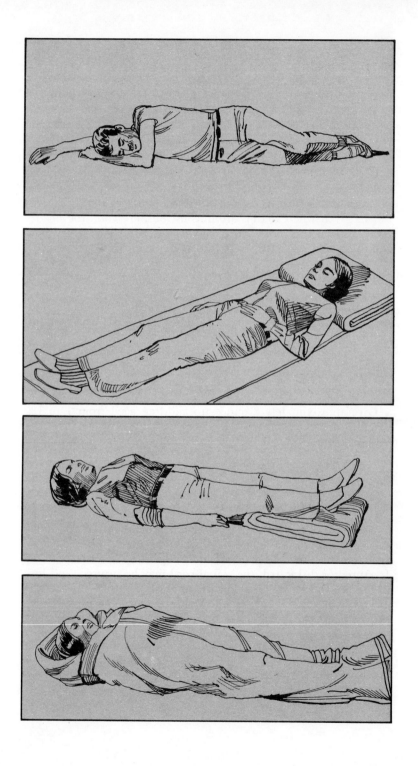

increased difficulty in breathing or experiences additional pain after his feet are raised, lower the feet again.

Keep the victim warm enough to avoid or overcome chilling. If he is exposed to cold or dampness, blankets or additional clothing should be placed over and under him to prevent chilling. No attempt should be made to add extra heat, because raising the surface temperature of the body is harmful.

Giving fluids by mouth has value in shock, but fluids should only be given when medical help or trained rescue personnel are not available within a reasonable time. However, fluids should not be given when victims are unconscious, are vomiting or are likely to vomit, or are having convulsions, since victims in such condition may aspirate fluids into the lungs.

Do not give fluids when a victim is likely to require surgery or general anesthetic, or when the person appears to have a brain injury or an abdominal injury.

Fluids may be given by mouth only if medical care is delayed for an hour or more and no contraindications exist. Water that is neither hot nor cold—preferably a salt-soda solution (containing 1 level teaspoonful of salt and ½ level teaspoonful of baking soda to each quart of water) should be given as follows:

- Give an adult victim about 4 ounces (½ glass) every 15 minutes.
- Give approximately 2 ounces to children aged from 1 to 12, and 1 ounce to infants of 1 year or less.
- Discontinue fluids if the victim becomes nauseated or vomits.

Spinal Injuries

Description and Characteristics

The backbone, or spinal column, is composed of 33 bones called vertebrae, in which the spinal cord is enclosed. If a vertebra, or one of the disks that separate the vertebrae, is fractured or dislocated, the spinal cord may be injured, and loss of motion and sensation below the level of the injury may result. Injury to the spinal cord should be suspected if the injured person is unable to move either his arms or legs after an accident or if he complains of numbness or pain.

With fracture or dislocation in the neck region, there is usually severe pain, spasm of the neck muscles, and difficulty in moving the head. There will be weakness and numbness below the level of the injury if the injury is slight, or paralysis and loss of sensation when damage is serious. Symptoms of fracture of the trunk region (upper and lower back) are similar to those associated with neck injury. There is pain at the affected site, which extends around the chest or abdomen or down the legs, along the course of the spinal nerves. There is also tenderness over the injury, muscle spasm, and weakness or paralysis and disturbance of sensation below the level of injury.

First Aid

If a spinal injury is suspected, extreme care should be taken to avoid any twisting, bending, or side-to-side motion of the victim's head and trunk. After rescue in a water accident, the victim should be kept floating in shallow water where possible, until trained personnel can be obtained. Needless to say, proper first aid must be given for other life-threatening injuries, such as stoppage of breathing or hemorrhage from an open wound. Keep the victim floating, with one hand supporting his shoulders and head while the other hand keeps his head immobile.

Burns

A burn is an injury that results from heat, chemical agents, or radiation. It may vary in depth, size, and severity, causing injury to the cells of the affected areas.

Classification

Burns are usually classified according to depth or degree of skin damage. Often the degree will differ in various parts of the same affected area.

First-degree burns are those resulting from overexposure to the sun, light contact with hot objects, or scalding by hot water or steam. The usual signs are redness or discoloration, mild swelling, and pain. Healing occurs rapidly.

Second-degree burns are those resulting from a very deep sunburn, contact with hot liquids, and flash burns from gasoline, kerosene, and other products. Second-degree burns are usually more painful than deeper burns in which the nerve endings in the skin are destroyed. The usual signs are greater depth than first-degree burns, red or mottled appearance, development of blisters, considerable swelling over a period of several days, and wet appearance of the surface of the skin due to the loss of plasma through the damaged layers of the skin.

Third-degree burns can be caused by a flame, ignited clothing, immersion in hot water, contact with hot objects, or electricity. Temperature and duration of contact are important factors in determining the extent of tissue destruction. The usual signs are deep tissue destruction, white or charred appearance (at first, possibly resembling a second-degree burn), and complete loss of all layers of the skin.

First Aid

The objective of first aid for burns is to relieve pain, prevent contamination, and treat for shock. The following chart gives the first aid advice for burns according to classification.

Burn	Do	Don't
First degree (redness, mild swelling, and pain)	• Use cold water application or submerge burned area in cold water. • Apply dry, sterile dressing. • Use additional home remedies as advised by physician.	• Apply butter, oleomargarine, etc.
Second degree (deeper than first degree, with blisters developing)	• Immerse in cold water. • Blot dry with sterile cloth. • Apply dry, sterile cloth for protection. • Treat for shock. • Obtain medical attention if severe.	• Break blisters. • Remove shreds of tissue. • Use antiseptic preparation, ointment, spray, or home remedy on severe burn.
Third degree (deeper destruction, with skin layers destroyed)	• Cover with sterile cloth to protect. • Treat for shock. • Watch for breathing difficulty. • Obtain medical attention quickly.	• Remove charred clothing that is stuck to burn. • Apply ice. • Use home medication.
Chemical burn	• Remove by flushing with large quantities of water for at least 5 minutes. • After flushing eye, apply sterile pad for protection. • Obtain medical attention.	

Sunburn

Sunburn is produced primarily by exposure to ultraviolet rays and may result in first- and second-degree burns. Deeper burns may result from careless use of sunlamps. Although sunburn rarely requires hospitalization, it may be incapacitating for several days because of pain, swelling, and such systemic effects as fever and headache. The time between exposure and the development of symptoms is usually from 4 to 12 hours.

First aid for sunburn is the same as for first- and second-degree burns. If later medical treatment appears likely, do not apply ointment to the sunburn. Any person with extensive sunburn (10 percent or more of the body surface in a child and 15 percent or more in an adult) should be seen by a physician. Likewise, persons with very deep burns with many large blisters should have medical treatment. If blisters break, apply a dry, sterile dressing.

HEAT STROKE, HEAT CRAMPS, AND HEAT EXHAUSTION

Excessive heat may affect the body in a variety of ways, which result in several conditions referred to as heat stroke, heat cramps, and heat exhaustion.

Definitions

- Heat stroke is a response to heat characterized by extremely high body temperature and disturbance of the sweating mechanism. Heat stroke is an immediate, life-threatening emergency, for which medical care is urgently needed.
- Heat cramps involve muscular pains and spasms due largely to loss of salt from the body in sweating or to inadequate intake of salt. Heat cramps may be associated, also, with heat exhaustion.
- Heat exhaustion is a response to heat characterized by fatigue, weakness, and collapse due to inadequate intake of water to compensate for loss of fluids through sweating.

Causes

Heat reactions are brought about by both internal and external factors. Harmful effects occur when the body becomes overheated and cannot eliminate the excess heat. Reactions usually occur when large amounts of water, salt, or both are lost through profuse sweating following strenuous exercise or manual labor in an extremely hot atmosphere. Elderly individuals, small children, chronic invalids, alcoholics, and overweight persons are particularly susceptible to heat reactions, especially during heat waves in areas where a moderate climate usually prevails.

Signs, Symptoms, and First Aid

Heat Stroke

Sign and Symptoms
- Body temperature is high (may be 106°F or higher).
- Skin is characteristically hot, red, and dry, since the sweating mechanism is blocked.
- Pulse is rapid and strong.
- Victim may be unconscious.

First Aid
First aid should be directed toward immediate measures to cool the body quickly. Take care, however, to prevent over-chilling of the victim once the body temperature is reduced below 102°F.

The following first aid measures are applicable whenever the body temperature reaches 105°F.
- Undress the victim and, using a bath towel to maintain modesty, repeatedly sponge the bare skin with cool water or rubbing alcohol; or apply cold packs continuously; or place the victim in a tub of cold water (do not add ice) until the person's temperature is lowered sufficiently.
- When the temperature has been reduced enough, dry the victim off.
- Use fans or air conditioners, if available, because drafts will promote cooling.
- If the victim's temperature starts to go up again, start the cooling process again.
- Do not give the victim stimulants.

Heat Cramps

Symptoms
- In the case of heat cramps, the muscles of the legs and the abdomen are likely to be affected first.

First Aid
- Exert firm pressure with your hands on cramped muscles, or gently massage the muscles, to help relieve the spasm.
- Give the victim sips of salt water (1 teaspoonful of salt per glass), half a glass every 15 minutes, over a period of about 1 hour.

Heat Exhaustion

Symptoms
- Approximately normal body temperature
- Pale and clammy skin
- Profuse perspiration
- Weakness
- Headache and perhaps cramps
- Nausea and dizziness (possible vomiting)
- Possible fainting (but probable regaining of consciousness as victim's head is lowered)

First Aid
- Give the victim sips of salt water (1 teaspoonful of salt per glass, every 15 minutes), over a period of about 1 hour.
- Have the victim lie down and raise his feet from 8 to 12 inches.
- Loosen the victim's clothing.
- Apply cool, wet cloths and fan the victim, or remove him to an air-conditioned room.
- If the victim vomits, do not give him any more fluids. Take him as soon as possible to a hospital, where an intravenous salt solution can be given.
- After an attack of heat exhaustion, the victim should rest and should be protected from further exposure to abnormally warm temperatures. It may be advisable for the victim to seek medical guidance before engaging in hard labor or physical exertion.

SUDDEN ILLNESS

Canoeists could encounter emergencies that are not related to injury but that arise from either sudden illness or a crisis in a chronic illness. Unless the illness is minor and brief (such as a fainting attack, motion sickness, a nosebleed, or a headache), medical assistance should be sought. Although sudden illness is not always urgent, sometimes it endangers a person's life, especially if associated with a heart attack or a massive internal hemorrhage. An important first aid measure in such an instance is to secure transportation of the victim to receive medical care as quickly as possible.

Many persons suffering from heart disease, apoplexy, epilepsy, or diabetes carry an identification card or bracelet that contains information about the type of illness and the steps to be followed if they are found unconscious. Search the victim (in the presence of witnesses) for such identification.

Heart Attack

Heart attack usually involves a clot in one of the blood vessels that supply the heart. The attack is sometimes called a coronary, since there is a loss of blood supply to a portion of the heart muscle. A heart attack may or may not be accompanied by loss of consciousness. If the attack is severe, the victim may die suddenly. The victim may have a history of heart disease, or the attack may come with little or no warning. Attacks with mild pain sometimes occur.

Signs and Symptoms

Signs and symptoms of a heart attack include—
- Persistent chest pain usually under the sternum (breastbone). (The pain frequently radiates to one or both shoulders or arms, or the neck or jaw, or both.)
- Gasping and shortness of breath
- Extreme pallor or bluish discoloration of the lips, skin, and fingernails
- Extreme prostration
- Shock (as a rule)
- Swelling of the ankles

First Aid

To give first aid after a heart attack has occurred—
1. If the victim is not breathing, begin artificial respiration.
2. Have someone call for a rescue squad equipped with oxygen and have the victim's doctor notified.
3. If the victim has been under medical care, help with the prescribed medicine.
4. Place the victim in a comfortable position. Usually, sitting up is the best position, particularly if there is shortness of

breath. However, the victim's comfort is a good guide. Use as many pillows as needed.

5. Provide ventilation and guard against drafts and cold.
6. Do not give liquids to an unconscious victim.
7. If you have been trained in cardiopulmonary resuscitation (CPR), and vital signs indicate CPR is needed, you should administer this resuscitation.

Stroke

A stroke (also called apoplexy) usually involves a spontaneous rupture of a blood vessel in the brain or formation of a clot that interferes with circulation.

Signs and Symptoms—Major Stroke

- Unconsciousness
- Paralysis or weakness on one side of the body
- Difficulty in breathing and in swallowing
- Loss of bladder and bowel control
- Unequal size of eye pupils
- Inability to talk or slurred speech

First Aid—Major Stroke

- Give artificial respiration if indicated.
- Maintain an open airway.
- Provide moderate covering.
- Position the victim on his side so that secretions will drain from the side of his mouth.
- Call a doctor for medical advice as quickly as possible.
- *Do not* give fluids unless the victim is fully conscious and able to swallow and unless medical care will be delayed a long time.

Signs and Symptoms—Minor Stroke

In a minor stroke, small blood vessels in the brain are involved. These usually do not produce unconsciousness, and the symptoms depend upon the location of the hemorrhage and the amount of brain damage.

The minor stroke may occur during sleep and be accompanied by symptoms such as headache, confusion, slight dizziness, ringing in the ears, and other mild complaints. Later, there may be minor difficulties in speech, memory changes, weakness in an arm or leg, and some disturbance in the normal pattern of the personality.

First Aid—Minor Stroke

- Protect the victim against accident or physical exertion.
- Suggest medical attention.

Fainting

Description

Fainting is a partial or complete loss of consciousness due to a reduced supply of blood to the brain for a short time. Occasionally, a person collapses suddenly without warning. Recovery of consciousness almost always occurs when the victim falls or is placed in a reclining position, although injury may occur from the fall. To prevent a fainting attack, a person who feels weak and dizzy should lie down or bend over with his head at the level of his knees.

Fainting is usually preceded or accompanied by extreme paleness, sweating, coldness of the skin, dizziness, numbness and tingling of the hands and feet, nausea, and possible disturbance of vision.

First Aid

- Leave the victim lying down.
- Loosen any tight clothing and keep crowds away.
- If the victim vomits, roll him onto his side or turn his head to the side and, if necessary, wipe out his mouth with your fingers, preferably wrapped in cloth.
- Maintain an open airway.
- *Do not* pour water over the victim's face because of the danger of aspiration; instead, bathe his face gently with cool water.
- Do not give the victim any liquid unless he has revived.
- Examine the victim to determine whether or not he has suffered injury from falling.
- Unless recovery is prompt, seek medical assistance. The victim should be carefully observed afterward, because fainting might be a brief episode in the development of a serious underlying illness.

Convulsions

A convulsion is an attack of unconsciousness, usually of violent onset. In an infant or small child, a convulsion may occur at the onset of an acute infectious disease, particularly during a period of high fever or severe gastrointestinal illness. Convulsions that develop later in the course of measles, mumps, and other childhood diseases are more serious and might reflect complications of the central nervous system.

Convulsions associated with head injury or brain disease, such as a tumor, an abcess, or a hemorrhage, often tend to be localized, with rigidity and jerking of groups of muscles instead of the whole body.

Signs and Symptoms

Convulsions are usually accompanied by—

- Rigidity of body muscles, usually lasting from a few seconds to perhaps half a minute, followed by jerking movements. (During the period of rigidity, the victim may stop breathing, bite his tongue severely, and lose bladder and bowel control.)
- Bluish discoloration of face and lips.
- Foaming at the mouth or drooling.
- Gradual subsidence.

First Aid

- Prevent the victim from hurting himself.
- Give artificial respiration, if indicated.
- *Do not* place a blunt object between the victim's teeth.
- *Do not* restrain the victim.
- *Do not* pour any liquid into the victim's mouth.
- *Do not* place a child in a tub of water.

If repeated convulsions occur, call for medical help immediately or take the victim to a hospital.

Epilepsy

Description and Characteristics

Epilepsy is a chronic disease, usually of unknown cause, usually characterized by periodic convulsions ("grand mal" seizures). The victim may be able to lie down quickly, or the family may be able to tell that an attack is beginning by the sudden paleness of the victim's face or by the person's behavior. Mouth-to-nose resuscitation in providing artificial ventilation for victims of grand mal seizure is effective. Because of the high incidence of expiratory obstruction created by the soft palate, mouth-to-nose ventilation is the only effective way in which these victims can be ventilated. The mouth-to-nose technique must be accomplished in such a way that the mouth is left open for exhalation. If the teeth cannot be separated, the lips should be parted to permit passive exhalation. Much research has been carried out on epilepsy in recent years, and excellent preventive treatment is available. For this reason, physicians should determine the type and cause of every episode and convulsion.

A milder form of epilepsy occurs without convulsions. There may be only brief twitching of muscles and momentary loss of contact with the surroundings ("petit mal" seizures). The victim may be seen staring fixedly at an object or off into the distance. This type of disturbance is less common than that which produces grand mal seizures.

First Aid

First aid for epilepsy is the same as for other convulsions, with the primary effort being made to prevent the victim from hurting himself.

First aid is as follows:
- Push away nearby objects.
- Do not force a blunt object between the victim's teeth. (If the victim's mouth is open, you might place a soft object, such as a rolled handkerchief, between his teeth.)
- When jerking is over, loosen the clothing around the victim's neck.
- Keep the victim lying down.
- Keep the victim's airway open.
- Prevent the victim's breathing of vomit into the lungs by turning his head to one side or by having him lie on his stomach.
- If breathing stops, give artificial respiration.
- After the seizure, allow the victim to sleep or rest. Provide privacy if possible.
- If convulsions occur again, get medical help.
- Do not allow a victim of convulsions to return to the water.

Prevention of Heart Attack and Apoplexy

The following measures may help to prevent a heart attack as well as apoplexy:
- Have a checkup every year after the age of 40.
- Control weight.
- Do not exercise strenuously if you are not used to exercise.
- Get adequate rest.

HYPOTHERMIA BY EXPOSURE TO COLD

Every person in a canoeing group has responsibilities to himself and to others. However, in outdoor travel away from civilization, a person's first responsibility and obligation is to his body—its warmth, its energy, and its protection.

Strange as it may seem, canoeists can perish in a very short period of time (as little as 6 hours) from the effects of hypothermia (reduction of normal temperature of the vital organs). Hypothermia can be brought about by strenuous muscle activity (which drains energy) in windy, cold environments. It is for this reason that canoeists should have a knowledge of hypothermia.

Characteristics and Effects

Cold kills in two distinct steps:
(1) Exhaustion and exposure to cold
(2) Serious hypothermic effects

The moment your body begins to lose heat faster than it produces it, you are undergoing hypothermia from exposure to cold. In step (1) two things happen: (a) You voluntarily exercise to stay warm and (b) your body makes involuntary adjustments to preserve normal temperature in the vital organs. Either response drains your energy reserves, contributing to exhaustion. The only way to stop the drain is to reduce the degree of exposure to the cold environment.

Step (2), serious hypothermic effects, will result if exposure to cold continues until your energy reserves are exhausted. Once cold reaches the brain, its effects deprive you of judgment and reasoning power. *You will not realize this is happening.* You will lose control of your hands. With this onset of advanced hypothermic symptoms, your internal temperature is sliding downward. Without treatment, this slide leads to stupor, collapse, and, finally, death.

Most outdoorsmen simply cannot believe that air temperatures between 30 and 50 degrees can be dangerous. (Most hypothermia cases develop between these temperatures.) Low air temperatures combined with wind can create a chill factor that is unbearable.

If clothing becomes wet because of perspiration, rain, or mist, the chill factors shown on the chart that follows will have rapid and fatal results.

WIND – CHILL FACTOR (INDEX)

DEGREES FAHRENHEIT DRY-BULB TEMPERATURE	CALM	5*	10	15	20	25	30	35	40
35	35	33	21	16	12	7	5	3	1
30	30	27	16	11	3	0	−2	−4	−4
25	25	21	9	1	−4	−7	−11	−13	−15
20	20	16	2	−6	−9	−15	−18	−20	−22
15	15	12	−2	−11	−17	−22	−26	−27	−29
10	10	7	−9	−18	−24	−29	−33	−35	−36
5	5	1	−15	−25	−32	−37	−41	−43	−45
0°	0	−6	−22	−33	−40	−45	−49	−52	−54
5	−5	−11	−27	−40	−46	−52	−56	−60	−62
−10	−10	−15	−31	−45	−52	−58	−63	−67	−69
−15	−15	−20	−38	−51	−60	−67	−70	−72	−76
−20	−20	−26	−45	−60	−68	−75	−78	−83	−87
−25	−25	−31	−52	−65	−76	−83	−87	−90	−94
−30	−30	−35	−58	−70	−81	−89	−94	−98	−101

(EQUIVALENT DEGREES)

COLD   BITTER COLD
VERY COLD   EXTREME COLD

* MPH

Prevention

Your *first* line of defense against hypothermia is to avoid exposure to cold. Do this by staying dry and avoiding the wind. Wet clothes lose about 90 percent of their insulating value. Wet clothes can extract heat from your body 240 times as fast as dry clothes. Wind drives cold air under and through clothing and it refrigerates wet clothes by evaporating moisture from the surface. Use your clothes properly before a hazard presents itself.

Put on rain gear *before* you get wet. Put on wool clothes *before* you start shivering. Wool is warm even when wet.

A great deal of body heat is lost through the head and neck areas. Therefore, it is essential to protect these areas from the cold. A woolen hat or knit cap will help to preserve body heat. Also, when extreme cold is encountered, a woolen scarf around the head and neck will not only retard heat loss but will also trap heat from exhaled air and will prewarm air being inhaled.

If you cannot stay dry and warm under existing conditions, using the clothes you have with you, *terminate* exposure. This is your *second* line of defense. Get out of wind or rain; go ashore and build a fire. Concentrate on making your camp as secure as possible, regardless of how temporary. Your canoe, when inverted on land, can provide some shelter. Never ignore shivering. If it is persistent or violent, you are on the verge of hypothermia. Make camp.

Making camp while you still have a reserve of energy will forestall exhaustion. Allow for the fact that exposure to cold greatly reduces your normal endurance.

Recognition and Treatment

It is wise to appoint a person to watch each member of your group for early signs of hypothermia. Make the best-protected member of your party responsible for calling a halt before the least-protected member becomes exhausted or begins to show symptoms of hypothermia.

Your *third* line of defense is the ability to *detect* hypothermia. If your party is exposed to wind, cold, and wet, *think hypothermia*. Watch yourself and others for the following symptoms:

- Uncontrollable shivering
- Vague, slow, slurred speech
- Memory lapses, incoherence
- Immobile, fumbling hands
- Frequent stumbling
- Drowsiness
- Apparent exhaustion; inability to get up after a rest

The *fourth* and last line of defense is the *treatment* of hypothermia. The victim may deny he is in trouble. Believe the symptoms, not the victim. Even mild symptoms demand immediate, drastic treatment. Get the victim out of the cold-producing environment. Strip off *all* his wet clothes and get him into a warm sleeping bag. However, if he is semiconscious or worse, try to keep him awake and give him warm drinks if he is able to swallow. An accepted and proven practice in survival, when the victim's life is in danger, is to have him stripped and put into a sleeping bag with another person (also stripped). If you have a double bag, put the victim between *two* "warmth" donors. Skin-to-skin contact is the most effective treatment.

CAUTION. Do not administer alcoholic beverages to a victim of exposure to cold, exhaustion, or hypothermia. Alcohol seriously hinders the ability of the human body to function properly in regulating the blood flow to conserve body heat in the vital organs (the body core temperature). The result could be a worsened condition of the victim.

A serious phenomenon associated with the rescue and treatment of hypothermia victims is *after-drop*. The extremities of hypothermic victims are frequently at or near the temperature of the surroundings. If the cold, stagnated blood within the extremities is allowed to flow too quickly back into the rest of the body, the result will be a further lowering of the core temperature. This could lower the temperature beyond the critical point and result in the victim's death.

The period immediately after rescue is most crucial, and rescuers must know how to treat hypothermic victims for prevention of after-drop. It is essential to apply warmth to the victim's body while keeping his extremities relatively cool. This warmth can take the form of a warm, sweet, nonalcoholic drink (given only if the victim can swallow), or warmth can be applied by using any of the methods mentioned earlier. Therefore, if a victim's body is warmed first, after-drop can be averted. In any case, watch for any depression of the victim's vital functions and treat him accordingly. All victims of hypothermia should be transported to medical attention as soon as possible.

IMMERSION HYPOTHERMIA

With the exception of immersion in waters warmer than from 70° to 75°, the main threat to life during *prolonged* immersion is cold or cold combined with the possibility of drowning. You can greatly reduce the latter threat by putting on a lifejacket.

The rate at which a person is affected by hypothermia varies from individual to individual. It has been shown that thin or slight persons show signs of hypothermia more rapidly than obese or robust persons. The one factor that is foremost is the environment: cold water. Unlike the effects described in the previous section, dealing with exposure to cold, immersion in cold water is an instantaneous reduction of temperature at the surface of the body rather than a gradual reduction.

Immediately after you enter cold water, it will be difficult for you to breathe normally. You should float quietly in a lifejacket or by clinging to a floating object. The discomfort should decrease. If you are not wearing a lifejacket, try to get one and put it on.

If there is no adequate floating object to cling to, inflate your outer jacket by trapping air inside it to provide a means of support with minimum activity. Effective positions to assume (while waiting for rescue) to conserve body heat and energy are shown in the following illustrations.

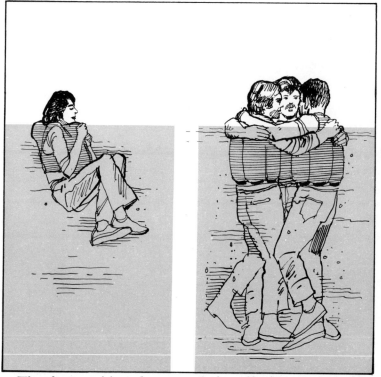

The above positions do not apply in swift river currents. See "Capsize Rescue" in chapter 7 for correct procedure.

If you fall into cold water, do not attempt to swim unless it is absolutely practical or necessary to do so—for example, if you are being carried by current toward danger, such as a waterfall or a dam, or if the distance to shore or safety is short. Even skilled swimmers are liable to drown suddenly if they attempt to swim any distance in very cold water, and few swimmers can cover as much as 200 yards in water near the freezing point. While floating in a lifejacket and waiting for rescue in cold water, do not exercise in the water in an attempt to keep warm. Exercising will actually have the reverse effect.

9

CANOE CARE AND REPAIR

A canoe, if handled with consideration, will remain in good condition for many years and will require only minimum routine maintenance. Most of the time, the canoe will be out of the water, where general deterioration can be rapid unless proper preventive measures are taken.

This chapter will help you successfully care for a canoe and make satisfactory emergency and permanent repairs. However, remember that the best source of repair information for a canoe is the manufacturer (if the company is still operating). Most manufacturers have lists of replacement parts and other materials for making all but the most extensive repairs. Many also have written instructions for the repair of specific canoes.

A thorough treatment of wood canoe repair and maintenance will appear in this chapter, since many manufacturers of wood canoes are no longer in existence. Many of the techniques discussed will apply to canoes built of both fiberglass and wood. It must be kept in mind, however, that methods of repair vary greatly among canoeists. Those methods mentioned here are reliable and time-tested, and although there are many other excellent and equally satisfactory procedures, they could not be included because of space limitations.

CARE IN STORAGE AND USE

In general, the following points can be applied to any canoe regardless of construction materials:

• Between periods of use, rack the canoe, *inverted,* off the ground and in the shade. If it is not practicable to put the canoe on a rack, turn it over, in the shade if possible. Great damage can result from long exposure to the sun. Protect the wood parts where they come into contact with the ground by placing flat boards or stones under them. Dry rot, particularly at the ends of the deck, can result from neglecting drainage and ventilation when the canoe is left in contact with the ground too long.

Aluminum canoes will also deteriorate when left on the ground, especially in highly acidic soil.

If the canoe is to be left unattended, lash it down to protect it from high winds and even secure it with a lock to prevent theft. In the latter case, keep accurate records regarding description and manufacturer's serial numbers. Obviously, no one should be permitted to sit on or get into a canoe that is resting on the ground. Do not leave the canoe right-side-up for extended periods, since rainwater left in it for a long period will damage it.

- Handle the canoe with care when carrying it, launching it, or lifting it out of the water. Avoid having it contact the ground or the dock.
- Observe proper techniques of boarding and debarking.
- Wear soft-soled shoes while using the canoe.
- While a canoe is underway, avoid contact with fixed or floating objects. Hitting them may seriously damage the craft.
- Avoid dragging the canoe through shallow water.
- Properly rack the canoe *inside* during the off season. If a wood canoe remains without even support over a long period, it will twist out of shape. A cover to protect the finish from dust and direct sunlight is desirable. The canoe should be cleaned thoroughly before storage. No weight should be permitted on it, and measures should be taken to prevent anything from falling on it. If the canoe is to be refinished before the next season, it would be better to plan this work for early spring, just prior to using the craft.

ROUTINE MAINTENANCE

Keep a good coat of marine or exterior spar varnish on all wooden parts of the canoe. Wherever there is a bare spot, moisture can enter the wood.

There are clear finishes other than varnish that are available. They are of the plastic or epoxy variety. Some manufacturers claim that their finishes have a life span twice that of varnish, and a more resilient surface. The problems in applying these resins are much the same as those in using varnish. The following paragraph applies to resins as well as varnish.

The absorption of water will add weight and cause general deterioration in wood. However, avoid varnishing the whole canoe when only a few spots need touching up. If succeeding coats of varnish are built up, before long, the entire finish will begin to crack, or "alligator." The cracks penetrate to the raw wood, and there is no cure for the condition but to remove all the old varnish and start over.

The first rule in the general painting or varnishing of a boat or canoe could well be that you should always sand off as much as you plan to put back on. If the interior is to receive a coat of varnish, sand and touch up the worn spots first. When these spots are dry, sand the entire interior (a fine garnet or aluminum oxide paper is recommended) and apply one coat, or two if needed, sanding well between coats. *Follow* the directions on the container for best results. Always sand with the grain of the wood. When the old varnish is to be completely removed from the interior, it can best be done with a remover. Use a type that will not retard drying of new varnish, since traces of the remover are bound to remain in the seams. Directions for using the remover will be found on its container.

The same general rule applies to maintenance of the exterior finish of the canoe. Although the interior is usually varnished, several types of finish are commonly found on the canvas. To reduce the dangers of blistering, peeling, cracking, and tackiness, determine the original type of finish and use the same for renovation. For example, use enamel on enamel, varnish base paint (deck paint) on varnish base, and airplane dope only on dope. The general rule has its exceptions. For example, aluminum powder paint is often applied over dope, and *then* paint of other colors is applied. When you are uncertain as to the original finish, test your selection on a spot about a foot square, and after a reasonable drying interval, check for "tack," adhesion, and the like.

Old, cracked finishes on the canvas can be removed, but in most cases it is better to recanvas the canoe. The cracks that develop in heavy coats of paint penetrate throughout the filler into the canvas, and if the condition has existed for some time, it is likely that the canvas has rotted under these cracks. Of course, the weight of the canoe has been increased by water absorption, and the result is a heavy, waterlogged craft, difficult to handle. However, if the canvas proves to be good under the accumulation of paint, it can be prepared for refinishing by removing the old paint with a remover (same type as recommended for the interior) or with a blowtorch. On heavy layers of paint, the latter method is preferable.

Some workmen report that to facilitate the removal of the finish, they soak the canoe by submersion underwater at least 24 hours. The moisture in the canvas, when vaporized by the torch, helps to loosen the old paint and filler and at the same time lessens the danger of severely scorching the canvas. To use the blowtorch method, remove the outwales, bang plates, and keel and invert the canoe over a support where there is good ventilation and no danger of fire. Use a blowtorch with a muzzle attachment that will give a fanlike flame and a broad knife (from $2\frac{1}{2}$ to 3 inches) for peeling off the paint. Start at the forefoot of the canoe and work toward your left if you are right-handed. Peel off the blistering paint immediately behind the flame as it is passed slowly over a small area 8 or 10 inches long, parallel to the keel line. The torch and knife must move across the surface in unison, because the paint will rebond if it cools. Peel off successive strips with the knife, lapping the cleared area above as you progress down toward the gunwale. Clear the next 8- or 10-inch section in the same way, and so on, until the job is finished.

CAUTION. When the outwales have been removed, there is always a chance that the edge of the raw canvas might catch fire and smolder unnoticed. Burns beyond the gunwale line could necessitate recanvasing.

Remove as much of the filler as possible as you burn and peel off the paint, because the cracks are there even though nearly impossible to see. Before repainting, use a commercial canvas filler, thinned down for deeper penetration, and build up a smooth surface before applying the first coat of paint. If you have decided to use dope, it can be applied without using a filler, but a more thorough removal of the old filler before application of the dope is necessary.

REPAIR

The information in this section will help you to satisfactorily make emergency and permanent repairs.

Wooden Canoes

Repairing Canvas-Covered Wooden Canoes

Holes in the canvas can vary in size from a small puncture to a tear many inches long. Punctures and very small tears can be repaired by filling them with waterproof liquid cement, letting

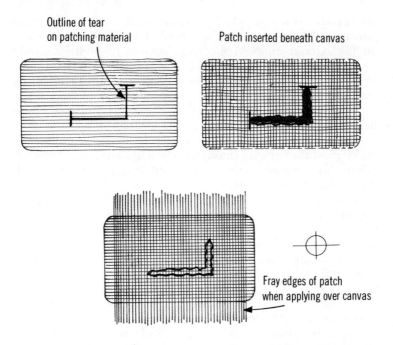

Outline of tear on patching material

Patch inserted beneath canvas

Fray edges of patch when applying over canvas

the cement dry, and applying a second coat. Larger repairs require a patch either over or under the hole, or both.

Make sure the canvas and the hull are dry when making the repairs. Prop open the lips of the cut for better ventilation and faster drying of the area. Use a lightweight piece of cloth with a close weave (broadcloth, muslin, etc.) and cut a patch that will extend an inch beyond the ends of the cut and about the same distance on each side. Place the patch on top of the tear and, with a pencil, trace the contour of the tear, which can be felt through the patching material. If the cut in the canvas is too small to permit working in a patch of this type, slightly enlarge the tear with a sharp knife. Impregnate the patch with a coat of waterproof liquid cement and allow the cement to dry, since the slight stiffness given to the material by the cement will make it easier to work the patch into position. Trim the edges and round the corners of the patch before inserting it under the canvas.

If the cut is on the turn of the bilge, spring in the hull by applying pressure a few inches from the tear in order to get more working room between the canvas and the planking. Line up the tracing on the patch with the tear in the canvas and carefully cement the patch in place. Because most waterproof liquid cement will "lift" the paint or varnish, try to avoid getting any on the exterior finish. A moderate amount of pressure should be applied to the repair while the cement is setting. Place a piece of wax paper over the repair to prevent sticking. In repairing large rips of a foot or more in length, use the same technique. It may be advisable to take a few stitches every 3 or 4 inches to help draw the lips of the cut together again.

After the repair has dried completely, fill in the voids between the edges of the cut with canvas filler or additional liquid cement. When this substance is dry, sand it and "touch it up" to match the original finish if you desire.

In certain instances it may not be possible to use the foregoing method. Cuts close to the stern or keel are hard to fix in this manner. When a patch cannot be placed beneath the canvas, apply one on the outside.

Occasionally, a portion of the canvas may be torn or worn off completely. The repair is made by filling in the void with canvas of about the same weight as the original.

To insure a perfect fit, prepare the filler piece by first giving it a priming coat of waterproof paint cement. Allow the cement to dry and then trim it with a razor blade or scissors to a size slightly larger than the hole. Place the material over the hole, mold the material to fit the contour of the canoe, and then, with a razor blade, enlarge the hole to fit the contour of the material. After the hole has been altered to fit the insert, cement a backing of light, strong material between the canvas and the hull. Cement the insert to the backing and finish with a lightweight patch on top.

Repairs to the canvas on a trip are usually of a temporary nature because thorough drying of the canvas is seldom practicable. However, the surface can be dried enough to permit some sort of an emergency repair. Waterproof adhesive tape or boating duct tape applied over the tear makes a good temporary repair. Makeshift jobs have been done with chewing gum, pitch from certain trees, wax from a dripping candle, and so forth.

Recanvasing Wooden Canoes

With the adoption of clear nitrate dope as canvas filler, re-canvasing a canoe has become a simpler task than it used to be. Special canvas-stretching tackle is no longer needed. Any person reasonably adept at ordinary handicraft projects can do the job with a helper. Each person needs a hammer, a pair of ordinary

CANOE CARE AND REPAIR

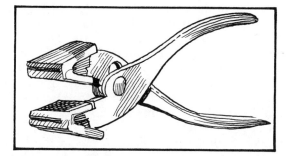

pliers, and a sharp pocketknife. If eventually more than one canoe will be recanvased, it will be worth while to have the jaws of the pliers widened to resemble webbing pliers. This may be done easily by having a 1/8-inch steel strap, about 3/4 inch wide by 1-3/4 inches long, welded to both sides of each jaw. Locking pliers, similar to those shown in the illustration above, can be purchased.

Canvas-stretching tackle is not needed because, although the canvas is put on only hand-tight, the dope filler shrinks it to a very snug fit. In fact, some persons have put the canvas on by using their hands, without pliers. You may apply several coats of the quick-drying dope in rapid succession on a good drying day. This means the filling job that used to take many days now takes a few hours at the most. Adding aluminum powder to the dope, bringing out the desired shade on the final coat, takes care of the coloring and finishing. The canoe could be used afloat the same day. (Clear nitrate dope and the appropriate thinner are available in gallon cans from aircraft maintenance supply companies and from some paint suppliers. It is not economical to put dope in smaller containers.) The following steps outline how the job is done.

1. Remove the outwales, bang plates, outside stems (if any), and the keel (if there is one). Save all these parts. If some are broken or damaged beyond repair, replacements will be necessary. With advance planning, you may have already made new parts, purchased these parts from the company that made the canoe, or had the parts made locally. If the screws are brass and in good condition, save them; otherwise, replace them with new brass or bronze screws of the same size.

2. Clinch, or remove and replace, all loose tacks in the planking. Use copper canoe tacks (available from canoe manu-

facturers) of the same kind and size as the old tacks. It is not necessary to replace these tacks as long as enough remain to hold the planking in place. The doped canvas will hold the planking tightly against the ribs, making excessive tacking unnecessary.

3. Replace any broken planking. Use cedar of the same thickness if cedar is available. Some canoe manufacturers will furnish it. Substitutes may be improvised from whatever material is available.

4. If there are broken ribs, repair or replace them. This work will slow up the total job, but broken ribs will be apparent from the beginning, and time should therefore have been allotted for this task. It is best done before the new canvas is applied.

5. Repair the stems with plastic wood or as described in the "Stem Repairs" section, or purchase new stems from the manufacturer.

6. Make any other necessary repairs to the wooden structure.

7. When all repairs are completed, sand the entire exterior surface. Make sure that no tack heads are protruding.

8. Lay the canoe, bottom up, on wooden horses or similar supports. Lay on the new canvas, centered and with equal overhang at each end. Number 10 white cotton duck canvas, 60 inches wide and 1 foot longer than the overall length of the canoe, is recommended, but much thinner material may be used if desired. If your canoe is unusually narrow, a 54-inch width may be adequate. Determine the necessary size by measurement, allowing a few extra inches to work with.

9. Stretch the canvas lengthwise, by hand, and hold it in the stretched position with one large tack at each end, driven partway into the stem at the forefoot. Do not stretch canvas enough to cause the single tacks to tear the canvas.

10. Start amidships, and, with someone working opposite you, pull the canvas down hand-tight and fasten it to the gunwale with large copper tacks (about ⅝ inch), driven partway in, at every third rib. Stop within 3 feet of each end. This is a temporary step to hold the canvas in position while the job of permanently tacking it on is undertaken.

11. Turn the canoe right side up. Work opposite each other and stretch the canvas carefully with pliers, using the gunwales as fulcrums.

Slide a small piece of angle iron along the inwale under

the pliers to protect the inwale from being marred. Fasten the canvas to the gunwales with two 5/8-inch tacks in every rib if the canoe is of open-gunwale construction. If it is of closed-gunwale construction, tack at intervals of about 1½ inches. Remove the temporary tacking as you go. Carefully observe the level at which the original tacking was done and duplicate it as closely as possible. If the nailing is too high, the tackheads may be in the way when the outwales are replaced. The tacking should proceed from amidships toward one end, stopping about 3 feet from the extreme end. It should then proceed in the same manner to the other end.

12. Turn the canoe bottom up. At one end, cut the canvas on the centerline from the end to the place where it has been tacked to the stem. Remove the tack.

13. Lay the canoe on its side. Move the supporting horses closer to the ends of the canoe so that the canoe will rest more securely. Pull the upper portion of canvas smoothly across the curve of the stem and start tacking it to the end of the stem at 1-inch intervals. Use small copper tacks (about 3/8 inch). If they do not hold well, try the larger size used at the gunwales. Tack to about midpoint of the curve and stop. Then bring the tacking at the gunwale along a couple of feet. Alternately work from both directions in this manner to assure finishing smoothly, with no wrinkles. Whenever a wrinkle appears, remove the tacks and straighten the canvas out before continuing.

14. With a pocketknife, trim off the surplus canvas at the end, but not along the gunwales. Turn the canoe over on its side and tack the other portion of canvas to the stem, on top of the first tacking. This tacking, however, should be at closer intervals (¼ inch if you are using the small tacks; ½ inch for the larger tacks). Trim the surplus canvas with care. Use a waterproof liquid cement liberally between these tacked portions. As an alternative, you could use airplane dope. If you use the dope, apply a thin coat to each tacked edge before doing the trimming, as an added measure to strengthen the fibers of the canvas so that the canvas will not shred at these edges.

15. Finish the other end of the canoe in the same way.

16. If you wish to do a little extra work, you can make a neat job of the ends by doing as follows: Cut a piece of muslin on the bias, making a strip about 1½ inches wide and long enough to cover the tacking done at the stem. Do the

cutting with pinking shears. Glue this strip on with airplane dope. Do the same for the other end of the canoe.

17. Apply several coats of dope, cut as desired with thinner. It is important to get good penetration with the first coat. Remember to color the dope with powder. Changing the shade with each coat will help to avoid "holidays," or gaps in your brushwork. There is no standard number of coats. Heavier canvas will take more dope to fill because its fibers are coarser grained. You may keep applying dope until you get a smooth finish if you desire. However, smoothness is not necessary from a utilitarian viewpoint. A total of 2 gallons of dope and 1 gallon of thinner will provide five or six coats, which are adequate. Sand lightly before the last coat or two. Routine sanding before each coat is probably unnecessary. Flow the dope on with a large brush, working rapidly, because it dries very fast. Keep the canoe out of the direct rays of the sun while putting the dope on, or it will dry almost too fast to enable you to get a smooth coat. Save a little thinner to clean your brush when you are done. If you let the brush harden, on the other hand, the dope and thinner should soften it.

18. After the doping is done, trim off the surplus canvas at the gunwales. Cut it exactly even with the top edge of the planking, otherwise you may have some of it in the way when you are replacing the outwales. You could have done this trimming before the doping job, but leaving it on until afterward provides protection against having the dope get into the woodwork of the canoe during application.

19. Put on the parts taken off originally, but consider the desirability of not putting the keel back on. If you elect to put it back on, puncture the canvas with an awl at each place where a screw hole appears in a rib along the centerline of the canoe. Put a thick coat of white lead on the canvas at each screw hole. Put the screws in place. Set the keel on, being careful to position it to match and line up with the screws. Tighten the screws.

NOTE. Some people have been successful in leaving off not only the keel but also the bang plates. With added care in using the canoe, no damage resulted.

Repairing Fiberglass-Covered Wooden Canoes

Occasionally, a fiberglass-covered canoe will become damaged. The damage might be a crack or a hole, or a piece of the bow may be damaged. A crack is relatively easy to repair. Sand the area about an inch on each side of the crack and apply a patch of the fiberglass cloth over the crack so that the cloth extends close to but never beyond the sanded area. After the first coat of resin is applied, feather the edge of the patch so that the patch blends evenly with the rest of the finish. Apply two more coats of resin, sanding between them. If the canoe has been painted, it will be necessary to remove the paint at the area where the patch is to be applied. When the coloring is in the resin, it is not necessary to try to remove anything. Just apply the patch after cleaning the area. A good patch job will hardly show.

If there is a deep gouge in the canoe, mix up some filler of fine sawdust and resin (even automotive putty will suffice) and fill the hole after any loose particles have been removed. While the filler is still soft, apply a patch of fiberglass cloth over the hole so that the cloth extends at least an inch beyond. Feather the edges of the cloth after the first coat and give the patch two more coats. If the hole extends right through the canoe, it will be necessary to fill it with fiberglass putty. So that the filler will not go through the hole and out the other side, place a backing on the inside of the hole. (See the section on molded fiberglassed canoes later in this chapter for illustrations.) The backing can be a piece of cardboard that has been coated with grease for easy removal after the filler has hardened. The filler can be home made old reliable sawdust and resin, or you can purchase commercial fiberglass filler or auto putty. The backing can be held in place by propping a stick from the opposite side of the canoe to the back of the cardboard on the inside or by stiff wires extending through the hole, which would be cut off and ground smooth when the patch has cured. From the outside of the canoe, fill the hole with filler and cover it with a patch that extends at least an inch all around the hole. Feather the edges after the first coat of paint resin and apply two more coats of resin. Then remove the backing.

Another repair job involving fiberglass is a bow that has been damaged by hitting an obstruction. If some of the bow is damaged and missing it can be built up with fiberglass putty and covered with a strip of fiberglass cloth. A broken rib can be repaired with fiberglass, and *then* the covering can be repaired.

Having found a broken rib, after you have removed the covering, remove a strip of the planking from both the left and the right of the rib. Clean and rough up the surface of the rib about 2 inches above and below the break. Give this area a prime coat of resin and let it harden. Cut one or two strips of cloth the exact width of the rib and 4 inches long. If the break is at a place where the rib is under tension, it will probably be best to apply two layers of 10-ounce cloth. Force the broken rib back into shape by extending a strip of wood from the left rib to the right rib, both above and below the break. Clamp these two strips in place with C-clamps.

Let the repair job harden overnight before removing the clamps. When replacing planking, you will have to sand down the underside of the planking where it fits over the damaged rib, since this area has been built up. Before tacking this planking at the broken rib area, you will have to drill small holes for the tacks; otherwise, they will not go through the fiberglass patch.

A problem that you might run into occasionally is finding tiny pinholes that you cannot fill. The difficulty is caused by an air lock: the brush rides over the holes but the resin does not fill the hole because air is trapped in the hole. This also happens if you use a spray gun and try to spray paint into a narrow crevice. Usually this problem can be solved with a brush, by lifting the handle of the brush straight up and poking the holes with the tips of the bristles. If that does not work, mix a little fine sawdust with some resin and paint it on slowly, or dab it on.

Fiberglassing Wooden Canoes

With the ever-growing popularity of synthetic cloths, such as fiberglass, very few wooden canoes are recanvased when the canvas cover is no longer seaworthy. Unless the owner insists on canvas, practically all canoes that are re-covered today are fiber-glassed. A canoe should last indefinitely after it is fiberglassed properly. Here are step-by-step directions on just how to go about it. (Bear in mind that no two people will give you exactly the same directions as to how the job should be done.)

Step number 1 is to strip the canoe just as you would if you were going to canvas it. This stripping would entail removing the outwales, keel, brass bang plates, and old canvas. Save all screws. You may find that the screws holding the bang plates on have had their heads filed smooth, so that no screwdriver slot is still showing. In this case, the screws would have to be replaced with new ones.

Place the canoe on two wooden horses, upside down. Check the planks and ribs and make needed repairs as explained under general repairs. Fill all space between the planks and also the indentations of the tack heads with plastic wood or auto putty. You may want to make your own plastic wood if much has to be used. It can be made by purchasing some clear nitrate dope from the nearest airport maintenance or paint shop and mixing it with very fine sawdust (similar to the type found in a hand sander that has a bag attached to catch the dust). Usually you can get this sawdust from a local cabinetmaker. Apply it with a putty knife. If you are planning on filling a large area such as a rotted deck section, you can make your own filler by using polyester resin and sawdust. Plastic wood made from nitrate dope should not be used in deep holes unless you build up one layer at a time, since it needs air to dry. Filler made from resin hardens by a chemical action and does not need the air. Fill any holes, indentations, or gouges that you find. Make sure to follow the stem curve around to the deck. It surely will need filling on the edges.

You should now sand the entire canoe smooth. After this, give it a prime coat of the polyester resin. Follow the directions on the can for mixing the hardener with the resin. It might be advisable to mix only about a half pint at a time at first, until you get used to the hardening time. Working in the sun is not advisable; if you must do so, you will find that the hardening time is greatly shortened, and you may find your brush caught in a pot of hard resin. Cold or cool weather will lengthen the hardening time. The best temperature for working resins is between 65 and 80 degrees. Since dampness adversely affects resin properties, working where humidity is high should be avoided. Therefore, if you are forced to work in a damp cellar, you may find that the resin takes considerably longer to harden. Do not get too ambitious at first, until you are familiar with the characteristics of polyester resin. The more hardener you use, the quicker the setting time; but too much hardener will make a brittle coat, and the finish will have a tendency to crack easily.

After the prime coat has sufficiently dried, usually overnight, sand it smooth again. Run your hand slowly over the canoe to detect any little rough spots that might snag the cloth when you put it on.

When you purchase the cloth, make sure it is at least 1 foot longer than the canoe. Most canoes require cloth that is 60 inches wide. A 10-ounce material is typical. Probably about 5 quarts of resin will be adequate. If the hardener does not come with the resin, make sure to purchase some.

Your next step is to lay the cloth over the canoe so that it drapes evenly over the gunwales on both sides and has an extension of about 6 inches over each end. Starting at the middle of the canoe, begin smoothing the cloth to your right and also over the sides of the canoe to the gunwale. Go slow and easy. You will usually find a ridge riding ahead of your hand. When you have smoothed the cloth to the end of the canoe to your right, go back to the middle of the canoe, where you started, and start smoothing the cloth to your left until you have reached the end of the canoe. You now have half of the cloth smooth. Go over to the other side of the canoe and repeat the same procedure.

At this point, before applying the resin, you should trim the surplus cloth that hangs below the gunwales. Again starting at the middle of the canoe at the side, start cutting the cloth just a little below the gunwale and toward the end. In this way you will protect the gunwale from the resin when you apply it. Go back and trim the rest on the same side and repeat on the other side. Save the scraps for any future patchwork. Now go to the end of the canoe and cut the cloth from the very end of the overhang from the middle to where the downward curve of the very end of the canoe starts. The cut should be about a foot and a half and will enable each piece to lap over the end, independent of the other piece. Do the same on the other end. You are now ready to apply your first coat of resin on the cloth. A paint roller can be used over most of the area, but a paintbrush is needed to work the sharply curved parts.

After mixing a batch of resin, go back to the middle of the canoe and start at the keel line, working to your right and also toward the gunwale. Soon you may notice that a small ridge has risen in the cloth where the roller left off toward the end of the canoe. You may also notice a small ridge as you approach the gunwale. This ridge will ride off the gunwale and disappear. The other ridge will also disappear over the end of the canoe as the end is reached. The stroke of the roller or brush is important. The main pressure on the implement should be toward the end of the canoe. On the back stroke, toward amidships, ease off a bit on the pressure. The same pressure on both strokes has a tendency to pull the cloth back and forth, and imperfections and poor adhesion may be the result.

Continue to the end of the canoe. Before lapping the cloth over the curve at the end, you must take the edge of the cloth on the side opposite where you are working and fold it back and hold it there with a tack so that it will be out of the way. Since you now have some surplus cloth on your side of the end of the canoe, you must trim it so that when you wrap it around the end of the canoe it wraps around about 1 inch. More than that will cause a great deal of puckering. Now wrap it around and apply resin. If the curve is not too small in radius, you have no problem. However, on some canoes, as you wrap the cloth around, you will notice that it has a tendency to pucker or bunch up in possibly two or three places. If this is the case, merely take scissors and cut the material right in the middle of the pucker and lap one edge over the other. The other side will cover the cut. You will have to sand the overlap on the other side.

An alternate method, rather than having the material overlap around the stern, is to trim the cloths on each side to leave the stem bare. Later, using strips of cloth cut on the bias, do the ends. Go back to the middle of the canoe and work to the other end in a manner similar to that described above. Do the other side in the same way. If you know that you cannot apply the resin to the whole canoe in one evening, cut the cloth along the keel and only do half. When you apply the second half, overlap the cloth along the keel line about 2 inches. Sand the overlap smooth before applying the second coat. After this coat has dried overnight, or sufficiently, you are ready for the second coat. However, you must first sand both ends where the cloth overlapped and also any sharp burrs that you may find. Again check by hand and look for irregularities. Be careful not to cut yourself on sharp burrs. You should be able to apply the first coat in about an hour and a half. The second coat will be much quicker. The first coat over the cloth can be clear resin.

After sanding and before applying the second coat, you must decide just how you intend to color the canoe. If you have a canoe in good condition you may want to just apply three coats of clear resin. In this case, you can see right through the resin to the planking. Sanding is necessary between coats. Another way of coloring is to put the coloring of your choice into the second and third coats, and the canoe will never need painting. Some people put coloring just into the third coat, but this is pushing your luck. Others would like their canoe a color for which they cannot obtain the color pigment. In that case, the canoe may be painted. You should tell your paint dealer that you are planning to apply the paint over fiberglass. Many people have little trouble with a good marine paint. Before applying paint, however, you should sand the canoe to remove the gloss.

Before you start replacing the outwale, keel, and bang plates, turn the canoe right side up and trim the surplus fiberglass cloth that extends beyond the gunwale. A wallpaper knife is excellent for doing this. A good procedure to follow in replacing parts is to replace the outwales first, then the keel, and finally the bang plates. The screw holes for the outwales may be punctured with an ice pick, but the screw holes for the keel and bang plates should be drilled. Make sure that the drill for the screw holes for the bang plates is smaller than the screws that are to be used.

Give the keel a good coat of seam cement before putting it back on. Since it will take a couple of days for it to bed down properly, even though the screws seem tight when you first put them in, you will be able to tighten them more the next day. Scrape off the seam cement that oozed from under the keel and paint the keel. It is also wise to put some seam cement under the brass bang plates where the screws go through. Do not put fiberglass over the keel. In many cases, it wears off from scraping and will leak.

You now should have one of the most durable canoes on the water.

Hull Repairs of Wooden Canoes

The ribs and planking of canvas-covered canoes occasionally may need repairing or replacing. Repairs to thwarts, decks, gunwales, and stems are sometimes necessary. This is particularly true of old canoes being rebuilt. Repairs that not long ago were considered impossible by the average person are now practicable through the use of laminations (thin strips of wood) bonded with easy-to-use, waterproof glues.

Damaged Ribs

For rib replacement with canvas or fiberglass on, first determine whether the rib or ribs must be replaced. If ribs are

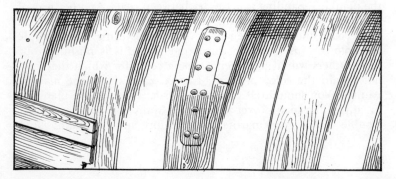

merely cracked, and not more than two or three are adjacent to one another, it may not be necessary to remove them. On the other hand, when just one rib has broken and has caused a marked bulge on the hull (usually at the turn of the bilge), it should be replaced before excessive wear occurs to the covering immediately over the bump.

To take out a rib, first remove any screws at the gunwales and keel, then carefully split out the rib with a screwdriver. Work the tacks up through the planking, using pliers. If small pieces of the planking are pulled through with the tackhead, press them back in place or fill the voids (when larger than $\frac{1}{4}$ inch in diameter) with plastic wood or resin putty (polyester resin and sawdust) so that they will not be felt through the covering after the new rib has been put in. With a hacksaw blade, clip off the nails that held the old rib in place at the gunwale if the canoe is of open-gunwale construction. On closed-gunwale canoes, remove the top and side molding strips first, and the nails securing the rib to the gunwale can then be pulled. Clean the area thoroughly, taking care that no old varnish ridges, splinters, etc., remain to prevent a good contact between the planking and the first laminations. The laminations should be of straight-grain white cedar, although good spruce, basswood, cypress, or other tough, nonbrittle wood may be used. Have the laminations sawed from a piece about 60 inches long and the same width as the rib. If they are made by a cabinetmaker, using a fine saw blade with little or no set to the teeth, more laminations of about $\frac{1}{16}$ inch will result in smooth contact between laminations. Place the canoe on a flat surface and block it in an upright position so that the bottom (or keel) directly under the repair areas is in full contact with the supporting surface.

Bend the first lamination into a horseshoe shape and, with the ends pointing toward the end of the canoe, slip it into place, working the ends up through the gunwale slots. Wedge the ends at the gunwales with a couple of screwdrivers after pressure is applied *downward* at the *tips* of the lamination to insure contact with the hull. If the wood was well selected and the laminations are not much over $\frac{1}{16}$ inch thick, it will not be necessary to steam or soak the strips to get a good fit without danger of breaking. Cut off the ends about 2 inches above the gunwales and mark for a taper that will match the taper of the adjacent ribs. This taper is usually only on the midship side of the rib. Remove the lamination and cut the taper with a sharp knife and a block plane, then use the first as a pattern for the two or three additional laminations that will make up the thickness of the rib. Do not attempt to bevel the edges or cut the ends to the finished length at this time.

Coat the planking and the bottom surface of the first lamination with a well-mixed plastic resin glue. Slip the lamination into place as before and wedge it temporarily at the gunwales. Avoid pressing it in with the hand at the turn of the bilge: there is less danger of breaking the lamination if pressure is applied downward at the tips. Moving the ends slightly forward or back may be necessary to secure a perfect fit. Next, coat the top surface of the first lamination and the bottom surface of the second, and slip the second lamination into place in the same manner. Thinner wedges will be necessary at the gunwales each time a lamination is added. They are inserted between the inwales and the last lamination. A small C-clamp can be used on open-gunwale canoes at the end of the adjacent rib to prevent the outwales from springing out, if there are no screws through them at that point. (On closed-gunwale canoes, use a C-clamp to hold the laminations in place and taper the *flat* side of the ends *after* the glue has set.) If the last lamination results in a rib slightly thinner than the original, build out the rib with a thin wedge between the inwales and the last lamination to maintain a uniform gunwale slot.

When all the laminations are in place and wedged, cut the ends to within an inch of the gunwales and tap them with a mallet or a hammer to be sure of contact with the hull. There is little danger of forcing them in too tightly because the canvas cover serves as backing; also, having the canoe resting on a smooth supporting surface will prevent any bulge from forming on the bottom. If the rib is wedged in too tightly, a bulge would first be noticed at the turn of the bilge. A tap on the gunwales next to the ends of the ribs before the glue has set will correct this.

Wipe off the excess glue with a moistened cloth. Cut a temporary thwart or crossbar to hook under the inwales next to the ends of the new rib and also one that will just catch the turn of the bilge. Pad the ends of the lower one to prevent scarring the rib, and force an upright between the two that will exert sufficient pressure to hold them firmly in place. Now fan out wedges between the lower cross member and the rib, using scrap pieces of the laminating material for this purpose. The slight spring from these strips will give enough pressure for a good glue joint.

If more than three ribs in one section have to be replaced, it is advisable to remove and replace every other one in the first

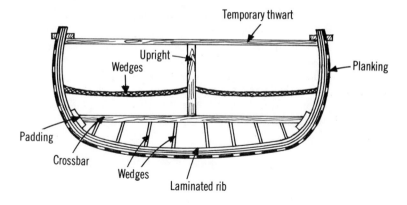

operation and then repeat the process on the broken ribs that were skipped, after the first ones have set. In this way, there is less danger of losing the original shape of the hull. Allow 24 hours for the glue to set thoroughly and then trim the ends flush with the gunwales and straight-bevel the edges with a sharp knife. A final sanding will slightly round the edge of the bevel, and the rib will be ready for varnishing.

If the canoe is to be recanvased as well, it is best to replace the ribs before removing the old canvas; but instead of pulling the tacks through the planking, clip them off flush with a pair of diagonal cutters. After the canvas has been removed, they can be easily pulled out.

When the canoe is to be recanvased, it is doubtless more practical to send an order to the manufacturer of the canoe for new ribs that can be put in while the canvas is off. When ordering from the manufacturer, give the serial number (as stamped on the inside stem) and the size of the canoe. Designate each rib needed, by counting from the end nearest the break toward amidships. If the serial number has been obliterated, measure the canoe, determining its overall length, its width at the widest point, and its depth amidships. Send this information with any other descriptive data to the manufacturer. He may be able to fill your order satisfactorily on the basis of this information.

An alternative is to make and bend the entire rib needing replacement yourself, or with local help. Clear, straight-grained spruce or cedar is recommended. Soak the ribs in boiling water if a steam box is not available, then bend them around the outside of the canoe and clamp them to the gunwales, not where they will be finally placed but two ribs closer to the end of the canoe, so that they will fit *inside* the canoe when finished. When they are dried to shape, put them inside in correct position.

In some cases it may be desirable to save the time and expense of putting in new ribs. If so, proceed as follows: (1) Remove the planking and tacks around the break. (2) Force the rib back to its original contour and hold it there with a strip of copper as shown in the illustration. (3) Replace the old planking with new.

Broken Planking

Broken sections of planking between ribs can be repaired with two-ply lamination without removing the canvas. Remove any loose pieces of the planking and trim the broken ends even with the edges of the ribs, but with a 45-degree bevel leading back under the rib. Insert a thin metal strip between the plank and the canvas while cutting the bevel, to prevent accidental puncturing of the canvas. The same type of laminating material recommended for the ribs is used for the repair. Sand two small pieces until their total thickness equals that of the original planking. After planing the edges down to the width of the space to be filled, cut a 45-degree bevel on one end and insert the lamination under one of the ribs so that the beveled ends are matching. Cut at right angles even with the edge of the other rib so that the first strip will fall into place. Prepare the second piece in the same way but with the beveled end locked under the rib opposite the first piece. Check for final fit, then remove the top piece and coat the contact surfaces with waterproof glue and fit the top piece back in again and apply pressure until dry. It is not necessary to glue the bottom lamination to the canvas, since the above procedure locks the patch in place.

When the canvas is off the canoe, replacing the planking is a simple procedure consisting of nailing on a new piece so that it

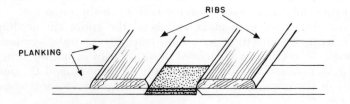

evenly abuts adjacent planking at the midpoint of a rib at each end. If two new pieces are on side-by-side, avoid having their joints fall on the same ribs.

Damaged Gunwales

Repairing a gunwale may involve one or more of a variety of possible procedures. An entire outwale or inwale strip might need replacing. You can easily mill this strip after taking measurements from the old piece. You can strengthen or repair a split, or "hogged out," gunwale by straightening or compressing the gunwale with a Spanish windlass around the canoe until the gunwale line is nearly straight, and then gluing and screwing a hardwood lamination to the underside of the inwale. One or two strips will correct a weak spot or a hogged condition; more may be needed to make a stronger repair for cracks or breaks. The laminations should extend a foot beyond the damaged area and can be up to $\frac{1}{4}$ inch in thickness. Use C-clamps to hold them in place, and do not release the windlass until the glue has set. Unless the gunwale has been badly splintered, it is seldom necessary to splice in a section. However, a section can be put in by lapping the joints (length of lap should be at least six times the thickness of the joint) and splinting with laminations beneath the gunwale. If the break has occurred at a seat or a

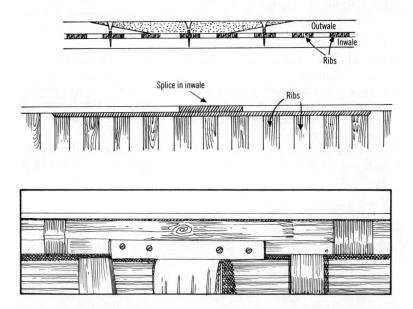

paddling thwart location, it is advisable to reverse the ends of the canoe by relocating the cross members.

In some cases, when a canoe is quite "run down" and appearance is not an important consideration, you can make repairs to broken gunwales with angle stock of aluminum or brass.

Cracked or Broken Stem

A cracked or broken stem that has not lost its original contour may be repaired without removing the bang plate or opening up the canvas cover of the canoe. Glue laminations to the inside face of the stem. Firmly press them up into place, and put in a tack or a small nail at the end of the stem to hold them there. When the glue has dried, remove the nail and "feather" the lamination into the stem.

If the break has altered the contour of the end, additional work will be necessary to make a permanent repair. After the inside curve of the stem has been reinforced with laminations, remove the bang plate, open up the canvas, and reshape the outside edge of the cracked or broken stem, using the ends of the planking as the contour guide. Work down small defects in the curve with a wood file; but on sharper breaks, plane the outside length of the stem down somewhat smaller than the original size. For a guide, mark with a pencil the original curve $\frac{1}{8}$ inch back from the ends of the planking and plane down to this mark, feathering out at the forefoot. Then build up the stem to the original size by gluing on several thin laminations. The laminations must be wide enough to cover the ends of the planking. After the glue has set, feather the laminations into the forefoot and taper the edges accordingly before resecuring the canvas.

When an old canoe is recanvased, the stems are often found to be split and rotted along the tack line. Follow the preceding directions for building up a new, solid surface to which the canvas can be securely fastened.

NOTE. When removing old brass screws, especially at the stems of a canoe, beware of getting small particles of glass into your eyes.

Damaged Breast Plate

The "decks," or breast plates, are very important structural parts of a canoe and are subject to considerable stress and strain. To repair a cracked or split breast plate, first release the outwales 3 or 4 feet from the tip of the breast plate. Pour waterproof glue down into the crack and draw the crack together with a large C-clamp or a carpenter's clamp until the glue has set. The breast plate area should be further strengthened by adding a short, narrow thwart a few inches back from the base of the breast plate. The thwart will prevent further outward strain on the breast plate and will also provide a good hand grip for short carries.

Carefully trim off rotted or otherwise damaged breast plate tips to provide for a lap joint and build them up with sections properly shaped and fitted. Since some inwale work is usually involved, the tips cut back beyond the breast plate repair. Then secure the prepared extensions of the inwale to the breast plate, and by lapping the joint, you can achieve a stronger and neater repair. Secure all sections by screws as well as with glue.

Broken Thwarts

If a thwart breaks, remove it and use it as a pattern to make a new one. It is not necessary to reproduce the curved surfaces of a typical canoe thwart, but length, angle of end cuts, and location of bolt holes should conform accurately to the original thwart to assure a precise fit. A thwart 3 inches wide with straight edges is suitable. When unfastening the old thwart, bear in mind that the diamond-headed bolts used on some canoes have an underflange and cannot be screwed out. They should be tapped up ¼ inch carefully (with nut on top of bolt) to clear the flange from the gunwale.

Split Planking

To repair split planking, apply a wood patch (softwood) to the inside of the planking, over the slit. The patch should be from ³⁄₁₆ to ¼ inch thick and about 1½ inches wide and should have a liberal coat of marine glue under it. Before applying the patch, drill a series of small holes about ½ inch from its edge. These holes should be just the right size to admit small brass or copper tacks long enough to go through the planking and the patch and to clinch over on the inside. Use a backing iron of some sort, held firmly against the patch while the nailing is done and in such a way that the tacks clinch over as they strike the iron.

Holes

To repair a hole, remove the affected section of planking, carefully cutting on the centerline of the adjacent rib on each side of the break. You can withdraw the tacks holding the planking to the ribs by cutting off their clinched ends on the inside of the ribs with a pair of side (or diagonal) cutters. Fit a replacement piece of planking of the same thickness (and of the same or similar wood) and nail it to the ribs. Renail the adjacent plank ends also. Use a good waterproof glue or seam compound at all joints.

Broken Ribs

To put in a new rib, use the lamination method or a prebent whole rib. Remove the old one by cutting off the clinched ends of the tacks and backing them out so that they may be grasped and pulled without damage to the planking. If necessary, the rib may be carefully broken up by splitting it with a screwdriver to aid in removing it. Nail the new rib in exactly as the original was nailed, using glue or seam compound between the rib and planking to insure that there are no leaks from the nail holes.

Doubled-Planked Canoes

Double-plank construction is rarely used any longer, and new pieces of planking or other repair materials are undoubtedly not available for specific canoes. However, the following information should help in the repair of a double-planked canoe.

- You can repair a small gouge in the planking with plastic wood or resin putty. If planking in the area is cracked or broken, but only to a minor degree, press it back into place and secure it by putting in some ½-inch copper tacks, clinching them in the same manner as that used in the construction of the canoe.
- When a section of broken planking must be replaced, make the new piece only slightly larger than the damaged area and only part of the width of the plank, to keep the repair as small as possible.
- If inside and outside are both damaged to the extent of needing replacement of planking, overlap the two pieces so that an inside joint and an outside joint will not coincide.
- Cut the replacement piece at an angle of 30 degrees across the grain of the wood. Put the replacement piece on the damaged area and, holding it firmly in place, cut deeply around it with a knife. Remove the copper tacks where the planking is to come out by cutting off the clinch on the inside and carefully pushing the tack out to where it may be grasped by the head and pulled. Finish cutting the old piece out, being careful not to cut the cloth lining. Coat the old cloth lining with slow-drying liquid marine glue. If it has been damaged, set a new piece of similar cloth on top of it and apply another coat of glue. Then put the new piece of planking in place and fasten it with

½-inch copper tacks driven through both layers of planking and clinched with a backing iron. Make an awl hole for each tack through the first layer of planking.

- When inside and outside pieces are both being put on at a damaged area, put the inside piece in place first and nail it to the outside planking that it overlaps. Then put the outside piece in place and nail it to any inside planking that it may overlap and to the new piece.

- Scrape off surplus glue and then wash off the remaining excess glue with a solvent. When the area is dry, smooth it with sandpaper or a file. You can remove hammer marks by applying hot water with a cloth.

- If there is a leak at a patch, you can stop it by forcing glue into the joints with a glue-saturated cloth. This method of stopping a leak is applicable to any area of the canoe.

It is apparent that bent-to-shape replacement planking from the canoemaker is especially desirable for inside patching because of the curved surfaces involved, due to the transverse direction in which the planking lies. The outside planking, being narrow and running fore and aft, does not need to be prebent but ought to be well wet on the outside when patching is done at a sharp curve. The lamination technique described for replacing ribs in a canvas canoe could be for inside patching. Make an effort to get cedar of the same type used in the canoe.

Molded Plywood Canoes

Repairs to gunwales, thwarts, stems, decks, and keel, if any, of molded plywood canoes should involve the same general procedures described for canvas-covered canoes. Repairs to the planking, however, involve somewhat different methods.

Damage such as minor gouging may be repaired with plastic wood or polyester resin putty and then should be varnished. A chipped-out piece of veneer may be glued back in place with plastic resin glue; in fact, several small pieces could be fitted back together like a jigsaw puzzle and glued in place. You must apply pressure evenly over these pieces. Even pressure may be applied by placing a piece of flexible board against the pieces and securing it tightly in place with a rope, or with clamps if possible (see illustration, page 280).

If two or more of the four layers of veneer are broken, you will have to replace one, two, or possibly all layers of veneer. Sometimes a blow on the outside of the canoe will break the inner layer and one or two of the layers beneath it without breaking the outside layer. In this case, carefully cut out the inner layer

at the area of the break and make a new piece to fit in its place. Apply plastic resin glue liberally to the inside of the replacement piece and to the underlying parts, working it into place. Then insert the replacement piece, holding it under pressure with clamps, if possible, or with an improvised rig. If the outside layer of veneer is also damaged but there is no definite hole, replace the outside layer also, in the same manner. The intermediate broken layers are in this way locked between the outside and inside face pieces.

When there is a definite hole in the canoe, you can repair it with a piece of plywood of the same material as the hull—the more plys the better. The edges of the hole must be carefully beveled, and the edges of the plywood patch also beveled, so that the patch will fit properly into place. Glue it into place under pressure. When the glue is dry, plane and sand the patch flush, as necessary. This type of patch is relatively simple to apply on the flat surface of the bottom but will be difficult on curved surfaces because of the necessity of molding the patch to the desired shape before fitting it to the hole.

An alternative is to employ the lamination principle used in replacing ribs. This principle involves separate replacement of each layer of plywood with a new piece of ⅟₁₆-inch veneer, cut to fit snugly in place. The pieces should be purposely cut in different sizes, with the face pieces larger than the underlying pieces, so that when they are all in place they will be glued not only to each other but also to adjacent veneer alongside the hole.

In any of the repairs described above, joints that have seams larger than desirable may be filled with plastic wood or a similar mixture of plastic resin glue and sawdust. You can smooth the area for varnishing with a file and sandpaper.

Fiberglass Canoes

Fiberglass boats are laid up in layers with the surface of the outside layer usually being gel coat. The gel coat is what gives the glossy, often colored, surface to the boat and provides some protection to the underlying layers.

Damage to an all-fiberglass canoe can range from superficial damage (loss of luster, scratches, abrasions, embedded dirt and grit, etc.) to extensive breaking apart of the hull.

Restoring the new look to a boat is a rather simple process of buffing after cleaning with acetone. Do the buffing carefully so as not to remove the gel coat, especially at the edges and corners. Once returned to a gloss, the surface can be waxed with an automobile body wax to protect the finish.

You can remove superficial scratches or embedded grit and dirt by cleaning, lightly sanding, and then buffing. Take care not to sand through the gel coat and to limit the area sanded to a small area surrounding the scratch.

You can repair scratches, air bubbles, nicks, and small holes that penetrate through the gel coat by cleaning and sanding to the depth of the damage. Then patch with the appropriate method mentioned in the following sections and smooth by sanding. Finally, apply the gel coat putty to the patch and finish to a smooth surface. If you do it properly, the repair will be almost undetectable. As with any other repair, seek out the assistance of a person with knowledge of such work who can help you do the job satisfactorily.

You can usually repair simple, nonpenetrating fractures by removing all damaged fiberglass and sanding the material surrounding the area by at least 2 inches from the actual fracture. Then apply patches of matting to build up the sanded area until the final patch, of glass cloth, overlaps the entire sanded area by about an inch. Wet all patches except the last one and void them of air bubbles. Since the last patch is cloth, you should

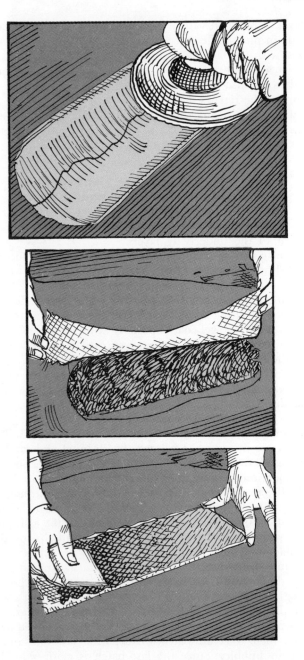

squeeze the entire unit. This action helps in restoring the original shape to the hull. Next, sand and apply gel coat, to give a neat finish to the repair.

Major breaks and punctures are repaired somewhat differently. Remove *all* damaged fiberglass from outside as well as inside the hull (where possible) with a power sander. Apply a temporary backing to the inside of the hull in such a way that the backing comes into contact with all edges of the hole. Lay up patches as done in the repairing and finishing of simple fractures. Once this process is complete, turn to patching the inside of the hull. The materials used should be comparable to those exposed by the sanding. At least two layers of glass should be built up and should cover an area that extends about 2 inches beyond the edges of the exterior patch. This area, of course, should be

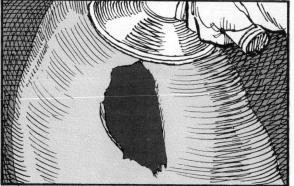

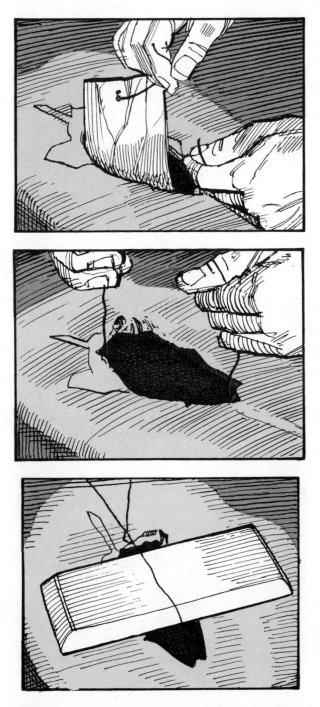

sanded smooth to prevent your injuring yourself if you come in contact with the area.

Any of the major breaks or punctures that occur to an area of the canoe that is accessible only from the outside, such as an enclosed flotation tank, can be repaired by using a form-fitted backup patch that is inserted in, and positioned through, the hole itself. This patch is made up on a piece of cardboard with wires attached to pull it firmly against the *inside* of the hull around the hole. When the patch has cured, seal the hole with a resin "putty" and rough up the surface when it has cured. Finish, as described earlier, with mat and cloth layup.

Although opinion varies on exactly how all phases of fiberglassing should be done, these directions show the kind of work that the novice can expect to do. Again, the novice should work with someone experienced in the kind of repair needed.

Aluminum Canoes

Repair Suggestions

Information and repair materials for use on aluminum canoes may be obtained from the manufacturer or his dealers. Here are some key facts selected from such material:

- *Do not use welding* in the repair of aluminum canoes, because the heat would leave a brittle area surrounded by a dead, soft area of larger dimension. Neither of these conditions is desirable.
- *If a rivet loosens,* tighten it by holding a heavy hammer against the outside head while striking the inside head with a smaller hammer to further peen (flatten) it over.
- *If a rivet is pulled out,* replace it with a larger one. A rivet can be removed by drilling or chiseling off the outer head and then punching out the remainder. This procedure must be carried out with care so as not to enlarge the hole or damage the skin of the craft.
- *If there is a leak along a rivet joint* and it cannot be exactly located, and no rivets are loose, use the marine sealer recommended by the manufacturer or his dealer, or use a known equivalent product.
- *To remove a large dent,* strike the bulged place firmly with your hand or foot or a rubber mallet.
- *To remove a small dent or a crease,* hold a cloth bag filled with sand against the hollow side and pound carefully on the bulged side with a rubber mallet. Work from the outside toward the

center and avoid striking too hard. A wooden block may be used instead of the sandbag, especially if a firmer backing is needed. Avoid use of a hard hammer, since too much pounding with it will thin the metal and will also make it brittle.

- *If the keel or the gunwales are bent,* block one side and pound the other with a rubber mallet until it is straight.
- *To stop the extension of a crack,* drill a $\frac{1}{16}$-inch hole at each end of it, then pound out the associated dent as described above. The hole will thus be nearly closed.
- *To temporarily seal a hole,* use duct tape, rags, a wooden peg, or almost any marine glue or cement.
- *To permanently repair a hole,* you can rivet an aluminum patch to the inside, using a gasket-and-seam compound between the patch and the skin of the canoe. The patch should overlap the crack or hole by at least an inch all around. Use $\frac{1}{8}$-inch rivets, located $\frac{1}{2}$ inch apart and $\frac{3}{8}$ inch from the edge of the patch. You can also make permanent repairs with a product referred to as an "aluminum plastic wood." It is

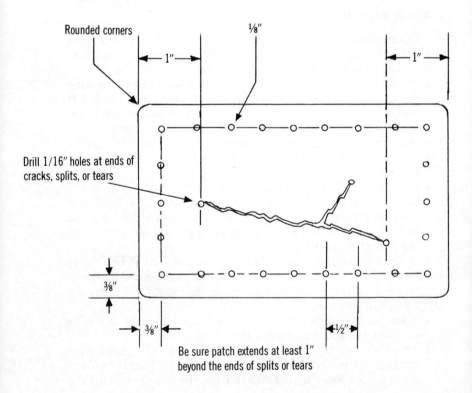

Rounded corners

$\frac{1}{8}$"

1"   1"

Drill 1/16" holes at ends of cracks, splits, or tears

$\frac{3}{8}$"

$\frac{3}{8}$" $\frac{1}{2}$"

Be sure patch extends at least 1" beyond the ends of splits or tears available from the manufacturer, from dealers, and from some automotive supply stores. For cracks and small holes, it may be applied directly to the bare, cleaned, and slightly roughened metal. For larger holes, it is probably best to apply it over a fiber patch as indicated in the instructions on the container. It is a paste and should be applied in thin layers. When the job is done, it may be sanded or ground to a bright finish.

Painting Suggestions

If you wish to paint an unpainted aluminum canoe, you can achieve satisfactory results as follows:
1. Clean the canoe with a household abrasive cleanser.
2. Wash the canoe with household vinegar, allowing the vinegar to remain on the canoe for 24 hours. Then wash the canoe thoroughly with fresh water and let it dry.
3. Apply one coat of a good aluminum primer and allow it to dry according to instructions on the container.
4. Apply two coats of a good marine enamel recommended for metal. Follow the application instructions on the container.

When a canoe is to be used largely in salt water, it should be purchased factory-painted. Factory-painted canoes receive special protective treatment before painting and a special paint requiring elaborate factory equipment for application. In addition, they are primed before being assembled. The priming gives protection to places that cannot be reached with a normal paint job.

When a factory-painted canoe needs repainting, clean it with a household-type abrasive cleanser and sand it with fine sandpaper. Any chipped or scraped areas should have their edges sanded smooth, but it is not necessary to remove the old paint. Repaint with a good marine enamel recommended for use on metal craft.

Canoes Made of Unreinforced Plastics

Because of the durability of the unreinforced plastics, such as ABS (arcrylonitrile-butadiene-styrene) or some similar material, repair is usually limited to eliminating dents and "wrinkles." Many canoes constructed of this kind of material that have been damaged by being wrapped around an obstacle have been successfully reshaped and used with few telltale signs of damage. Repair is usually accomplished by careful application of heat to the damaged area and gentle pushing back into shape.

Punctures of an unreinforced plastic hull are most difficult to repair satisfactorily. Even the manufacturer would be hard pressed to complete an adequate repair.

Polyester resin does not adhere properly to this material and therefore cannot be used for repair. However, if the outer layer of vinyl is sanded off, epoxy resin seems to adhere adequately.

Paddles

Occasionally a paddle is broken, and usually it is discarded. However, practically all broken canoe paddles can be repaired. Perhaps the worst type of break is straight across, but this kind of break can easily be repaired and made as good as new. To repair a wooden paddle, first glue the broken pieces together with some wood glue, or you might use polyester or epoxy resin. Scrape or sand all varnish above and below the break for about 9 inches. Remember that varnish penetrates wood rather deeply, so make sure you remove it all. If your resin does not harden and remains sticky, it is because you have not removed all the varnish. Next give the area that you have cleaned a coat of resin and let it harden. Cut some fiberglass strips about 2 inches wide. Start at least 6 inches above the break and wind the cloth around the paddle, painting on the resin as you go along. Overlap the layers as you wind, so that there are at least two layers everywhere. Proceed toward the break and 6 inches below the break. When the resin is dry, do what sanding is necessary and put on two more coats of resin.

You can repair a hollow aluminum shaft by sawing off the distorted position around the break, then inserting a tight-fitting hardwood plug about 4 inches long. This plug should be glued in and the shaft wrapped with fiberglass (as with a broken wooden paddle). The resulting paddle will be an inch or two shorter than before it was broken.

To prevent the tips of a wooden blade from either splitting or burring over from using it to push off with, it might be a good idea to fiberglass the tip. This is best accomplished as described in chapter 3.

Emergency Repair Kit

On a long trip, you should take an emergency repair kit. The contents of the kit should be appropriate for the types of craft used on the trip. For example, if the canoes are all aluminum, only repair materials for aluminum should be taken. The same would be true for each kind of canoe on the trip. Generally speaking, the basis for the kit should consist of a roll of heating duct tape, some scraps of glass cloth, a pint of polyester resin with enough hardener, a sharp knife or scissors, a putty knife, sandpaper, and a few paper cups for mixing. Other useful items are paper towels, a paintbrush, and lacquer thinner (or acetone).

Most splits, cracks, and small punctures can temporarily be taken care of with duct tape. This emergency repair work will keep the canoe serviceable until a more appropriate location for further repair is reached.

10

RIVER CANOEING

This chapter deals directly with the subject of the river, the hazards of the river, and the techniques of skillful and safe river canoeing. Other pertinent information, such as equipment, clothing, and general safety, is covered in chapters 6, 7, and 11 in this text.

The subject of river canoeing has been written about for many years. However, within the past decade there has been a marked increase in interest and in reference material. Because of this fact, it would be difficult to list the better books for fear of leaving some out. Readers should be critical about some of what they might read, however. Older books imply that a canoeist learns only through years of experience, but this assertion is no longer true. Today, people are taught refined skills and clever tactics for specific recognizable and recurrent situations. It is extremely difficult to improvise by yourself what so many people have spent the past 10 years developing.

As a novice, you may learn some of the necessary skills from this chapter or from organized courses, but do not think you will then be a skilled whitewater canoeist. A talking acquaintance with canoeing techniques is not enough. You must practice approved strokes and the required special tactics, and you must train your eye to read the water to evaluate existing conditions. If you are new to river canoeing you must develop judgment through practical experience. Development of this judgment is best attained by paddling and practicing with an experienced group.

You should join a whitewater club. Even if the club does not give formal instruction, you will be safer and will learn more among canoeists who are more expert than you are. As you follow the leader, you will observe his decisions and will learn to understand them. You will naturally make some mistakes but will then get a firsthand appreciation of rescue skills. Undoubtedly, the rescue skills you use will be derived from those principles expressed in chapter 7. You should review these principles and practice them under supervision prior to venturing onto a river.

If you do not find an experienced club in your area you should form a group of your own and learn with others. It must be emphasized that you should practice the skills in safe situations before you apply them where they are really needed. You should be encouraged to "play the river"; and remember that you are out for fun, and fun is not measured in miles traveled but in hours spent in safe rapids. You should not rush through rapids but stay and play at forward ferries and eddy turns before going on to look for the next fun spot. When you really need these skills, they will then have been practiced and perfected.

You should also read other canoeing books. A different point of view will sometimes help, but you should be very wary of old notions and possible misstatements.

PADDLE STROKES

A thorough review and practice of flatwater skills will aid you in putting the following information to effective use. Every skill used on flatwater is useful at some time for the varied demands of the river canoeist. All the strokes should be mastered. However, when running rivers, you must carry out each tactic in the one way that is best for the particular situation. Automatically and without hesitation, your paddle must move into action with the proper and appropriate stroke, even though your conscious thought is preoccupied with whether there is a rock under a certain wave or whether you can reach the safety of the eddy beyond. There is no time to think whether to use a draw, a pry, or some other stroke. All that must be automatic. Habit must produce the one best way, not some alternative way of accomplishing the same end.

As a whitewater paddler, it is especially important for you to make your strokes continually more effective through practice. Partly, you must make decisions faster to allow more time for action. This will give you more time to move your paddle, so that you can take more strokes in the time gained. The techniques learned must be perfected in accordance with your physique, so that you get the maximum effectiveness from your strength. In this regard, every prospective river paddler should review the basic paddling strokes described in chapter 6. Also, the braces and sweeps should be reviewed, since they are utilized very heavily in river canoeing.

TACTICS AND TECHNIQUES

At the very heart of river canoeing are those special tactics with which you can attempt to outwit the river and can play the river currents so that they help you to place your canoe just where you want it. The steering tactic of lake canoeing is as obvious as following your nose. However, the tactics of river canoeing are not obvious; they are unexpected and are sometimes even counter to instinct. Having a mastery of tactics, from full understanding to practiced skill, is the only way to make the rapids safe. Even the general canoeist should learn the variety of tactics early in his canoeing career, before conventional maneuvers become too deeply ingrained in his mind.

Running Position

When the "captain" (the stern paddler) shouts "Okay!" he means do nothing, as opposed to "Forward!" "Back!" "Left!" or "Right!" It is important that you know how to "do nothing" well. Today the canoeist coasts with his paddle vertical in the water, about a foot from the canoe, ready to go in any direction. Holding the paddle across the chest is obsolete because it takes too long for the paddler to initiate action. However, in severe wave plunging, some compromise position may be better; and in treacherous spots, the low brace position may help you anticipate the next problem.

Paddling Without Switching Sides

For years, paddlers have correctly been taught that the sternman should paddle on one side and the bowman on the other, and that they should not shift sides haphazardly. However, paddlers should learn to do *all* the strokes on *either* side. Then, both can switch periodically for a rest, but not indiscriminately while running a rapid. In modern heavy-water canoeing, a canoeist must know that his partner will stick to his own paddling side, ready to brace if the need arises. For solo canoeing, there is still an argument concerning changing sides, but for tandem canoes, the need for changing sides is past.

The Art of Reading Fast Water

There is beauty in fast water. The patterns and colors are a painting, and the sounds are a symphony. This you must discover for yourself. In addition, once you learn some common aspects of river rapids, you will be more able to see rocks where none are visible and to see clear passages where only chaos greets the untutored eye.

The first factor you should consider with moving water is its tremendous power. Coasting through a river rapid at 5 miles an hour may seem tame to the beginner, but the conditions are deceiving. An analysis of a hazardous situation will help to illustrate the river's power: Suppose a 15-foot canoe is pinned on a rock perpendicular to the 5-mile-an-hour current. The force of the water on the canoe is the area that the canoe presents to the water (15×2) times the water velocity squared (5^2) times 2.8—or 2,100 pounds holding the canoe against the rock! Suppose the water is only up to your thighs and you try to stand in it. An application of the above mathematics shows that a 100-pound force will be pressing against your legs. These facts should convince you that the water could work for you and not against you. You will see, then, that if you are going to pursue this sport, you must learn properly and not just blunder in.

"Still waters run deep," and, conversely, fast waters run shallow. This statement is a fundamental bit of common sense. Consider two places on the same river. Where the river is deep and wide, the current is slow. Where the river becomes shallow, the current must run faster to pass the same volume of water. Once you have the feel of a stream on a particular day, you can deduce the depth from observations of width and velocity.

294

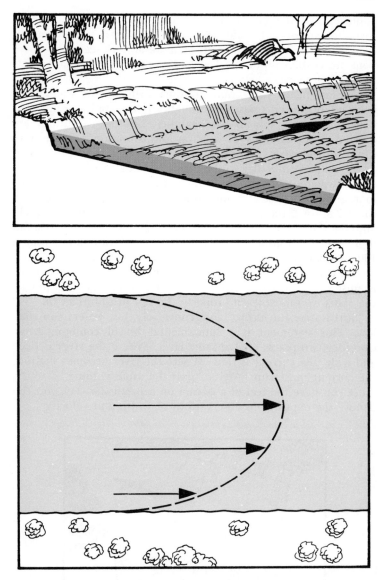

The water velocity is not consistent all across the river. Friction slows the water along the banks. Also because of friction, the water flows fastest on the surface in midstream, except when making a bend. This is why you must back ashore when landing, or the current differential will spin the canoe about. The result

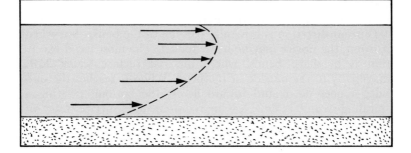

of the current differential from surface to bottom will be that a person in the water will be tumbled headfirst unless he keeps his feet and hips at or near the surface. As shown in chapter 7, this is the basic reason for you to keep your feet and hips up, but secondarily, it helps by keeping your legs pointed downstream, thus providing the best protection against your hitting some obstacle.

Any time water flows around an object, it sets up back currents and whirls collectively. This resulting action is called an eddy.

Eddies are the extreme case of current differentials. Behind a large rock, the current may be entirely still, or even flowing upstream in a reversal. The surface of the eddy can have a current upstream that is quite violent, while right beside the rock, the main current rushes by at full speed. Here the current differential is abrupt; you will hear it called the eddy line or even the eddy

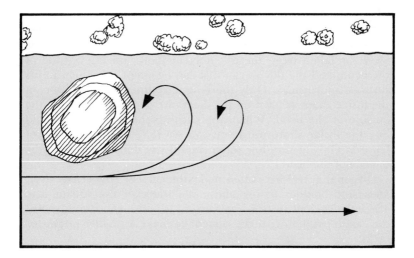

wall. This eddy line, or boundary, marks the area between the main current and the eddy water.

Current direction is generally parallel to the banks, but when it is not, the novice may be badly fooled. The most usual exception is in sharp bends, where the fast surface water flows diagonally to the outside of the bend. When it reaches the outside, it goes down and inward across the bottom, creating a spiraling secondary flow, leaving room for more surface water on

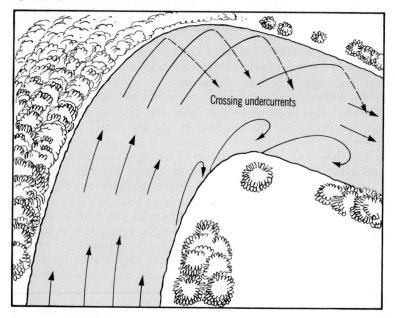

Crossing undercurrents

the extreme outside of the bend. All too often, there are large waves or fallen trees due to undercut banks on the outside of the bend, and the novice canoeist can be swept into them to his surprise and dismay. Only the boundary line layer of water on the inside shore (shown on the diagram) does not end up at the outside of the bend. When approaching the bend, you should hug the inside shore until you can see if the outside is free of hazards. Only at very low water should you deliberately seek the outside of the bend.

Diagonal gravel bars often make the current flow across river, and large boulders rising above the water of the stream may affect the current in this way also. In general, you should point the canoe parallel with the current to make a smaller target for rocks.

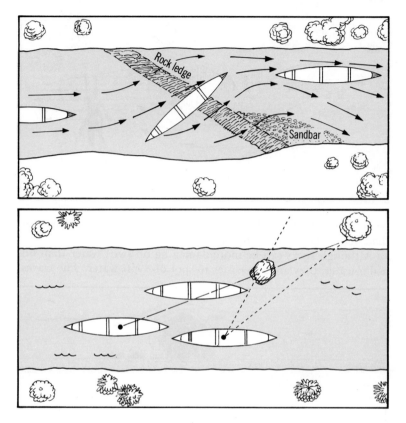

In a turbulent rapid, it may be difficult to tell when your canoe is being swept sideways and is not headed the way it is pointed. You must, therefore, learn to sight obstacles (rocks, waves, bridge piers, tips of fallen trees, etc.) against the background. If the alignment stays unchanged, the canoe is on a collision course with the object. You must then take action to avoid the obstacle.

When the water meets a solid ledge, it is turned aside, and the action of the water will help to carry your canoe clear also. However, when the water goes on through the obstacle, beware! Sometimes it is pouring over a ledge or a dam, and you must be careful to see that you are not swept over too. The most common and most dangerous example is where the water flows through the branches of a fallen tree. Watch for such an obstacle on the outside of river bends, especially on swollen rivers. If you do not

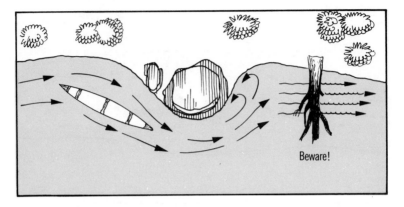

want that 2,100-pound force pinning you on the branches, you had better stay clear far in advance.

   Although rocks can be more damaging on swift water than on calm water, they are also easier to spot on swift water. The waves

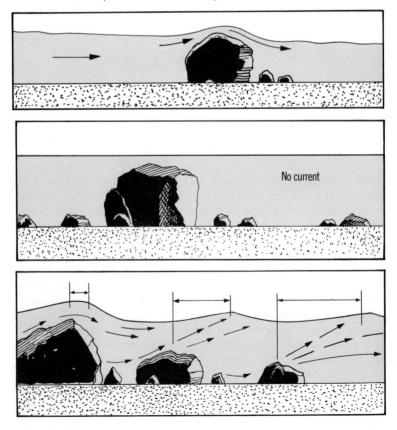

reveal the rocks' hiding places. If a rock is close to the surface, the water follows the contour of the rock as it pours across, and a raised convex "pillow" appears on the surface of the water. Remember, however, that the pillow is stuffed with rock. If the surface wave appears farther downstream from the rock producing it, the rock is fairly deep in the water, and the canoe can safely pass over it. Therefore, on still water, rocks close to the surface are not readily apparent.

As the current becomes swifter, the pillow over the rock will be followed by one or more scalloped standing waves, which are much easier to spot than the pillow. You will learn that such scalloped waves generally mark the channel. However, when they occur unexpectedly in a fast stretch, the bowman must look intently for that trace of a pillow at the start that says, "Don't run these waves."

In very powerful currents, a souse hole appears behind the pillow. Even when you can run over the pillow in a very large-scale example, the canoe may not be able to climb out of the souse hole, even if it has full forward speed and a full splash cover. Souse holes at high water should be avoided.

Low-level dams or weirs across rivers are especially hazardous.

Their smooth construction creates reversals beneath the surface
that are difficult or impossible to escape from without aid. This
type of backwash holds canoes and people for unreasonable
lengths of time.

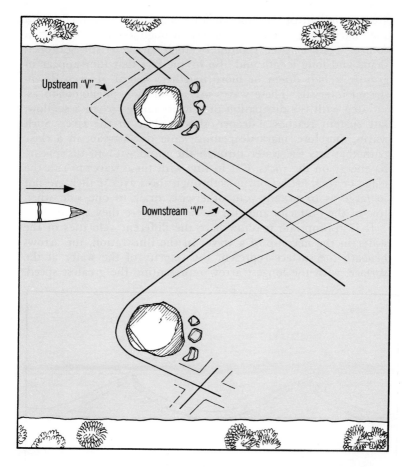

Dangerous currents and powerful forces are created by water-falls. Many paddlers, some experienced, have narrowly escaped serious injury or death by drowning from venturing beyond the limits of safety with regard to dams and waterfalls.

Note that in the above illustration, the V pointed upstream has a rock at its tip. A downstream V is nothing more than the joining of two upstream V's, and so it marks the course between two rocks. The downstream V often has a slick and glassy ap-pearance. It is most inviting and is usually the correct course. You must also look for other signs in the watery turmoil after the side V's meet for the assurance that it is runable. Watch out for pillows. Look for standing waves.

Standing waves, or "haystacks," mark deep water and are the

greatest delight of the canoeist. Like all river waves, these stand stationary while the water rushes through on its downstream course. They may be spotted by their characteristic scalloped shape and long length and also by the fact that they appear in groups, a half dozen or more together, spaced at even downstream intervals. These waves are a vibration phenomenon associated with the dissipation of velocity energy when a shallow, fast current reaches a deeper, slower place in the river. Such waves, therefore, mark deepening water downstream in a clear path that lets the water through the rapid without dissipating its energy on the rocks. Get in line with these waves to run the ledge or rock field. Continue through the waves if they are not so large as to swamp you; otherwise, draw to one side when free of the obstacles and run the waves where they are small.

It is appropriate to show here the different velocities of the water in the makeup of a wave. In the illustration, the arrows beneath the surface represent the velocity of the water at the surface, with the longest arrow representing the greatest speed.

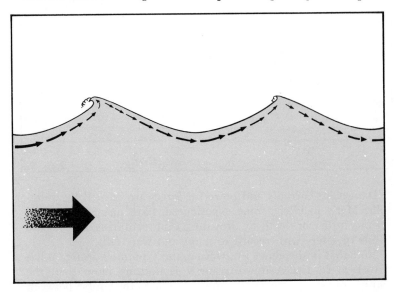

Needless to say, if your canoe broadsides the crest of a wave, it could very well come to an almost abrupt stop, thus causing a hazardous situation.

An interesting and useful precautionary rule should be observed: when you are in rough and turbulent water and see a nice quiet spot, avoid it like the plague. As you shoot past, sneak a look back and you will probably see that a hidden rock with water pouring over it protects the quiet spot.

The teacher of river canoeing will show his students pure examples of the various waves so that they may learn the wave shapes to watch for. However, in practice, these phenomena may be jumbled and hard to recognize. When you have learned the information in this chapter, you must still train your eye. First scout from shore, because you can often see rocks clearly from the side and from below although they are almost invisible from the approaching canoe. As you dodge past pillows and avoid the quiet spots, look back a moment to see if they were as bad as you thought. So it is that you train your eye until you know, without scouting, where the rocks are, and thus you will develop a feeling for where the current is going and why. In this regard, rapids lose their look of impassable chaos and become orderly.

Steering

Conventional steering has its place in slick or slow water. Where there is plenty of room, the sternman does almost all the steering, and the bow paddler usually provides forward power only. Where the channel becomes narrow and tortuous, there is not room for the stern to swing wide and push the bow in a new direction. Here the bowman must steer his end of the canoe, drawing or prying as required, usually without the need of commands from the stern. However, as the current becomes swifter, this practice becomes increasingly hazardous. When dodging rocks, the canoe may not be headed the way it is pointed but will be moving sideways with the current. The bow may be in the portion of the water going to one side of the rock and the stern in the portion going to the other side. A canoe sliding sideways, even slightly sideways, makes a target for a rock. Also, consider the consequences of a canoe's being pinned broadside in a swift current. Whether rock-strewn rapids will be "cemeteries" or "rock gardens" to you depends on your knowledge of the right tactics.

The following two sections describe tactics most used with conventional (open) canoes. Slalom (decked) canoes and kayaks, which turn much more easily because of the rocker, are generally steered around obstacles, and it is only occasionally necessary to resort to the following tactics.

Parallel Sideslip for Rock Dodging

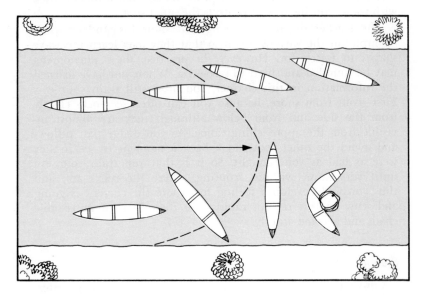

One alternative to steering around a rock is simply to sideslip the canoe. The canoe stays parallel to the current at all times but it slides to one side and coasts past the rock. The bowman sees the rock first and makes the decision to go right or left. He draws or pries, and the sternman counters with the opposite stroke—a pry for a draw and a draw for a pry—to move his end of the canoe in the same direction. There is no need to shout out a command. From the bowman's action, the situation, though unseen, is evident. The bowman puts his end of the canoe where it belongs and the sternman keeps his end directly upstream. The often-heard statement that a canoe must have forward motion or steerageway is pointedly refuted in river canoeing. It is far safer to go slower, relative to the rocks, than to go at the same speed as the water, since less shipping of water in the waves will result. Going slower also permits you to simply slide the canoe one way or the other to let it coast past the rocks. Going slower also allows more time for planning and execution of maneuvers. A canoe with flat bottom and shoe keel, or no keel at all, is obviously better for maneuverability. A round bottom, a V bottom, or a small keel are features of lake canoes. If you plan to use your canoe on rivers as well as on lakes, you had best avoid these latter features.

It may occur to you that a canoe is not well streamlined when moving sideways. If the problem is that there is a substantial distance between the notch in an upstream ledge of rock and that in a lower ledge, you will not make it by sideslipping. Sideslipping is for short dodges. You undoubtedly will not make it by paddling forward either, since even with oversteering you will only be swept broadside over the lower ledge. You had better learn to back ferry, as explained later in this chapter. For decked boats, it is probably better to turn completely upstream and ferry across. This action offers the most power in a more familiar paddling attitude.

Eddies

The eddy may be a welcome spot for resting, for waiting for other members of your party, or for planning your strategy on the next stretch of river to be encountered. However, there is a hazard involved in crossing an eddy line. The differential between the main current and the eddy water will have the tendency to spin the canoe end for end as the opposing currents act on the craft. Also, as the current is being entered, it will tend to suck down the up-current side of the canoe. Both of the actions described will tend to roll the boat, flipping unwary paddlers into the water. The paddlers can counter this rolling tendency by leaning the canoe away from the current to be entered. This action presents the bottom of the canoe to the current, and if properly done, it should aid in making the turn and assist the paddlers in maintaining optimum stability. The amount of lean will depend on the differential between the eddy water and the main current. The greater the differential, the more the canoe will have to be leaned. Also, the greater the differential, the faster the resulting action will be.

An additional characteristic of the eddy line is its thickness. If the river is deep and fast and the obstruction is large, the eddy line will be more of an "eddy wall," often being more than 2 feet wide. This eddy wall is composed of many diverse currents and must be crossed quickly and with determination.

Back Ferry To Move Across the Stream

The use of the back ferry is limited. The solo paddler will find that the following principles apply, but the execution is often difficult, since he must control both ends of the boat and back paddle simultaneously. The back ferry is, however, best used in putting to shore without the canoe's cartwheeling (spinning end for end) as it enters the slower current.

The commands of the stern paddler are the key to the maneuver. He sees the angle of the canoe best and therefore directs the maneuver. The back ferry is initiated with the sternman's calling, "Back!" Both paddlers back paddle the canoe to check its speed before it reaches an appropriate spot, which could be a rock at the head of an eddy. At the proper moment, using a draw or a pry, the sternman swings the stern in the direction of the shore toward which he wishes to move. In the case of a pry, the canoe will pivot faster if the paddle is started exactly under the stern. After this maneuver, the bow will be pointed away from the shore toward which the canoe is moving.

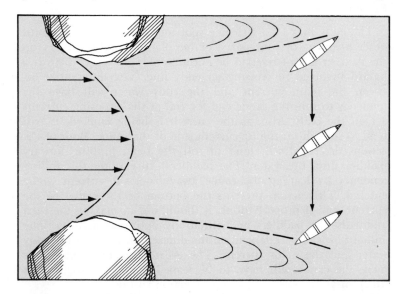

An angle of about 30 degrees with the current is ideal. If the turbulence causes a loss of angle, the stern paddler can pry the stern over again. If the stern is swept off to too large an angle, the bow paddler is commanded to go right or left, whichever moves the bow toward the shore to be reached and thus straightens the angle with the current.

Forward Ferry

For a forward ferry, point the bow upstream and paddle forward. The forward ferry is more instinctive, easier, and more powerful than the back ferry. You must spin the boat to point upstream before starting the maneuver. The ferry is carried out with the paddlers' backs downstream, and the canoe must be spun downstream again after the crossing is achieved before continuing downstream. Of course, current differentials are used in spinning the canoe. Despite its simplicity and directness, a good forward ferry from an eddy through a fast jet and into an eddy on the other side involves more skill than a back ferry. It is practiced over and over when you play a river.

The trick is to get up speed before breaking through the eddy line into the fast current. The angle with the current must be very slight before entering the current, and the speed must be high enough so that the whole canoe is in fast current before the angle gets out of control. The result is spectacular. Not only does the canoe's momentum carry the craft well across the fast jet but also the inertia of the canoe causes the current to push the craft across as it accelerates the canoe downstream. This is a precision tactic, and one paddler must be ready to throw a quick paddle brace if the angle gets too large, until the whole canoe is in fast water and can be driven forward again.

If you are ferrying in large waves, position the canoe on the upstream face of a wave. Gravity will pull the canoe upstream (downhill on the wave) while the current tries to push it back downstream. Done properly, the maneuver results in a stalemate, and you can move straight across by angling the boat slightly, even in extremely fast water.

What ferry angle is best? What angle of the canoe moves it farthest across the stream for a given slip downstream? If the river is slow, there is no real problem. If it is fast, with waves, and you are in an open boat, you may not want a big angle of attack with respect to the current. Traveling straight across the current is a large attack angle of 90 degrees. The key to the whole problem is whether or not you can paddle faster than the current. If so, just about any angle is acceptable for attaining a desired spot.

If the current is flowing faster than you can paddle, it is best to head upstream of the intended goal. You can always bear off to get there. A 30-degree angle is a good generalization in most circumstances, especially for novices. Note, however, that when the current is very fast, you should paddle almost straight across. (Likewise, a swimmer should swim straight across.)

If you are attempting a forward ferry in a very fast jet of current and your intended angle gets away from you, do not fight to correct it. Just drive straight across, letting the eddy on the other side turn your bow upstream again. The maneuver will look like an "S" turn, and you will have to use a canoe lean and a paddle brace at both ends.

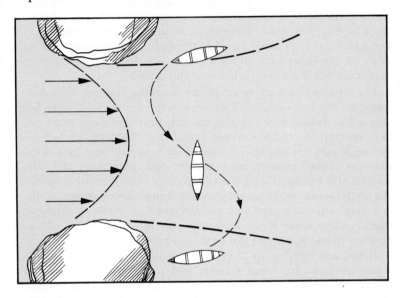

Another consideration is that of driving hard straight across if a trough can be used. Again, the paddlers should be prepared to brace when needed.

From Back Ferry to Eddy Turn

The back ferry represents the cautious and cagey side of all

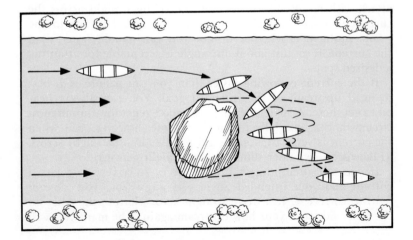

canoeists. It is consistent with slowing down in places where you might hit rocks and slowing down to ride over large waves in an open canoe. It is absolutely necessary that paddlers master the back-paddling tactics. However, there is also a dynamic forward paddling brand of advanced whitewater canoeing. When the current becomes powerful, the waves become large, and the souse holes open up, you must "shift gears" from back paddle into forward drive. Your drive must be such that its momentum will carry the canoe up the big waves, lest it should slide back down into the trough or souse hole and be swallowed. If you try to back into an eddy, the current tries to pull the canoe out and onward. If you drive forward into an eddy, the momentum carries the canoe in, and the river current helps by pushing it in. This is the eddy turn. It is, then, not primarily a turn but a way of going from a powerful current into an eddy. The turn is a compulsory consequence. The eddy turn does not replace the back ferry; it is for different river conditions. It requires skill and much practice.

Eddy Turn

In a tandem situation, the stern and bow paddlers must work together to provide the best possible angle of attack, then drive to get into the eddy, and then brace and lean the canoe for stabilization. The canoe must come from farther out in the river than the eddy line and so have forward momentum toward the eddy. The stern paddler sets up the entry point, and as the

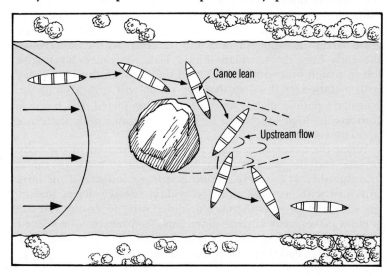

Canoe lean

Upstream flow

bow cuts into the eddy line, the person paddling on the inside of the turn braces and leans the canoe to the inside.

In the following examples, a pry is preferred in carrying out some maneuvers. A word of caution: do *not* use a pry on the downstream side of the canoe if the water is shallow. Instead, use a cross draw to avoid the possibility of "tripping" over the paddle if it should catch on the bottom of the river.

Suppose the stern paddler is paddling on the left and wants to enter an eddy behind a rock also on the left. Both paddlers drive forward, and the stern paddler gauges it so that the bow knifes into the eddy just below the rock. As the bow cuts in across the eddy line, the stern paddler leans the canoe to the left with a low brace. At the same moment, the bow paddler initiates a cross draw, so that his blade is in the eddy water.

The whole canoe will then spin quickly around the bow paddle blade. The bow paddler must permit the canoe to lean into the turn by allowing his right knee to ride higher than his left. The canoe will skid sideways in turning. If it is not leaned far enough, it will be caught by the water and spun to the outside of the turn. After a moment of possible turmoil, the bowman returns to his paddling side, then drives forward to bring the canoe well in to the eddy behind the rock. The maneuver consists of three skills blended into one for the bowman (forward drive, cross draw, and drive) while the sternman leans out, reverse sweeps, low braces, and then drives. Once the canoe is in the eddy, the bow paddler must shift his weight and brace for the lurch as the stern enters. If, however, the sternman is paddling on the right as the canoe approaches the left eddy, he must allow the canoe to be leaned by riding with his right knee high as he drives the canoe forward into the eddy. As the bow crosses the eddy line, the bowman should lean the canoe far to the left in a high brace and should hold the canoe in the eddy water with a stationary draw so that the canoe will spin around the bowman's paddle blade. As the turn is completed, the bowman converts his high brace to a forward stroke and pulls the canoe up to the rock.

When the canoe is paddled solo, the differential in the eddy current and the main river current is used to turn the canoe into the eddy. If the eddy current is strong enough and the boat will turn without assistance, the paddler simply drives toward the eddy and permits the current differential to do the rest.

For a rather weak current differential, a stroke may be needed to help turn the boat. This stroke is normally the *forward,* or *power,* stroke. Paddling side is not a factor.

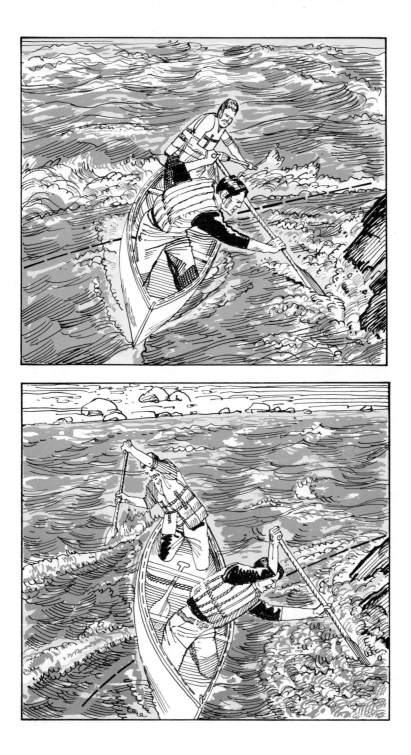

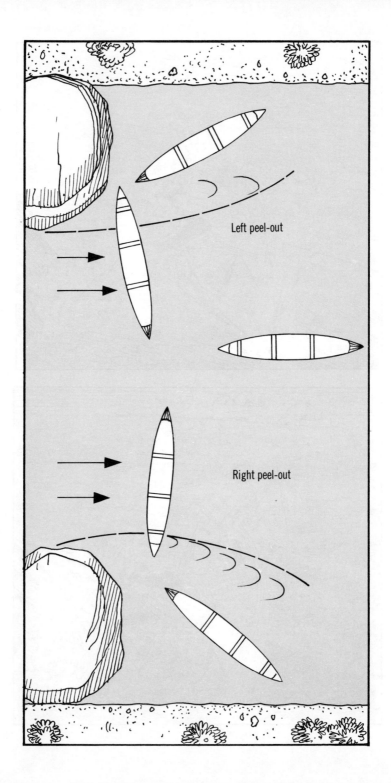

Left peel-out

Right peel-out

The Peel-Out

Once the canoe is in an eddy, it is necessary to have a maneuver to get out of the eddy. This maneuver is the peel-out and is the same as the eddy turn, except, of course, that the canoe is coming out of the eddy and turning downriver.

In tandem paddling, the principles of the peel-out and the bow and stern duties are the same, and the canoe lean is again to the inside of the turn.

It is interesting to compare the peel-out with the "advanced" forward ferry, because they both start in much the same way but end in very different ways. The peel-out has a large angle with the eddy line, has momentum across the eddy line, and is initiated on a wave crest or on the downstream face of a wave whenever possible. If the forward ferry is made onto very fast water or is poorly done, the bow is swept down as in a peel-out, and the canoe will capsize unless it is leaned downstream and braced. The bowman should use a low brace for a moment and then go back to paddling forward. However, in the peel-out, he wants the bow to turn downstream and uses a high brace, if paddling the downstream side, while the stern paddler drives forward into

the main current. With the bowman paddling on the off-side, the stern paddler low braces and leans the canoe into the turn. The bow paddler will drive hard to bring the canoe out of the eddy and will assist in turning the canoe downstream with either a pry or a cross brace, as shown.

The solo paddler, turning toward his paddling side, will high brace and drive hard. If paddling on the off-side, he will cross draw and brace, then drive fully into the main current.

It is interesting to note that a canoe simply cannot drift out of an eddy, because the current will catch the bow quickly and, at best, the proper angle will be lost.

Playing the River

The tactics described above all require practice. Shorten your mileage plans, have more fun, and learn more canoeing. Many people will find a two-or-three-hundred-yard stretch of river and play it a half day or more, moving from eddy to eddy, practicing everything they know, and pushing themselves slightly beyond their ability.

With proper safeguards (shore rescue, etc.), a group of paddlers can find a good-sized hole (very large eddy) within most of their capabilities and play it over and over, approaching it from many angles and using varied tactics. What better practice can you get under reasonably safe conditions?

SAFETY

The emphasis that whitewater canoeists place on safety is in itself an admission of the potential hazards. The novice is sometimes scared off by being told of the tons of force of the water or the deadly numbing effect of icy water. Experienced paddlers do not intentionally scare off people, because they believe their sport to be safe. They simply want novices to resolve at the start to become good whitewater paddlers so that the uninitiated too will find canoeing a safe sport.

Unfortunately, whitewater canoeing has a public reputation for being extremely dangerous. Every dramatic mishap makes all the newspapers. The public concludes that rapids are all dangerous and that only fools venture into them. It is now known that canoes are not "tippy," although some canoeists are. The canoe and the kayak can travel in certain kinds of water too dangerous for other boats. Most rapids are not dangerous unless ignorant canoeists make them dangerous. If you are going to paddle whitewater, you owe it to yourself and to fellow paddlers to be a safe whitewater canoeist.

Fundamentals of Safety

Whitewater skills are the most important ingredient for whitewater safety. All the chapters in this text up to this point contribute to your safety, and ample practice of the skills taught will help to keep you out of trouble.

Judging your own capabilities accurately, being able to realize your limitations, and resisting the temptation to venture beyond those limitations are the first steps in safely paddling rivers. First, however, there is a safety code that every paddler or potential paddler should learn thoroughly. This code was written by expert whitewater paddlers from coast to coast. It is worthy of careful study and full adoption as your own safety code. Experienced canoeists, when reading of whitewater fatalities, note that many of these rules were broken simultaneously—although, of course, the reporters describing the incidents do not know it. This text can do no better than to quote verbatim the safety code of the American Whitewater Affiliation.

Hazards of High Water

When a river rises above its normal level because of heavy rains, storms, or spring runoff, or when a dam releases large quantities of water periodically, it becomes a hazard to any kind of navigation. The forces produced by the increased volume of water are enough to uproot trees and change the shape and configuration of the river bottom. These increased forces play havoc with canoeists who are not prepared to cope with them. What was an easily runable river for you one week can be hazardous the next. The spring runoff is a typical time to expect rivers to be above their normal level and the water to be extremely cold, thus increasing the potential hazard.

Any time there is *any* question in your mind regarding your safety and that of your companions, the canoe trip should be terminated or not even attempted.

American Whitewater Affiliation Safety Code

Personal Preparedness and Responsibility

1. **Be a competent swimmer,** with ability to handle yourself underwater.
2. **WEAR a lifejacket.**
3. **Keep your craft under control.** Control must be good enough at all times to stop to reach shore before you reach any danger. Do not enter a rapid unless you are reasonably sure you can safely navigate it or swim the entire rapid in event of capsize.
4. **BE AWARE OF RIVER HAZARDS AND AVOID THEM.** Following are the most frequent **KILLERS.**
   - **High water.** The river's power and danger and the difficulty of rescue increase tremendously as the flow rate increases. It is often misleading to judge river level at the put-in. Look at a narrow, critical passage. Could a *sudden* rise from sun on a snowpack, rain, or a dam release occur on your trip?
   - **Cold.** Cold quickly robs one's strength, along with one's will and ability to save oneself. Dress to protect yourself

from cold water and weather extremes. When the water temperature is less than 50°F, a diver's wet suit is essential for safety in the event of an upset. Next best is wool clothing under a windproof outer garment such as a splashproof nylon shell; in this case, one should also carry matches and a complete change of clothes in a waterproof package. If, after prolonged exposure, a person experiences uncontrollable shaking or has difficulty talking and moving, he must be warmed immediately by whatever means available.

- **Strainers.** Brush, fallen trees, bridge pilings, or anything else which allows river current to sweep through but pins boat and boater against the obstacle. The water pressure on anything trapped this way is overwhelming, and there may be little or no whitewater to warn of danger.

- **Weirs, reversals, and souse holes.** The water drops over an obstacle, then curls back on itself in a stationary wave, as is often seen at weirs and dams. The surface water is actually going **upstream,** and this action will trap any floating object between the drop and the wave. Once trapped, a swimmer's only hope is to dive below the surface where current is flowing downstream, or try to swim out the end of the wave.

5. **Boating alone** is not recommended. The preferred minimum is three craft.

6. **Have a frank knowledge of your boating ability.** Don't attempt waters beyond this ability. Learn paddling skills and teamwork, if in a multiple-manned craft, to match the river you plan to boat.

7. **Be in good physical condition** consistent with the difficulties that may be expected.

8. **Be practiced in escape** from an overturned craft, in self-rescue, in rescue, and in artificial respiration. Know first aid.

9. **The Eskimo roll** should be mastered by kayakers and canoers planning to run large rivers and/or rivers with continuous rapids where a swimmer would have trouble reaching shore.

10. **Wear a crash helmet** where an upset is likely. This is essential in a kayak or covered canoe.

11. **Be suitably equipped.** Wear shoes that will protect your feet during a bad swim or a walk for help, yet will not interfere with swimming (tennis shoes recommended). Carry a knife and waterproof matches. If you need eyeglasses, tie them on and carry a spare pair. Do not wear bulky clothing that will interfere with your swimming when waterlogged.

Boat and Equipment Preparedness

1. **Test new and unfamiliar equipment** before relying on it for difficult runs.
2. **Be sure craft is in good repair** before starting a trip. Eliminate sharp projections that could cause injury during a swim.
3. Inflatable craft should have **multiple air chambers** and should be test-inflated before starting a trip.
4. **Have strong, adequately sized paddles or oars** for controlling the craft and carry sufficient spares for the length of the trip.
5. **Install flotation devices** in noninflatable craft, securely fixed and designed to displace as much water from the craft as possible.
6. **Be certain there is absolutely nothing to cause entanglement** when coming free from an upset craft; i.e., a spray skirt that won't release or tangles around legs; lifejacket buckles or clothing that might snag; canoe seats that lock on shoe heels; foot braces that fail or allow feet to jam under them; flexible decks that collapse on boater's legs when a kayak is trapped by water pressure; baggage that dangles in an upset; loose rope in the craft, or badly secured bow/stern lines.
7. **Provide ropes to allow you to hold onto your craft** in case of upset, and so that it may be rescued. Following are the recommended methods:
    - **Kayaks and covered canoes** should have 6-inch-diameter grab loops of ¼-inch rope attached to bow and stern. A stern painter 7 or 8 feet long is optional and may be used if properly secured to prevent entanglement.
    - **Open canoes** should have bow and stern lines (painters) securely attached, consisting of 8 to 10 feet of ¼- or ⅜-inch rope. These lines must be *secured* in such a way that they will not come loose accidentally and entangle the boaters during a swim, yet they must be ready for immediate use during an emergency. Attached balls, floats, and knots are *not* recommended.
    - **Rafts and dories** should have taut perimeter grab lines threaded through the loops usually provided.
8. **Respect rules for craft capacity** and know how these capacities should be reduced for whitewater use. (Life raft ratings must generally be halved.)
9. **Carry appropriate repair materials:** tape (heating duct tape) for short trips, complete repair kit for wilderness trips.
10. **Cartop racks must be strong** and positively attached to the vehicle, and each boat must be tied to each rack. In addition,

each end of each boat should be tied to car bumper. Suction cup racks are poor. The entire arrangement should be able to withstand all but the most violent vehicle accident.

Leader's Preparedness and Responsibility

1. **River conditions.** Have a reasonable knowledge of the difficult parts of the run, or if an exploratory trip, examine maps to estimate the feasibility of the run. Be aware of possible rapid changes in river level and how these changes can affect the difficulty of the run. If important, determine approximate flow rate or level. If trip involves important tidal currents, secure tide information.

2. **Participants.** Inform participants of expected river conditions and determine if the prospective boaters are qualified for the trip. All decisions should be based on group safety and comfort. Difficult decisions on the participation of marginal boaters must be based on total group strength.

3. **Equipment.** Plan so that all necessary group equipment is present on the trip: 50-to-100-foot throwing rope, first aid kit with fresh and adequate supplies, extra paddles, repair materials, and survival equipment if appropriate. Check equipment as necessary at the put-in, especially lifejackets, boat flotation, and any items that could prevent complete escape from the boat in case of an upset.

4. **Organization.** Remind each member of individual responsibility in keeping group compact and intact between leader and sweep (capable rear boater). If group is too large, divide into smaller groups, each of appropriate boating strength, and designate group leaders and sweeps.

5. **Float plan.** If trip is into a wilderness area or for an extended period, your plans should be filed with appropriate authorities or left with someone who will contact them after a certain time. Establishment of checkpoints along the way at which civilization could be contacted if necessary should be considered. Knowing location of possible help could speed rescue in any case.

In Case of Upset

1. **Evacuate your boat immediately** if there is imminent danger of being trapped against log, brush, or any other form of strainer.
2. **Recover with an Eskimo roll if possible.**
3. **If you swim, hold onto your craft.** It has much flotation and

is easy for rescuers to spot. Get to the upstream end so craft cannot crush you against obstacles.

4. **Release your craft if this improves your safety.** If rescue is not imminent and water is numbing cold, or if worse rapids follow, then strike out for the nearest shore.

5. **Extend your feet downstream** when swimming rapids to fend against rocks. **Look ahead.** Avoid possible entrapment situations: rock ledges, fissures, strainers, brush, logs, weirs, reversals, and souse holes. Watch for eddies and slackwater so that you can be ready to use these when you approach. Use every opportunity to work your way toward shore. [*Also, the Red Cross recommends that you should* never *stand up in fast-moving current or in a chute unless the water is too shallow for swimming. Try to get into an eddy or slow-moving water* before *standing up.*]

6. If others spill, **go after the boaters.** Rescue boats and equipment only if this can be done safely.

International Scale of River Difficulty

(If rapids on a river generally fit into one of the following classifications but the water temperature is below 50°F, or if the trip is an extended trip in a wilderness area, the river should be considered one class more difficult than normal.

CLASS I   Moving water with a few riffles and small waves. Few or no obstructions.

CLASS II   Easy rapids with waves up to 3 feet, and wide, clear channels that are obvious without scouting. Some maneuvering is required.

CLASS III   Rapids with high, irregular waves often capable of swamping an open canoe. Narrow passages that often require complex maneuvering. May require scouting from shore.

CLASS IV   Long, difficult rapids with constricted passages that often require precise maneuvering in very turbulent waters. Scouting from shore is often necessary, and conditions make rescue difficult. Generally not possible for open canoes. Boaters in covered canoes and kayaks should be able to Eskimo roll.

CLASS V   Extremely difficult, long, and very violent rapids with highly congested routes which nearly always must be scouted from shore. Rescue conditions are difficult, and there is significant hazard to life in event of a mishap. Ability to Eskimo roll is essential for kayaks and canoes.

CLASS VI   Difficulties of Class V carried to the extreme of navigability. Nearly impossible and very dangerous. For teams of experts only, after close study and with all precautions taken.

11

CANOE TRIPS AND CAMPING

Nearly everyone who has ever stepped into a canoe has conjured up a vision of what a wilderness trip would be like. Many believe it would be like a trip back in time—to relive, at least in part, those days when a person would venture into the wilderness to survive for weeks on his own ingenuity and ability.

Canoe trips, voyages, camping expeditions, or whatever you might want to call them, are natural steps in the development of all-round canoeing knowledge. These trips take you away from people, the pressures of daily routine, and the drudgery of earning a living. They put you into a different and exciting way of existence. With proper planning, there is rarely a cause for concern as to whether or not you will come through safely. The independence and self-reliance involved in such adventures are what many people require to round out their life.

CAUTIONS TO BE OBSERVED

The primary consideration facing you if you intend to take a canoe down a river or into the wilderness for an extended period of time is that of your own limitations. These limitations, once you recognize them, will dictate most aspects of your canoe trip. Limitations, of course, must be coupled with a knowledge of the hazards, which could involve such factors as remoteness of area to be canoed in, size of river or lake area, class of river, and probable temperature of water to be encountered.

Are you physically fit? If you are a diabetic, if you have a heart condition, or if you have other physical handicaps or weaknesses you should consult your doctor before attempting any such trip.

Are you skilled enough to cope with potential hazards and accidents? Do you have adequate emergency first aid knowledge and background? Ideally, each person in your party should be first aid trained. However, no party should venture out without there being at least one person in the group who is certified in the completion of first aid training and who has practiced first

aid under conditions similar to those that will be encountered.
All the aforementioned items should be carefully considered
prior to the planning stage of a canoe trip.

PLANNING

Included in the preparation of an enjoyable and successful
trip are the following subjects in a logical sequence:
1. Selection of your traveling companions
2. Selection of locale and route
3. Selection of necessary equipment
4. Preparation of food and cooking gear lists
5. Selection of leader
6. Preparation for possible emergencies

Traveling Companions

Choose your party carefully. Make sure that your group is
experienced enough to handle the class of river to be run, with
its normal hazards and possible accidents, or that they could be
adequately at home in the wilderness.

A party of six (or three canoes) is the minimum for safety.
Never travel *alone*. If a person in the party is injured, the others
can often assist him to safety. If the injury is serious, there will
be enough people to stay with the victim while at least two go
for help. It is dangerous for one person to go for help alone.
Information regarding emergency first aid in the event of injury
or illness is given in chapter 8.

Your traveling companions should be people who, in their
attitude toward others, have a natural pride in doing their share
of work and are willing to help fellow paddlers. If you have a
feeling that a certain person will not fit in, discuss your feeling
with the others and determine whether that person should be
discouraged from taking part. The problem of keeping a party
together is minimized if great differences in stamina and temper-
ament of the individual members are avoided. Someone must always have the least stamina, and certainly that person deserves
the consideration of his more robust companions; but if his
stamina is far below the party average, this weakness then becomes a hazard.

There are times when an unfortunate disparity of tempera-
ment among casual acquaintances cannot be foreseen. It is for
this reason that the organizer of a trip should know each indi-

vidual in the party well enough to insure sharing and conviviality.

The above considerations are not as important for a 1-day trip as they are for several-day voyages. The longer the trip, the more important these considerations become.

One fundamental principle often overlooked is that all members of the party should agree on the purpose of the trip. There should be only one emphasis, such as serious fishing, exploring out-of-the-way spots, floating with the current and relaxing, or pursuing some other special interest.

Locale and Route

Once the group members are decided upon, they can begin planning the route and the duration of the trip, remembering, naturally, to keep the trip within the capabilities of everyone in the party.

You must make careful plans, especially if the river or the route are new to all. Consult with the government agency having jurisdiction over the area in which you will be traveling, such as the U.S. Forest Service, the Bureau of Land Management, the U.S. Park Service, and a variety of other federal and state, and perhaps local, agencies. Contact local people or special-interest groups that know the area. Also, check for stream, wilderness, or river guides published by paddling clubs.

Make sure that put-in and take-out spots are convenient for your group as well as for those people whose land you must cross. Also, be considerate of landowners when making a portage. If you ever have the misfortune of venturing onto the land of an angered resident, you will not soon forget the experience. Remember those who may want to make the same trip some other time.

Necessary Equipment

In making up an equipment list, try to include every item that you feel is necessary for the enjoyment of your trip. Then you must shorten this list by eliminating those items that are not *absolutely* necessary. Remember to take only equipment that is in good shape.

The duration of the trip (in hours or days) and the length of possible portages will inevitably dictate the quantity of equipment to be taken. The lighter the pack on a portage, the more enjoyable the portage. Perhaps a good motto is, When in doubt, leave it out.

All equipment other than paddles, fishing poles, Coast Guard approved lifejackets, heaving line, etc., should be fitted into packs. The packs should be waterproof, much the same as the rubberized duffel bags that are available through army-navy stores.

Varieties of relatively inexpensive, lightweight, sturdy, weatherproof tents are now available, with good and not-so-good features. Your choice will depend on duration of trip, size of group, forecasted weather, and purpose of trip. Perhaps a tent will not be necessary at all.

The amount of clothing to be carried and worn is always a concern to the canoe camper. Clothing worn on a canoe trip should protect the wearer from sun, wind, and rain or, in the case of winter canoeing, against cold water and biting winter air. It should be adaptable for protection against insects.

Footwear is *very* important. It must be flexible enough to curl comfortably into the many necessary sitting and kneeling positions, yet sturdy enough to give comfort and support on the portages to be expected. Heavy leather boots are cumbersome and offer little advantage; they could even be a hazard in deep, swift water if a capsize should occur.

A good quality foul-weather suit will provide sufficient protection against rain and wind. Such a suit has the added feature of having both pants and parka, either of which could be worn independently if the need should arise. The use of ponchos should be avoided; they offer little protection from the wind and are bulky.

The following list should give you some idea of what is desirable for river or lake camping and touring. However, you should use great care in the selection of equipment for *your* trip.

Personal Gear

Shoes
Underwear
Hat
Heavy wool socks
Pants
Handkerchiefs
Belt
Foul-weather gear
Mittens
Extra pants, socks, shoes, underwear, etc.
Swimsuit
Sleeping bag
Pack
Knife
Ground cloth
Toilet kit
Notebook and pencil
Matches in waterproof case
Camera and film
Lifejacket
Fishing gear
Insect repellent
Paddles
Toilet paper
Elastic eyeglass holder and an extra one
Spare eyeglasses
Bailer and sponge

Emergency Kit

Compass
Maps
Flashlight
Concentrated food
Whistle
Extra waterproof matches
Salt
Fishhooks and line
Adhesive bandages and aspirin
2-inch gauze bandages and sterile dressings

Community Gear

Cooking utensils (including packable type of stove)
Tent
Extra paddles
Canoe repair kit
Large first aid kit
Maps and compass
River guidebook, if available
Rescue rope
Bushman's saw
Extra fresh water

You should keep the extra equipment dry and should pack it in waterproof plastic bags within the large pack. This precaution usually insures that there will be dry clothes. Use protective measures to avoid loss or breakage of personal items such as eyeglasses or pocketknife.

Food and Cooking Gear

As with equipment, you must take into consideration the weight factor of food and cooking gear, with regard to the length of the trip. It is wise to list those items that seem to be needed for the trip as much in advance of the trip as is practical.

As time for the trip grows shorter, so should the inventory of necessary items. Remember, the question is not what you can use but what you can do without.

A party of eight on a multiple-day trip with four canoes could easily get by with the following gear:

Nest of pails (3-gal., 2-gal., 1-gal., ½-gal.)
Two 12-inch skillets with folding handles
One 4-qt. tea or coffee pot
One 4-qt. grease can with top
Plates, cups, knives, forks, and spoons (eight of each)
Two large serving spoons
One pancake turner
One carving knife
Salt in waterproof container
Laundry soap
Five dish towels
A rubberized canvas bag for carrying all of the above

Because menus must take into account individual likes and needs, all members of the group should be involved in the menu planning. Although some members of the group may be accustomed to a skimpy breakfast, care should be taken to assure that all members of the party receive ample food to last them through the noon meal. Suggested breakfast items are applesauce, omelets, toast, oatmeal, stewed fruits, biscuits, honey, fruit juices, pancakes, various breakfast meats, and potatoes. These can be prepared with little effort into delicious and nutritious meals.

Since the middle of the day is occupied with activity (paddling, portaging, fishing, etc.), a quick, energizing lunch, requiring no campfire and little preparation, is best. Possibilities are—

Sandwiches, prepared meats (salami, etc.)

Dried fruits and nuts, cookies, hard candy, biscuits or crackers, honey, malted milk tablets, and dried beef

Beverages can be made up from packaged products. However,

they should be thirst-quenching. A pinch of citric acid powder dissolved in cool water is a real thirst-quencher.

Dinners are undoubtedly the mainstay of the three daily meals. Due to their ease of preparation, soups are probably the best to serve as the first course of any dinner. Spaghetti, creamed meats, instant potatoes, varieties of vegetables, stews, and many other dishes can be prepared and can be extremely tasty if care is taken.

The following are suggestions that may be useful if you are planning a menu for a trip of 4 days or more:

- The food must be of a minimum weight yet must have adequate food value. (From 3,000 to 4,200 kilogram calories per day are required by an active person on a vigorous canoeing trip.) Light weight of equipment is attained primarily by using dehydrated foods and secondarily by selecting food with a high caloric value. About 2¼ pounds per day of such foods are required for each person. The breakdown is as follows:

Starches (precooked)	.45 lb.
Sugar	.45 lb.
Nuts (shelled)	.15 lb.
Dried fruits and precooked vegetables	.30 lb.
Fats and fatty foods	.15 lb.
Protein	.75 lb.
Beverage materials	To suit
Flavoring and condiments	To suit

- Food should be readily digestible and should be balanced between fat, protein, and carbohydrates.
- Good keeping qualities and easy packaging are essential. Cans and bottles are undesirable because they add weight and bulk. Food that can be placed completely in waterproof bags, tied at the top, can be carried easily.
- Food must be easy to prepare quickly, with simple equipment. For this reason, it is desirable to take precooked foods that can be eaten cold if something should happen to the stove or if a fire cannot be made for some reason. Because the boiling point of water decreases with altitude, the cooking time doubles with every 5,000-foot increase in elevation—something many people forget.
- Strenuous activity in dry high-mountain air causes more perspiration and attendant loss of salt than is frequently realized. This loss must be replaced by extra salting of food.
- Vitamin sufficiency for trips of 4 days or less is not essential; however, enough vitamins *must* be taken along to avoid complications during extended trips.

CANOEING

- If an adequate supply of drinkable water is not at hand, water must be taken along in containers.

Selection of a Leader

Must a leader be selected immediately? Perhaps it is best to select a leader after most plans have been made. In this way, the organizer of the trip will be able to observe the individual group members working together and can suggest to the group the person best suited to lead the trip.

For a leader, the group should agree on a person who has spent considerable time in a canoe on rivers and who has had actual training and experience in river touring. Do not make the mistake of selecting a leader only for his canoeing ability.

It is really not formal leadership that is required. The leader should be someone who can easily take over when a crisis arises or, more importantly, can recognize potential danger and help to avert a crisis. In these cases, he should be given full authority and the respect of the group.

The form of the leadership will be determined by the length of the trip and the experience and stamina of the individuals in the group. Whatever form the leadership takes, the party should respect it—and the leader should, in turn, respect the members of the party.

Above all, *do not attempt* a trip on any river, stream, or lake without *competent* leadership.

Preparation for Possible Emergencies

Included in the planning phases of any trip should be the notifying of relatives, friends, and river-area authorities—or all three—of your intentions. The notification should include the dates and duration of the trip, where the put-in and take-out points are, and the names and home telephone numbers of the individuals in the party.

First aid training is a must. No trip should be attempted without having someone in the party who is trained and experienced in first aid.

Each person in the party should swim well enough so that he will not constitute a hazard to himself or others. *All* persons should be required to wear lifejackets while on a river or a rough lake.

Everyone in the party should have the ability to rescue personnel and equipment in case of a capsize. It is wise to have a session in rescue procedures prior to the trip. This practice helps in reducing confusion in time of emergency.

The weather for your trip is important. If there are predictions of a storm, or if water conditions are unsafe, the trip should be cancelled or at least delayed. Safe travel on rivers requires moderately good weather conditions. Bad weather can make a trip tough or even calamitous. Fog or snowstorms can slow you markedly or even stop you. High water on rivers often proves disastrous. Sudden changes in weather can produce impossible conditions while you are out on a trip.

Hypothermia (exposure to cold), including immersion hypothermia (cold effects of water), is discussed in chapter 8. Hypothermia and its effects on the human body should be understood by all those venturing into the outdoors *before* they go.

First aid, artificial respiration, and other emergency lifesaving measures are also discussed in chapter 8. This information, however, should not be considered as a substitute for a first aid course.

GETTING READY

Careful selection of pack, pack frame, or rucksack will enable you to take all of the necessities for the trip. Such selection will also help in portaging, since these items will fit the person using them most comfortably. Duffel bags are also used, and their selection is a matter of individual preference.

When packing all of the necessities, you will probably carry all of your personal gear plus some of the community equipment. You should place all gear carefully in the rucksack in such a way as to pad hard items so that they will not dig into your back and to place items needed during travel in a convenient location. Also, when packing, remember to keep the center of gravity low and close to the body; the pack must not sway in fast turns or have a tendency to go over your head in case you fall.

A pack with a rigid frame is easier and quicker to pack; and heavy, irregularly shaped articles can be placed close to your body without sticking into your back. The frame also allows for ventilation between your body and the pack, thus reducing an uncomfortable buildup of moisture due to perspiration.

Since water is a deterrent to comfort in canoeing, you should

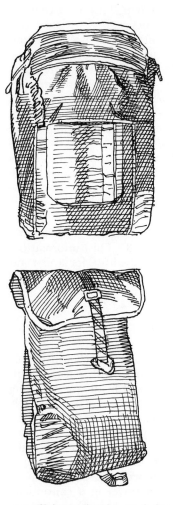

put all items in the pack into individual watertight plastic bags
to help insure against getting them wet. The pack should also
be of the waterproof variety.

Once the pack is ready to go, put it on and walk around with
it until you are sure it feels as comfortable as possible. If it is
uncomfortable, even in the slightest way, rearrange its contents
until it feels right.

Put sleeping gear into a watertight bag and tie the bag to the
top of the pack or pack frame, since sleeping gear usually does
not have much weight.

Keep the canoes, paddles, lifejackets, and other gear, such as fishing poles, together until the time of transportation to the put-in place.

Lash fishing poles securely to the canoe under the gunwales. You can usually jam paddles into one end of the canoe and securely tie them to the thwarts or seats.

You can put drinking water into containers at the last minute. Of course, if drinkable water can be had while on the trip, you can leave additional water behind.

Packing the food so that it will fit neatly with other things in the canoe and will be easy to carry on portages is a task requiring thorough knowledge of methods. You can also give consideration to its arrangement in the food pack, with regard to accessibility, so that food for a specific meal may be found without handling the entire supply.

Before leaving home, the leader should obtain the latest weather forecast and river condition report. This is easily taken care of by a telephone call to the local weather service or forestry service, or some similar agency.

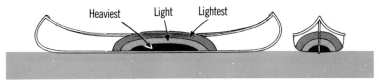

Heaviest   Light   Lightest

LOADING THE CANOE

After the putting-in, pack the canoes with provisions and equipment. Place packs in the midship section of the canoe. By trial and error, you can make adjustments so that the canoe will be trimmed evenly.

If the weather is damp, you can wrap the packs and provisions in a sheet of plastic or a tarp. Usually, it is not necessary to tie this wrapped material in, since it will float if it is as watertight as it should be. In case of upset, it would most likely float free of the canoe, thus facilitating the rescue of the canoe—a very important factor in heavy water conditions. There are, undoubtedly, some instances in which you would want to tie everything into the canoe, but these seem too remote to mention.

Secure spare paddles to the canoe with very light string or by some other method that permits immediate release but prevents loss of the paddles in case of upset. It is wise to always tie nonbuoyant items, such as fishing poles or binoculars, to the canoe.

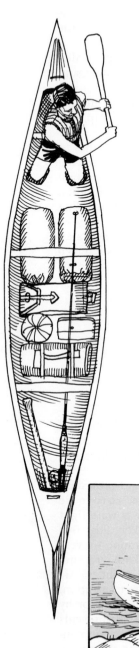

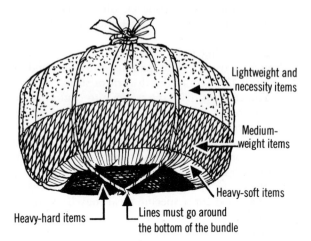

Lightweight and
necessity items

Medium-
weight items

Heavy-soft items

Heavy-hard items

Lines must go around
the bottom of the bundle

ROUTES OF TRAVEL

Routes of travel can be simplified if you obtain a topographic map of the area to be traveled in and learn to read it properly. Topographic maps show nearly everything of importance to the canoeist, especially the elevation contour lines, which will help to identify rugged, steep terrain to be avoided. Guidebooks, when used with the maps, are also of great value.

Occasionally, while traveling through wooded areas on flatwater, you could easily become confused about proper route selection due to minor flooding from heavy rains or excessive runoff during spring thaws. Flooding can cause overflow where there is a dam at the end of a lake and can cause an expansion of the shoreline into brush and timber. Flatwater riverbanks can also be expanded in much the same way. To find the main channel, check the topographic map, look for telltale signs of current, and watch for openings through the treetops made by the main channel.

Being properly prepared prior to venturing into the wilderness is one way to avoid the discouragement of getting temporarily lost and wasting valuable time.

BACKPACKING AND PORTAGING

A knowledge of the methods of carrying a canoe, discussed in chapter 4, is the basis for efficient portaging. The easiest methods are those using the commercial-type yoke or the improvised padded thwart. A load that is too heavy will be dangerous and is unnecessary. Of course, participants should be willing to do at least their share in portaging in keeping with their capacity for heavy work. Frequent stops for rest should be taken if they are needed, and time should be taken for recreation. A portage should not be a contest of speed and strength. Backpacking and portaging require common sense. If you are inexperienced and not strong, admit it and start by carrying only half the load that you will carry a little later on, and make two trips. When you are tired, stop and rest. Do not try to keep up with the next person, who might be in better shape than you and more advanced in his knowledge of the outdoors. Your companions will think more of you if you have a willing attitude and insist on resting when tired. They would rather go a little more slowly than carry you too. Portaging can be a very enjoyable and rewarding experience if you go about it properly.

Finding the portage is one of your first problems. On large lakes, a map is probably necessary. Portages on smaller lakes can usually be found without much trouble, and portages on the rivers are often easier to find, since the trails or blazes generally can be seen.

Portage trails are usually marked by blazes, signs, or other indications left by previous canoes. Keep a sharp lookout. Often it is good if you can scout an apparent route in steep terrain prior to moving equipment and supplies.

When a portage trail is found and your party is ready to land, there is a definite procedure for disembarking. If the landing space is small, only one canoe at a time should land, with the bowman stepping out and steadying the canoe. The sternman passes the duffel to the bowman, then steps out himself. The canoe and duffel are put together in a safe, out-of-the-way location with the paddles lashed to the canoe and ready for portage. The two canoeists return to the landing to assist the other canoes.

When all is ready, an experienced person with map, compass, and a light load should lead the way. On long portages, a rest every 10 or 15 minutes is a necessity. To avoid rolling the canoe down and up again, rest it in the crotch of a tree wherever possible.

When walking, do not step on roots, because they are slippery and often cause serious falls. A good rule to follow is not to step on anything that you can step over, such as rocks or logs. This precaution saves energy and avoids losing your balance, slipping, or falling. An injury in a remote area would be serious and would spoil the trip for all concerned.

To hurry through a portage invites accidents. It also puts a burden on your fellow portagers and causes unnecessary fatigue and discomfort. Help one another and stay together. Rest at regular intervals and take time to enjoy each other, the wilderness, and the trip. A great touch and a fine gesture is to have someone keep insects away from you and to swat that fly on your neck when you are carrying a canoe or have your hands full.

At the end of the portage trail, make sure that everything that was off-loaded for the portage has arrived and that nothing has been lost or left behind.

When everything is reloaded into the canoes and all is ready, the party can start out once again as a unit.

TRACKING, LINING, AND WADING

When a stream is too fast for successful upstream work, it will be necessary to carry around the difficult places or to tow the canoe upstream. Towing the canoe is called tracking and is often done with long lines. The upstream line should be rigged bridle fashion to lead out from the forefoot of the canoe (see chapter 7). This arrangement will assure that this end of the canoe will at all times ride lightly, free of the grip of the current. A second line is tied to a downstream thwart. One canoeist working both lines or two canoeists, one on each line, tow the canoe along in deep water while walking along the bank or wading in shallow water if the shore is obstacle-cluttered. The towing is accomplished by letting the current hit the inshore side of the canoe at a slight angle, keeping the canoe headed away from shore as it is pulled upstream. You can keep the canoe at this desired angle by adjusting the relative lengths and pulls on the two lines. In mild circumstances, the same task may

be done with the regular bow and stern lines. Sometimes only the upstream line is used, and the second person keeps the canoe offshore with the tip of his paddle.

When water is too dangerous to run, you can carry the canoe around the bad stretch or line it down through. Lining is the opposite of tracking, in respect to the direction in which you are moving the canoe, but the rigging of lines (e.g., upstream line leading from forefoot) and the handling principles are the same. Work the lines, one against the other, to put the canoe in the right position in respect to the current so that it will be carried downstream, clear of the alongshore obstructions, but will be

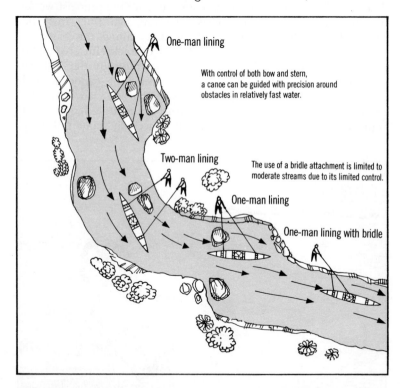

One-man lining

With control of both bow and stern, a canoe can be guided with precision around obstacles in relatively fast water.

Two-man lining

The use of a bridle attachment is limited to moderate streams due to its limited control.

One-man lining

One-man lining with bridle

under control at all times. The illustration depicts tracking or lining as done by either a solo paddler or a tandem crew.

If when going upstream you encounter rapids against which progress cannot be made, and yet shallow water makes wading possible and safe, it is an easy matter to step out and wade up through, towing the canoe along. It is necessary to tow from the upstream end, and it will be helpful if you lift lightly on the end rather than lean on it, so that the current will not catch it. When you encounter very shallow and rocky stretches while going downstream, follow the same procedure. Wade, holding the upstream end, and guide the canoe down with the current.

CAMP SETUP

It is not possible to give exact specifications for an ideal campsite, since much depends on terrain, climate, and type of shelter to be used. However, the following points can be used as general rules of thumb:

- Freedom from hazardous occurrences, such as rising river and falling trees or falling rocks from loose hillsides or ledges
- Availability of drinkable water—Sometimes you must bring drinking water with you.
- Protection from wind—Timber is the best wind protection.
- Firewood—Having a campfire saves fuel if small stoves have been brought along and adds a comfortable evening atmosphere.
- Warmth of location—Lowest temperatures usually come on clear, quiet nights. On such nights, flat valleys are the coldest spots in mountain areas. A sheltered bench 100 or more feet above the valley floor will frequently be 10 or 15 degrees warmer than the valley. Also, your camp should be placed to get the morning sun.
- Routes of retreat—Since a storm or some other more serious hazard may arise, you should make sure that a safe route of retreat exists.
- Time—The most ideal campsite prepared in the dusk or dark will not compare with a camp set up in daylight—completely cozy, with fire crackling, supper steaming, and sleeping bags ready when night falls. You can enhance the pleasures of a trip if you start your camp-making early.
- Scenery—Whenever possible, set up the camp in a location offering all the above features *and* the most beautiful scenery possible. No one should miss the opportunity of letting his imagination loose as he looks at the moonlight on trees, river, lakes, mountains, or snow-covered peaks. The effect is not decreased by having all but your nose and eyes in a warm, snug sleeping bag.
- Lightning—Hilltops, tall trees, and large, open areas are

especially susceptible to being struck by lightning. Avoid them when setting up camp. Aluminum canoes, especially, attract lightning; therefore, to use one for shelter in an electrical storm is foolhardy.

- Limited area—At times, you may be forced to make camp where comfortable space is at a premium, such as a relatively narrow canyon or a heavily bushed location. All efforts, in this situation, should be directed to the security and safety of the group and equipment. Packs could be suspended from trees. Canoes should be secured high and dry. Freedom from danger and accessibility of retreat should receive first consideration.

The campsite in the illustration below typifies an ideal camp setup.

Some improvised shelter arrangements are shown in the following illustrations.

More and more canoeists, when traveling through marshland areas or swamps, are utilizing the kind of shelter shown in the illustration.

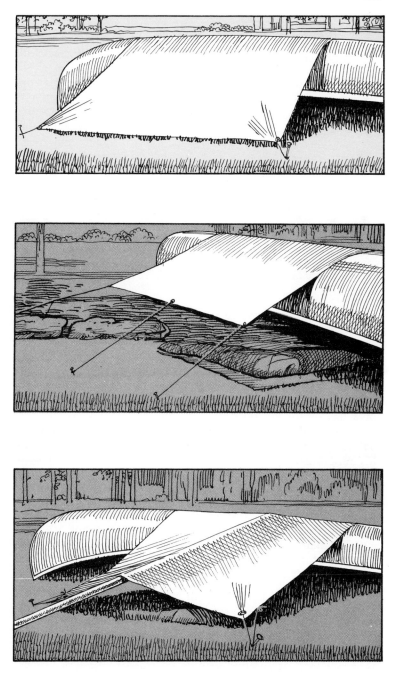

This is a good idea for marshlands, swamp areas, and very protected inlets on lakes. It should not be used around moving water.

THE FOREST AND ITS CONSERVATION

If you plan to go into forest areas, whether nearby or remote, for a day or for extended periods, you should understand the importance of the forest and its conservation. The following material from a Department of Agriculture bulletin * points up this importance.

The forest itself is beautiful and useful, and has played a vital part in the development of the human race. . . . The history of the United States is staged against a forest background.

As the country expanded . . . communities sprang up subsisting mainly upon the bounty of the forest. Each decade saw more and more forests cut away with an extravagance born of the idea that the forests of America were inexhaustible.

The forests have been and still are one of the nation's most important natural resources. Not only do they play a leading

---

* *Our Forest Resources*, Agriculture and Information Bulletin No. 131, U.S. Department of Agriculture, Forest Service. (*Adapted*)

part in the economic and industrial life of the nation today, but they also serve us in many other ways. By checking the rains and melting snows, they help to prevent erosion and floods and to insure a steady flow of water for power and domestic use; they are the source of many products besides lumber; they produce forage for domestic livestock; they are the home of much of our game and wildlife; they furnish innumerable opportunities for recreation; and they make this country a more pleasant and beautiful place in which to live. If we were deprived of forests, we would suffer economically, physically, and esthetically. It is therefore important that we handle our forest wealth so that it may be used to fill our countless needs and at the same time continue as a permanent natural resource.

A review of the literature, including government pamphlets, dealing with the use of forests for recreation reveals quite uniform rules for conduct in regard to the conservation of the forests. In general, these rules are as follows:

• Build your campfire close to the water's edge and on a spot where you have scraped away all leaves, moss, lichen, deadwood, or other flammable material in a circular area 10 feet in diameter. Drown the fire with water before leaving camp, even if you will only be away for a few minutes. Mix the ashes thoroughly with water. Merely pouring water on top of the fire is not sufficient, since live coals may not be reached and may start a forest fire after you are gone.

The U.S. Forest Service states that 9 out of 10 forest fires are started by man, so remember that you cannot be too careful. On a dry and windy day it might be best not to light a fire at all, unless it is at the very water's edge, and it would be advisable to put up a stone barrier at the onshore side of the fire. Under normal conditions, build fires where others have built them before you. This is a general rule in national forests and national parks. Be aware of and abide by local regulations that pertain to campfires. In the many wilderness areas that do not permit campfires, a small portable stove would suffice.

• Dispose of garbage and trash by burning them in your campfire where such a practice is permitted. Unburnable refuse must be carried out with you in the interest of ecology.

• Leave the campsite cleaner than when you arrived, if possible. A National Parks information folder expresses outdoor cleanliness and good manners as follows: "Let it not be said, and to your shame, that all was beauty here, until you came."

- Make sure you know the regulations about smoking. Generally, smoking is restricted to times when you are afloat, or in the cleared campsite area. When in doubt, consult a ranger, or use your best judgment.
- Do not pollute the ground or the water. Never throw any refuse of any kind into the water, and do not clean fish in the water. The latrine area should be a good distance away from the water and from the open campsite area. Excrement should be buried promptly.
- Abide by applicable regulations regarding cutting wood. Usually only dead and fallen wood should be cut, and trees and shrubbery should not be defaced. On the other hand, the cutting of wood is a matter of location.

12

COMPETITIVE PADDLING

This chapter deals with the organized sport of canoeing in its major specialities. Competitive canoeing as an organized amateur sport in the United States is governed by the American Canoe Association (ACA), which conducts divisional and national championship races each year. The ACA also selects team members for the World Championships every 2 years (whitewater) and for the Olympic Games (flatwater) when they are held.

In order to protect the amateur status of competitors, those persons who want to conduct competitive events should write to the ACA for guidance. This will eliminate the chance of any paddler's losing eligibility for further development as a top amateur competitor.

Informal races are often conducted in camps, schools, and recreation agencies and by various clubs and organizations not affiliated with the organized sport of canoeing, as a part of instruction and recreation.

Organized competition for sailing canoes (see chapter 14) and canoe poling (see chapter 13) is also sponsored by the ACA. Canoe poling competition is conducted as a slalom race, with rules and regulations resembling those mentioned in the section on slalom competition.

GETTING STARTED

The best way for the novice to get started is for him to associate himself with a person already competing, or with a club. The American Canoe Association conducts various clinics at its base camp and in different parts of the country, to help develop talent. A knowledge of paddling techniques, good physical condition, and skill in the use of specialized craft are all necessary in any form of competition. In Olympic flatwater competition, the use of specialized craft may be the most difficult aspect. The novice should always start competing in the standard types of craft, and as his abilities improve and develop, he can gradually shift to the more specialized types of craft.

River competition is an exercise in strength, stamina, and paddling techniques. Added to the competitor's problems beyond flatwater racing is the art of properly reading the varied currents found on rivers. Selecting the fastest possible course down the river is perhaps the most difficult part of river competition. Miscalculating the current or not placing the boat in the proper part of the current can result in the boat's being turned into an eddy, thus wasting valuable time.

Since absolute control of the craft is necessary at all times and in any river situation, strength is a must in order to develop the needed control.

Nearly all paddling clubs participate in some form of training and racing. The novice should join a club in order to take advantage of the expertise of the members, to learn about the different types of craft, and to utilize the resources of the club for training.

Paddling with precision on flatwater is one thing, but in a fast-moving river it becomes more difficult. Many competitors use the winter season to develop control, in pool sessions with slalom gates hung above the water, or they practice on a quiet stream or pond. Later they progress to more rapidly moving water and advance to whitewater.

The novice racer should begin in shorter races held on easy rivers and should go on to the more strenuous and difficult races as his abilities develop, under the guidance of a more experienced competitor. The opportunities for the novice in river racing are widespread, since this is one of the most popular forms of canoe competition.

OLYMPIC FLATWATER COMPETITION

History

Competitive racing on flatwater was well established in the United States when it was first introduced into the Olympics in Europe in 1924. The XIth Olympiad in Berlin, in 1936, saw canoeing introduced as an official part of the games. The classes of competition then included F-1 and F-2 (folding kayak), K-1 and K-2 (rigid kayak), and C-1 (Canadian canoe). The races covered distances of 1,000 and 10,000 meters.

Events

Today the Olympic canoeing events include those for women (K-1W and K-2W) and men (K-1, K-2, K-4, C-1, and C-2). The women's events cover a distance of 500 meters, while the men's events cover both 500 and 1,000 meters (except the K-4, which is held only at 1,000 meters).

Although these are the only events currently used in the Olympic Games, there are other events included in national championship competition and international competition. Other events usually will include senior, junior, juvenile, and master, in K-1W

(5,000), K-1 (10,000), C-1 (10,000), K-2 (10,000), C-2 (10,000), C-4 (1,000), K-2W (5,000), and K-4 (10,000). International competition includes the Continental Championships and the Pan American Games, as well as any other competition in which two or more nations compete.

Craft

The craft used in the Olympic competition have evolved into
a highly specialized design that only slightly resembles the typical
canoe. They are constructed of laminated wood veneer, although
some are made of fiber-reinforced plastics. These craft are long
and narrow, with rounded and pointed ends. Their speed potential is a function of their length-to-beam ratio and the amount
of wetted surface of the hull. The longer and narrower the hull,
the greater its potential speed. Stability, paddler comfort, turning ease, and strength have all been minimized to produce a craft
with the greatest possible speed potential and the lightest weight.
The design of these craft has become standardized.

Course

An Olympic course is laid out as nine straight lanes, marked by buoys, with start and finish lines clearly indicated. Sheltered water, with no current and of sufficient depth to provide fair canoeing conditions, is required. There should be at least 9 feet of depth. If it is not possible to have such a depth, a uniform depth is necessary for the entire course. Courses of up to 1,000 meters (straight courses with no deviation) must provide lanes 7 meters wide. Courses of over 1,000 meters must provide sufficient clear width of 5 meters for each boat. There should be a place for the finish judges and timers, with a clear view of the finish line. The starter must be located at the starting line, and a referee in a motorboat must follow the competitors.

Race Procedures

The paddlers are each assigned to their lanes by the clerk of the course and told when to report to the starter. The start is a

standing start, with each competitor responsible for properly positioning himself at the starting line.

The starter starts the race as soon as he feels that all craft are in a fair position. Any paddler unable to control his craft at the start is disqualified.

The object is to get from the start to the finish in the shortest possible time. The first boat across the finish line wins. If it is necessary to have two or more heats for a final, the elapsed times are used as qualifying factors for the finals.

WILDWATER COMPETITION

Wildwater competition, which is a relatively recent development in canoe sport, consists of three basic forms: open-canoe whitewater, wildwater using decked canoes, and marathon competition.

For the purpose of this text, a race on a river with suitable whitewater challenges using "open," or undecked, canoes will be termed a wildwater race. The craft used in this competition meet the ACA specifications for open canoes.

A wildwater race also utilizes decked canoes and kayaks with spray skirts. The procedures for using either craft in competition are the same.

Marathon competition is covered later in this chapter.

Events

The classes of competition include the five ICF recognized events in wildwater: K-1, K-1W, C-2, C-2M, and C-1. Open-boat races include C-1, C-2, C-2M, C-2W, and other events held at the race chairman's discretion.

Craft

In an open-boat wildwater race, virtually any type of canoe is eligible, but the most successful types usually have generous freeboard and are long, narrow, and light in weight. The ACA has established measurement specifications for these craft and designates three different length classifications: short (less than 16.5 feet), medium (between 16.5 and 18.5 feet), and long (over 18.5 feet). The decked craft in wildwater competition are designed along the same general principles but are fully decked and must meet the ICF specifications.

Course

There is no specified length for wildwater races, although they are generally in the range of from 3 to 7 miles ICF and 5 to 20 miles for open canoes. A wildwater site must have a course of at least 1.86 miles and must be of Class III difficulty or greater. In no case (for ICF decked-boat races only) is a portage allowed in a wildwater race, and the course must be navigable throughout its length. Some open-canoe whitewater races include a portage. It is desirable for there to be general public access at both the start and finish of the race course. Permission from land-owners is necessary; and, if possible, there should be areas for spectators along the race course, particularly at the finish. The Open Canoe National Championships use a site that has a variety of water conditions (flatwater, moving water, and rapids up to Class IV) and a portage.

Race Procedures

Each competitor is assigned a starting time in advance, as his entry is received, and he receives the time and the race number at registration or at the competitors' meeting, prior to the race.

It is each competitor's responsibility to be at the starting line, ready to start, at the assigned time. This requirement is very important, since the race starts at the assigned time whether the competitor does or not. Competitors are started at established intervals, usually 30 seconds or 1 minute, with a short break between classes. In this way, 120 boats or 60 boats can be started in 1 hour.

At the finish, the times are recorded as the paddlers cross the finish line, and the elapsed time is calculated by using the difference between the starting and finishing times. The lowest elapsed time wins.

There are safety crews stationed at any especially difficult and hazardous spots. Also, a sweep boat follows the last competitor to make sure that all paddlers are off the river at the end of competition.

SLALOM COMPETITION

Slalom competition is conducted for both decked and open canoes in separate races. The organization of a slalom is a complex logistical and administrative problem, requiring the help of several people to insure that the race runs smoothly. Slaloms may be held on flatwater as well as on whitewater. They may also be held for canoe poling, using similar organization and rules.

History

Whitewater paddling was promoted and organized in the United States in the thirties by the Appalachian Mountain Club. In 1949, in Geneva, Switzerland, the first Slalom World Championship was held. The North American debut was in 1953, on the Brandywine Creek in Delaware. In 1958, on the West River in Vermont, the first national championship was organized. Until 1962, standard canoes were used, then the sport was dramatically changed with the introduction of the fully decked canoe designed in Europe for whitewater slalom racing. These first fiberglass boats, designed for maneuverability, fully decked, and built to the minimum specifications, revolutionized the sport of whitewater paddling.

In 1962, there were two major U.S. slaloms. Today, there may be one or more every weekend of the paddling season, all across the country.

Events

Events include the five recognized ICF classes: C-1, C-2, C-2M, K-1, and K-1W plus C-1W and C-2W in the United States. Other classes may be added at the race chairman's discretion.

Craft

Slalom craft are built to meet specifications for minimum length and beam, as follows:

Type	Length	Beam
C-1	4 meters	.70 meters
C-2	5 meters	.80 meters
K-1	4 meters	.60 meters

Slalom craft are usually low, short, narrow craft, with either rounded or flat bottoms with a great deal of rocker. A true slalom boat is built to be as light as possible and is constructed of fiber-reinforced plastic.

All craft must be unsinkable and must be equipped with flotation bags and either end lines or grab loops at each end for safety. Paddlers must wear helmets and lifejackets. A slalom for open canoes does not require paddlers to wear helmets. There are no specifications for open slalom canoes at this time. However, definitive specifications will probably be developed in the near future.

Course

A slalom site should have public access and good vantage points for spectators. The object is to negotiate a numbered series of narrow gates in order, from the starting point to the finish in the shortest time, without touching any of the gates. Since touching a gate or missing one will add a penalty time to the score, it is necessary to go through the course with precision as well as speed.

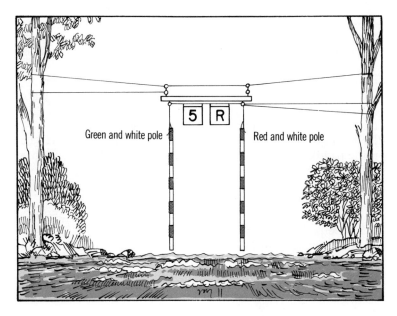

Green and white pole

5 R

Red and white pole

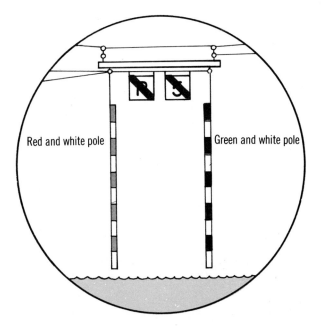

Red and white pole

Green and white pole

A course can be set up on any body of water from flatwater through Class V rapids, depending on the intended level of competition. The course should be no longer than half a mile, with a maximum of 30 gates. A gate consists of a crossbar hung on a wire, with two poles and the gate number hung from it. The poles—one green and white and the other red with white horizontal stripes—are at least 1.2 meters (4 feet) apart. An "R" after the gate number indicates a "reverse" gate, which the paddler must go through stern-first. The red-and-white poles will be on the paddler's left as he goes through and the green-and-white poles on his right. The back side of the gate number has a diagonal line through it. If the gate is a reverse gate, the back side of the "R" has a diagonal line through it also.

The course is designed to present a challenge to the abilities of the competitors to read and use the moving water.

The following illustration is an example of the kind of maneuvering necessary to negotiate a series of gates on a slalom course.

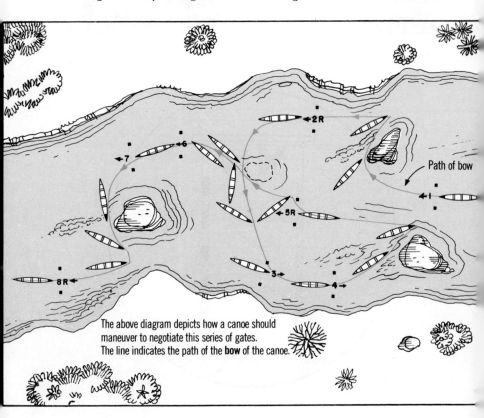

Path of bow

The above diagram depicts how a canoe should maneuver to negotiate this series of gates. The line indicates the path of the **bow** of the canoe.

Race Procedures

Paddlers will be assigned a starting order for each class of competition, rather than a specific time at which to start. The start is from a fixed position next to the starter. The paddler must get his body and boat through each gate in the proper order and direction. For each gate, a paddler may receive one of the following penalties: 10 seconds for touching a pole from inside the gate while going through the gate in the proper order and direction; 20 seconds for touching the gate from outside or touching both poles from inside the gate followed by negotiating the gate; and 50 seconds for not going through the gate in the proper order or direction or for another technical violation.

The object is to negotiate the course in the shortest possible time with as few penalties as possible. The competitor's score is his elapsed time plus all penalties. A competitor is permitted one official practice run and two race runs on the course. Of the two race runs, the poorer score is discarded, and the better of the two scores is his official score for the purpose of determining the race results. The lowest total score wins.

MARATHON COMPETITION

Today the term "marathon" is generally meant to apply to a race held on still or moving water over a long distance. Distances covered in a race tend to be about 20 miles, but sometimes the distance is as little as 6 miles or as much as 50 miles. As in a downriver race, the object is to get from the start to the finish in the shortest possible time. It is sometimes difficult to make a distinction between a marathon and a downriver race. Sometimes, a marathon has a massed start of all competitors and is held on relatively flat water or in easy rapids, as contrasted with the wildwater race.

For many years the ACA sanctioned the marathon and championship programs, but in 1958, the United States Canoe Association (USCA) was established to undertake the administration of marathon canoeing. Today, both the ACA and the USCA are cooperating in the sponsorship and organization of marathon competition in the United States.

Events

Today's events in marathon competition are predominantly tandem races. In order to be sanctioned by the USCA, a marathon race must offer at least C-2M, C-2W, C-2 Junior, C-1, and K-1 competition. Other classes may be added at the discretion of the race chairman.

Craft

There is no standardized design for marathon canoes, but they are designed to meet certain specifications. For example, if maximum length were 18½ feet (or 222 inches), minimum width at a 4-inch waterline would be .14375 times length, or 31.9125 inches. Standard types of canoes may be entered in separate classes of competition. The competitors usually paddle from a sitting position on a lowered seat, with the paddler braced into the canoe. The canoes have low ends and little freeboard. In some instances, spray decks may be permitted, such as the improvised plastic one shown in chapter 3, which is taped on.

Course

Normally, any distance may be covered, but as a general rule, a distance of 20 miles is desirable. The start and finish lines should be well marked. The course should include a variety of water conditions such as a lake, a stream, rapids, and even a portage (although it is not necessary).

Race Procedures

As the competitors register at the race site, the canoes are inspected and the paddlers' race numbers are issued. (Many large races conduct preregistration for competitors.) As with wildwater racing, competitors start at predetermined time intervals. In races with a great number of competitors, classes start separately, or competitors are even started in heats. In such cases, starting times for all boats must be accurately recorded. Finish times are recorded for each boat at the finish, and the elapsed times are calculated. The lowest elapsed time wins. The last boat down the course is followed by a safety boat to make sure that all paddlers are off the course and safe.

RULES AND OFFICIALS

Generally speaking, the following sections will give you some idea of the rules and personnel used in organized amateur competition. The specific details of race organization, race rules, and design specifications for boats and equipment have not been included in this chapter because of frequent changes in procedures and rules made by either the International Canoe Federation (ICF), the USCA, or the ACA.

Rules

The majority of rules concern the equipment and its specifications. This, of course, includes the craft and paddles as well as wearing apparel required by the specific rules governing the competition. In addition, rules of conduct while competing are included. For instance, no interference with other craft on the course is permitted, and no assistance may be given that enables a competitor to gain an unfair advantage over other competitors. However, there are rules stating that if another competitor is in danger, others are required to render assistance.

In most flatwater events, a paddler who is clearly out of control of his craft at the starting line may be disqualified. Crossing over a lane line is also considered interference and is reason for disqualification.

Race Officials

Race officials are the key to a successful competition. The number of officials necessary for any particular competition depends upon the type of competition, the number of entries, the level of the competition (i.e., interclub, regional, national, or international) and the type of course. The following officials are usually found at any large competitive event: race chairman, registrar, clerk of the course, recorders, referees, judges, timers, announcer, safety and first aid crew, measurement committee, and protest committee to handle any protests that might arise. Although all these officials are useful, races have been held with only a fraction of them being used.

13

POLING

THE POLING CONCEPT

Poling was considered an essential part of canoemanship by the voyageurs and the pioneers of early American river travel. In later years, the total concept was all but lost with the use of the car shuttle, as more and more paddlers became downstream canoeists. However, with the upsurge in canoeing in recent years, the poling concept has been revived in many parts of the country. Moreover, due to the availability of new materials used in making poles and canoes, poling is constantly being refined.

Poling is the fastest way to move a canoe upstream by human power. Newcomers attending poling events are surprised to learn that this is true. The experienced poler is able to continue his ascent in all but the swiftest cascading rapids. But even there, he uses the eddies, works his way up behind boulders, or probes his way through the shallows near shore. His progress continues, while the paddler must battle the current, give up, or resort to tracking or portage.

Canoeing seems to attract the independent type of person, and he can add to his independence by taking up the pole. With little or no preparation, he can drive to the put-in, pole upstream, and float back at his own leisure. He need not worry about driving expense or car shuttle. Learning the art of poling can open up many streams to a former downstream paddler. If he has a yen to pioneer uncharted or unfamiliar streams, he can do so without worry over much detailed planning, distance of travel, time of take-out, unexpected portages, or water level. If he encounters any of these problems, he can simply turn around and drift back.

While poling in the standing position, the canoeist learns the river from a new perspective. With a higher view than a paddler, the poler is better able to see the river bottom and the life therein. He acquires a more accurate picture of the river and learns more about its currents and movements. On long downstream cruises, the paddler can find poling a welcome relief from a continual paddling position. After acquiring experience, he can alternate by poling first on one side and then the other, thus putting more muscles into use as well as covering greater distances, whether canoeing upstream or downstream.

The canoe pole must not be thought of simply as a tool that the poleman applies to the river bottom in order to propel his canoe. It has many other uses, e.g., it can be used in the manner of a double-bladed paddle when the poler finds himself in water too deep for poling. With its long length, the pole affords enough catch to quickly move the canoe whether the canoeist is in the standing or the sitting position. While the canoeist is poling in the standing position, the pole can be used in the same manner as the aerialist's balancing bar. It is also used as a snubbing device to slowly bring the canoe down and through rough and rocky rapids. When the paddler finds himself hung up on logs or boulders, the pole can supply the needed grip on the river bottom for shoving off. This is especially true in deep, icy, winter water, when the paddler prefers to remain in his canoe and not jump into the water to release it. Also in cold weather, the pole is a useful implement for moving the canoe over shallow water to the shore, thus allowing the poler to step ashore directly from his canoe without getting wet. The pole has also been used as a lean-to spine, as a tent pole, or, on certain occasions, as a means of warding off wild animals. It is highly recommended for all canoemen, since it can be carried out of the way and bent around inside the canoe, whether the canoe is on the river or on the roof of a car.

STABILITY FROM A STANDING POSITION

If you are a beginning poler, it is very important for you to know how stable a canoe is when you are in the standing position. This position is highly recommended, since poling is not nearly as effective from the kneeling or sitting position.

To learn, get into a canoe on a warm day with pole in hand and situate yourself in still water about 2 or 3 feet deep. Be prepared to get wet, and have someone standing nearby. Hold the pole in the middle and keep your knees loose and flexible. Remember that the pole will help you to keep your balance. Start rocking the canoe from side to side and gradually increase this action to the turning-over point. Do not hold back and worry about dumping, since you should be prepared for it. Consequently, in a matter of minutes you will quickly know the stability limits of the canoe, and the result will be a more relaxed and comfortable feeling, since these limits are far greater than non-polers realize. Knowing the turning-over limits of the canoe will help you recognize just how safe poling is from the standing position. You will learn more quickly and will considerably reduce the initial anxiety period and the time wasted on timid and ineffective strokes. Many beginning polers do not allow themselves enough time to overcome this anxiety period, nor do they attempt to discover the stability limits; therefore, they give up and never learn the art of poling and its full effectiveness. It would be wise to note that many experienced polers, when first boarding their canoe, will rock it a bit in order to get the feel. Therefore, if you take some time out from paddling and follow these instructions, you will soon become a safer and more effective poler.

CHARACTERISTICS OF POLES

Poles can be made in several different ways and with a variety of materials. Even those quickly hacked out of the woods may prove useful; however, a top-quality pole is highly recommended, since it can last for many years and can greatly enhance performance. Poles can readily be obtained from lumber yards or aluminum suppliers. They should be about 12 feet long and 1 inch in diameter. However, the diameter will depend on the type of material used. A strong, light, semiflexible material is best. Either a clear, straight-grained wood, such as spruce, or a light, flexible ash is first rate if it can be found. If no other materials are available, the more common woods such as maple and pine can do the job. These woods can be strengthened by being wrapped with fiberglass tape and then being saturated with polyester or epoxy resin. However, depending on the kind of woods used, sufficient fiberglass wrappings to increase the strength can make the pole too heavy.

With the exception of highly expensive poles that are filament-wound, aluminum poles are the best. Yet in selecting an aluminum pole you must be careful that you choose the proper alloy. Although somewhat more expensive than most wooden poles, aluminum poles are both strong and light and can last a lifetime. They are presently being used by most of the top national polers. Since the pole is metal, many polers do not bother attaching a metal shoe or spike. The aluminum ends do not wear or split like wood and they grip relatively well against rocky river bot-

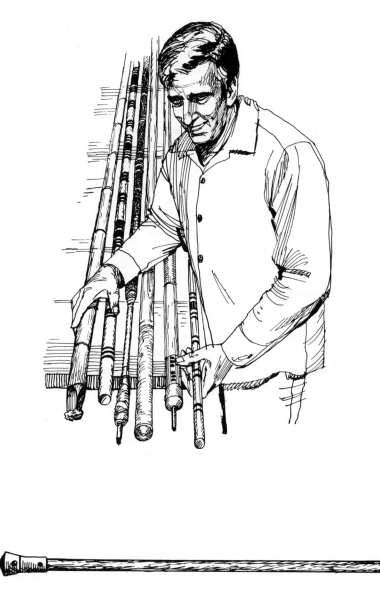

toms. Nevertheless, it would be wise to add a shoe and spike if you want the best in performance. It is important for you to select a pole that will conform to the current American Society of Testing Materials specifications. This will assure that the pole will be light enough to float (if plugged on both ends), strong enough to withstand the strain, and flexible enough to bend sufficiently and spring back into shape. Request a 6061 T-6 round or drawn tube, 12 feet in length and 1 inch in diameter, with a .058-inch wall thickness. Many manufacturers make tubing that weighs between .200 and .230 pounds per lineal foot. Note that the total weight of such a pole will be less than 3 pounds.

Aluminum poles should be plugged at both ends, so that they will be watertight and will float. Plugs are usually made of wood and are driven into the end of the pole approximately 1½ inches and cut off flush with the end of the pole.

Poles can be painted bright red, bright green, brown with several white or yellow stripes, etc. Evenly spaced stripes, 1 foot apart, can tell you the exact depth of the river while the contrasting stripes can aid you in quickly locating the pole if it is lost overboard. The paint (which helps preserve a wooden pole) also prevents the metal of a nonanodized aluminum pole from rubbing off on your hands, while at the same time the painted pole seems to fit better into the overall canoe scene.

SHOE AND SPIKE ATTACHMENTS

Shoes and spikes added to the pole can not only enhance the poler's performance but also can greatly add to the life of the pole. They should be designed so that they give the kind of grip the poleman desires but do not catch onto rocks or ledges. Due to constant erosion, most rivers have either rock, sand, or gravel bottoms, which make them highly suitable for poling. The experienced poler knows that most streams having soft or muddy banks can offer a solid grip a short distance from the shoreline. Therefore, it is best to have some type of spike attachment on the pole. On rivers, lakes, and swamps, with relatively soft bottoms, the crow's foot or duck's bill attachment can offer the needed grip.

Wooden Pole

Wooden poles can be fitted with all the shoe and spike combinations shown in this section. The pole diameter should be from 1¼ to 1½ inches and should be made from a nonsplintering, straight-grained, knot-free, lightweight wood.

Aluminum Pole

Aluminum poles can be purchased from metal supply houses, but see to it that they rigidly conform to the material specifications (see section on characteristics of poles). All types of pole ends can be attached to the aluminum pole with minor changes in size and configuration. However, it is important that the shoe and spike are not so heavy that the whole pole will sink if accidentally dropped overboard.

Sawtooth Shoe

The sawtooth shoe is made of a high-impact-resistant metal with a sawtooth edge filed so that the sharp corner of the tooth is at the extreme outside tip. When the teeth are sharp, this shoe performs well on slick slab rock, gravel, and most other river bottoms. This shoe can be kept ready for use by continual sharpening with a triangle file. It is wise to apply a safety-type cap over the sawtooth shoe when the pole is not in use.

Nylon Shoe and Spike

The nylon shoe and spike can be turned on a lathe by a machine shop and can be made to fit over any size of aluminum or wooden pole. It performs as a one-piece spike, shoe, and gravel-guard combination. The impact resistance of nylon or similar types of plastic is well known, and nylon's abrasive resistance is excellent.

Quick-Jab Shoe and Spike

For the quick-jab stroke, the section of the pole exposed to the water when the pole is dragged forward should have the smallest cross section possible, to minimize water resistance and to allow for instant return to the next jab position. The illustration of the shoe in this chapter is one example, and there are many variations. The extension rod should extend down from the pole from 24 to 30 inches and should be turned from aluminum in one piece and screwed or force-fitted to the pole. Although this shoe can be used for general purposes, it is most effective against a fast rapid less than 3 or 4 feet in depth.

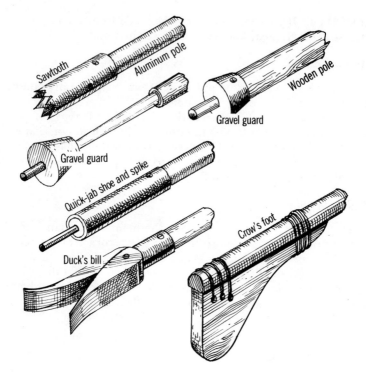

Gravel-Guard Shoe

The gravel-guard type of shoe is used only on a wooden pole and consists of a piece of aluminum, brass, or steel tubing about 1 foot long, tightly fitted over the pole. After the tube is applied, a hard steel rod from ¼ to ⁵⁄₁₆ inch in diameter and 7 inches long can be used as the spike. A hole slightly smaller than the spike can be drilled into the pole end. The hole should then be wetted, thus allowing the wood to swell so that the steel rod, after being driven into the hole, will not come loose. The spike should not extend more than 2 or 3 inches down from the end of the pole.

Duck's Bill

The duck's bill is used in lakes, swamps, rice paddies, or in some rivers having soft sand or mud bottoms. It is commercially manufactured and is constructed of steel stampings and an aluminum casting. It can be fitted to a wooden pole having a diameter of 1¼ inches. Also, it may be used with aluminum or wood poles having smaller diameters by utilizing metal sleeves. The stampings are hinged so that they fan out away from each other when driven into soft sand or mud, thereby exposing a large flat area for an effective catch. They are commercially available from a large Midwest mail order house at a nominal cost.

Crow's Foot

The crow's foot is used for the same purpose as the duck's bill but does not nearly equal the same degree of effectiveness. However, it can also be used as a rudder, near the end of the stroke, to assist with the steering. It should be constructed of a hard wood 1 inch thick and about 9 inches long. The final shoe can be varied but should approximate that in the drawing. The pole should be slotted to receive the crow's foot with a snug fit. Then it can be wired on to hold it in place. Holes drilled to receive the wire should be staggered across the grain for strength.

Boathook

Boathooks (not shown) can also be adequate as pole shoes. They can be purchased from some marine suppliers, and the hook can be removed so that the socket forms the pole shoe. Although they are almost complete upon purchase, they are not very effective and are difficult to attach to aluminum poles.

BASIC POLING STROKES

The very basic poling strokes can be easily understood, but as you gain experience, it is important for you to realize that a canoe will move and turn in a different manner or direction if there is the slightest alteration in grip, stance, foot position, hip swivel, etc. For example, you can execute a left turn from the left side while moving slowly and probing directly out to your left from the stern. Yet this same application made from the middle of a fast-moving canoe will result in a right turn. Also, changes in directional pressure applied by your hands against the pole can result in the canoe's turning to the right instead of the left. More simply stated, you can apply the pole out to the left, resulting in a left turn, or you can direct the poling force toward the canoe by pulling yourself toward the pole with your lower hand and outward with your upper hand, thus making a right turn.

After learning the basic turns, you will soon find yourself

poling along while instinctively applying opposite directional force with your hands onto the pole in order to steer the canoe. Also, you will discover that normal turns can be made without the need of probing out and away from the canoe. You then transfer leverage pressure, through semistiffened arms, body, and legs, down through your feet to the hull, and this action will result in a turn. The position and placement of your feet, as well as the selection of which foot receives and transfers the leverage force, can determine which way the canoe will turn, even though your hand application may still be the same. When you attempt to make a left turn, there are many inhibiting factors that can cause the canoe to turn right instead: speed of canoe, direction of current, wind direction and velocity, etc. In addition, such factors as weight distribution, whether the canoe is being poled solo or double, and improper hip motion must be taken into account.

Although the explanation may seem complex, it should help you to understand the strokes described and to realize that there is more to it than meets the eye. For example, if you attempt one of the strokes described and the canoe seems to be heading right instead of left, you should determine which of the many factors caused this action. But, most important, you will be thinking and reasoning, therefore not only learning the basic strokes but also using them in combination to achieve desired results.

You should learn the strokes mentioned here with the understanding that not only are they highly effective but also they may be performed in numerous other ways. In some instances, each stroke or turn mentioned is only one of many ways of achieving similar results.

Although the paddler is concerned with the relationship of his boat to the water, the poler has an added factor to consider: he must also relate his poling to the river bottom.

The intention here is to describe some of the basic and most effective strokes used in cruising and some of those most frequently used by top polers in competition.

The basic poling strokes are relatively simple. Much can be learned by situating your canoe in shallow water, applying your pole at different angles, and making a mental note of the results. As a beginning poler, you should attempt the basic strokes from the standing position, realizing that it will take time to greatly reduce the uneasy feeling of standing in a canoe. Learning the basic strokes can be compared to paddling. As you become more experienced in poling, you will develop strokes that may seem too difficult to the beginner. Just as the sculling stroke may seem magical to the novice paddler, the quick-jab stroke can seem mystifying to the beginning poler.

There are those who will not attempt poling because it may seem too risky. This reluctance is understandable, since even learning to ride a bicycle may appear unsafe to the novice rider. However, there is no doubt that poling is far safer than bicycling, because it involves fewer moving hazards and also offers a softer landing in an accident.

The most basic and most commonly used stroke is the hand-over. It is chiefly used for poling straight ahead. (The poling stance varies, depending on whether you are with or without duffel, maneuvering or cruising, or heading upstream or downstream). If you are poling solo you should generally take a stance near the stern and almost face the side of the canoe. Your feet will be about 2½ feet apart and at a 45-degree angle with the keel line. While poling on the left side, you can simply place the pole down into the water against the bottom and then "climb" with your arms, one hand over the other, until you have nearly reached the end of the pole. Then you return, or toss the pole

back through your hands to the original position, for the next stroke. If you are a beginner, it is important for you to note that after the pole is set against the river bottom, the upper half of the pole should remain open for "climbing." After the canoe has picked up speed, make the thrusts a few feet forward of the first few thrusts. If the thrusts are made too far forward or toward the stern, you are not in position to perform the number of hand-overs necessary to utilize the full power of this stroke. Polers should carry their stroke back behind them far enough to take full advantage of the power of this stroke. After a short while, novices should feel comfortable enough to utilize a full stroke.

BASIC TECHNIQUES

Right Turn

While you are poling on the left side, the right turn is the most difficult of the two turns. However, if you are a beginner, it is not too difficult if you execute it while standing amidships. You simply place the pole out to the left and forward of your stand-ing position. The farther it is out to the left and in front, at a 45-degree angle, the sharper will be the right turn.

After you have some experience you can make normal right turns from the stern while the pole strikes the river bottom in the normal course of a stroke. This action is especially effective against the current, and there is no need to cross the pole to the opposite side of the canoe. You apply pressure against the pole and toward yourself with your lower hand while pushing against the pole with your upper hand. This action will transfer the stress through your body and legs to your feet, resulting in pres-sure against the hull and a right turn. Although this may seem complex at first, it is actually performed in a natural manner while the pole touches the river bottom in the process of making a stroke.

The sweep stroke is similar to the paddle sweep. It is mainly used in water too deep for poling against the bottom. In order to turn right, you simply put the pole out to the left and sweep it toward the stern. The canoe will turn in relation to the depth and power of the sweep: the deeper and more powerful the sweep, the sharper will be your turn.

After some experience, you will acquire the habit of placing the pole back and at an angle, automatically modifying your thrusts and therefore steering the canoe.

Left Turn

The left turn from the left side is the easier of the two turns. From the stern, you make a thrust to the left and a few feet out from the canoe. This action will force the stern to the right and the bow to the left, resulting in a left turn. The degree and speed of the turn can be increased by thrusting with additional power and farther out to the left. The left turn can be performed while you are situated in the middle of the canoe, by applying the same stroke but farther astern of your location.

For the beginner in most cruising situations, when only slight turns are needed, the pole may be trailed in the water at the end of the poling stroke.

Another way of turning left is by dragging the pole (see "Stopping With Pole") on the left side and holding it down firmly. The canoe will turn left but it will also slow to a stop.

At first, while poling on the left side, you may find it useful to apply the pole straight out to the right in order to turn left. However, you will soon find that this method is difficult and cumbersome, allowing for only slow forward progress.

As you become more experienced, you will automatically place the pole in the proper relative position in order to steer the canoe in the direction you desire to go. Therefore, it is highly recommended that at first you stand in the canoe in shallow water, apply the pole at different angles, and note the direction in which the canoe turns.

Stopping With Pole

There is one most effective way of stopping a canoe, whether going upstream or downstream. This is known as dragging. You jam the pole down and a few feet back of the poling position and continually apply downward pressure with your hands and the weight of your body against the pole. The pole shoe will drag against the river bottom until the canoe comes to a stop. While you are poling against the current, this maneuver is not too difficult; however, while you are poling or snubbing down through a fast rapid, you must take a firm grip and apply continual weight and pressure to the pole. While you are checking or stopping (slowing forward momentum), the canoe will have a tendency to turn to the poling side. In order to keep the canoe straight, you can make several powerful dragging strokes by extending the pole out and to the left with both hands (if you are poling on the left side) and then by dragging the pole with your right hand. If your arm, body, and leg muscles remain rigid, you can transfer the resulting leverage pressure through your feet to the hull of the canoe, thus holding the canoe straight and on course. In most situations, a metal point and shoe can greatly aid in the effectiveness of this stroke.

Kayak Stroke (With Pole)

The stroke described here is similar to the basic kayak stroke; that is, you can hold the pole in the center of the canoe and take alternating strokes on both sides. This stroke is especially effective if you find yourself suddenly in deep water and are unable to probe to the river bottom. Also, you can use this stroke when you have no time to reach for a paddle; or you may realize that the pole may be as effective as a paddle in that particular situation. And finally, as a change of pace on a downstream cruise, an experienced poleman will pick up his light aluminum pole and use the pole-paddling stroke for long distances while seated in his canoe. Many single-blade paddlers are surprised to note that they are being overtaken by polers using such a kayak stroke.

The important point to remember is that although poles are round and seemingly offer little resistance as compared to the paddle blade, their great length presents not only ample resistance but also greater adjustable leverage to the water. This resistance and leverage, plus the quick double action of the kayak-type stroke, results in considerable forward speed.

Snubbing (Setting Downstream)

Snubbing or setting (slow and deliberate movement of the canoe, using a pole) is a defensive type of operation used in maneuvering while poling downstream. It should not be confused with poling downstream. An example of snubbing is the working of a canoe down through a rough, boulder-strewn rapid while using eddies or slower water and avoiding the main current. On the other hand, poling downstream is used to give a change of pace from paddling or to aid in the overall progress of the canoe.

In *snubbing,* you stand near the middle thwart and up two or three steps toward the leading end of the canoe. But when *poling* downstream, or upstream, you usually stand near the trailing end of the canoe. Snubbing can save you the time of lining downstream (see chapter 11) and the difficulties in portaging. Furthermore, snubbing can see you through certain types of rapids that may prove too risky if you are paddling in an open canoe.

In snubbing, you stand facing forward with the pole in a ready position, pointed downstream. If the canoe drifts slowly, you need not be concerned with the position of your feet, but as the current increases, even a light forward thrust can jar the pole loose from your hands. Therefore, you should be positioned, similar to the position for upstream poling, at a 45-degree angle to the snubbing side. For example, if you are snubbing on the right side, your left foot should be forward and to the left of your right foot. If the bow drifts too far to the left, you should set the pole forward against the bottom on the left side and hold that position until the bow swings back. Conversely, if the bow drifts too far to the right, you should probe forward to the right side.

You should stand from one to three steps forward of the middle of the canoe in order to place your weight toward the bow to assist in holding the bow pointed downstream. In downstream maneuvering situations, you will still be near enough to the middle of the canoe to step back, thus effectively using the hand-over, dragging, or turning stroke when needed.

You should set the pole forward and remove it, allowing the canoe to drift downstream. Then you alternately apply and remove the pole in relation to the power of the current. If the current is slow, you should not snub frequently but should allow the canoe to drift over longer distances. Generally speaking, it is important to snub the canoe in such a manner as to allow a slow rate of descent, especially in maneuvering situations. If you perform this stroke properly, the canoe will not be swept out of control by the current, and the pole will not be knocked from your hands.

When snubbing, it is wise for you to use your feet to assist in steering the canoe. While your pole is set forward, you can transfer the resisting force through your body and legs by applying direction and transferring this force with your feet to the hull of the canoe.

If you find that the current is too swift and you are unable to stop the canoe by snubbing, you can step back to the middle of the canoe while allowing the pole to drift back just astern of your body. At this time you can quickly apply the powerful dragging stroke, thus bringing the canoe to a stop. Again you can return to snubbing.

In the illustration, the stern paddler has snubbed the canoe to a temporary stop, and the bow paddler is using the paddle to help hold the canoe in line with the current. This is a typical procedure for a tandem crew.

Draw Strokes

While you are poling on the left side and standing near the middle thwart, you may sideslip the canoe to the left by reaching several feet out to the left and setting the pole against the river bottom. You should then apply reverse hand pressure by simply pulling in with your lower hand and pushing out with your upper hand. If you hold the pole spike against the river bottom, the canoe will move toward the pole or to the left. If you want to sideslip to your right, you may simply push the pole against the bottom, directly out to the left. The canoe will move to the right if you are standing directly between the bow and the stern.

The draw strokes are far more difficult if you are standing either in the stern or the bow. This kind of poling requires experience, since you must apply reverse hand pressure relative to the current and the direction in which you want the canoe to move.

ADVANCED POLING SKILLS

The more complicated poling strokes may seem confusing if you are a beginner, and they should be attempted in rapids only after you have experience and feel comfortable and relaxed in the standing position. At first you should try them in slow and shallow water, but it will take time before you can use them with a high degree of effectiveness.

Holding Stroke

The holding stroke may be compared to the double low gear of a truck. Its purpose is to enable you to slowly inch your way forward or to hold your position against a powerful rapid. As with the quick jab or straight jab, you hold the pole at a length where it strikes the river bottom. You do not move your hands up the pole but hold them in one place and about 30 inches apart. The holding stroke can be used when all other strokes have failed and may well be the final alternative before you give in to the overpowering current. You usually make very short, quick thrusts, either just holding your position or slowly inching the boat forward. You may use the stroke as a short respite before slowly inching forward and then changing (similar to shifting into a higher gear) to a powerful hand-over, hand-over switch, or quick jab for a final attempt.

As shown in the illustration, the poler holds on for a short rest after poling up over a 2-foot dropoff. By alternating his strokes and avoiding the main current while using the eddies, an experienced poleman can proceed upstream over very difficult sections of the river.

Hand-Over Switch

The purpose of the hand-over switch is to drive the canoe up through a stiff, fast rapid or to attain maximum forward speed. You stand facing the bow of the canoe, using a lightweight pole from 14 to 16 feet long. You perform the stroke in the same manner as the basic hand-over; that is, after the catch is made, you quickly pass one hand over the other in the manner of climbing, except that you do not return the pole back to the same poling side. When you have climbed your hands to a point within a foot or two from the top of the pole, you thrust the upper end of the pole down on the opposite side of the canoe for the next catch. Then you repeat the hand-overs and thrust the upper end back over again to the original side. You continually switch from one side of the canoe to the other. However, for steering purposes, you may make two or more strokes on the same side.

The great advantage of this stroke is that more powerful hand-overs can be made, and less time is lost between strokes. The main problem is that the pole is constantly being switched from one side to the other. However, this switching is tiring. Also it is relatively easy for you to strike the pole against the canoe, resulting in the pole's being knocked from your hands. Although this stroke requires much practice and a high degree of dexterity and coordination, it can furnish the experienced poler with his most powerful stroke.

Quick Jab

The quick-jab stroke is used to move a canoe upstream through a fast, shallow rapid. It can be performed with most 12-foot poles but is best executed with a pole having a 3-foot-by-$\frac{3}{8}$-inch steel rod extension on the shoe.

In making the quick jab, you stand facing the side of the canoe.

Unlike the procedure used in the other climbing strokes, you do not climb your hands or move them up the pole. Instead you hold them in one place and at a length where the pole strikes the river bottom. You make a jab against the bottom and sweep the pole about 2 feet straight forward against the current, and it is immediately in position for the next quick jab. Do not remove the pole from the water but only lift it a few inches off the river bottom before sweeping it forward. The most important thing to remember is that the jabs are executed continually and at a very rapid rate of two or three per second. The main disadvantage of this stroke is that it is not too effective in water with a depth exceeding 3 feet. Moreover, it cannot be used continually over long distances, since it requires constant fast and strenuous effort. But again it must be remembered that the stroke is used primarily over short distances (perhaps from 20 to 70 yards) to conquer the fast, shallow sections of a difficult rapid.

Although experience is always helpful, the quick jab is not as risky as the hand-over switch. It can be practiced by the beginner, since the pole is always held near the river bottom and can assist him in his balance.

Windmill Stroke

This stroke is less tiring than the other strokes for long poling situations, whether you are cruising upstream or downstream. It can be thought of as similar to the overdrive gear in a car, yet it is still effective against most rapids. The windmill stroke should be performed with a lightweight aluminum pole. You stand facing the side of the canoe with your feet from 24 to 32 inches apart. You revolve the pole in the manner of a windmill, except that after every 180-degree turn you make a thrust before the next 180-degree revolution. When you are poling on the left side, you revolve the pole in a clockwise direction, and from the right side you revolve it in a counterclockwise direction. Unlike the action used in the basic hand-over stroke, you do not climb your hands up the pole. You hold the lower and upper hands about 2 feet apart. The lower hand remains almost in the same place while turning and controlling the pole. Immediately before the thrust is started and immediately after the prior thrust has struck the river bottom, apply downward thrust with your upper hand while holding onto the pole. At this time you again regrip in the same place with the lower hand, which automatically had

CANOEING

untwisted during the stroke. Just before you remove the pole from the river bottom, take your upper hand off the pole. Then your lower hand will send the pole into its next 180-degree revolution. Although both hands assist each other, the lower hand is the controlling or steering hand, and the upper hand applies the major part of the downward force.

The windmill stroke becomes highly effective when the degree of dexterity is such that you can control the pole and quickly revolve it to the next thrust. With this stroke, since little time is spent in repositioning or returning the pole, the overall progress of the canoe is greatly increased. The forward momentum is almost continually carried; thus the canoe does not suddenly "die," or slow down. Moreover, there is little loss due to drag while the pole is being removed from the water.

Spin-Around (180-Degree Turn)

The spin-around, or 180-degree turn, is also known as the crash turn. The first part of this stroke is performed in the same manner as the dragging stop. That is, you must jam the pole down a few feet back of your poling position (on the left side if you wish to turn left and on the right side if you wish to turn right). With your upper hand you apply force against the pole, while at the same time you pull in with the lower hand toward your leg that is nearer the stern. You hold your upper body and legs stiffly, therefore transferring the force to your feet. Your foot that is closer to the bow forces the bow to swing toward the poling side while your other foot applies pressure in the opposite direction. If enough pressure has been applied, the canoe will continue to turn until you have turned it in the desired direction. That is, you can stop the canoe at 60, 90, 180, or 240 degrees, or you can make a complete 360-degree turn if you so desire. The turn can be made whether you are heading upstream or downstream or in any direction in regard to the current. It is easier to make the turn downstream with the current than it is to turn upstream against it. The 180-degree turn can best be made downstream with a keel canoe with the poleman standing in the stern. The turn can be best made upstream

with a keelless canoe with the poleman standing in the middle.
Remember, however, that the best overall maneuvering position
is near amidships. Since your feet are straddling the center of
the canoe at a 45-degree angle to the left, with one foot toward
the bow and the other toward the stern, while you are facing
the poling side of the canoe, the foot pressure can be applied
in opposite directions with little resistance. The reason for this
is that one foot is exerting force toward the pole and the other
is directing force away from it.

Although this turning stroke is effective, it can halt your forward progress, especially when you are poling against the current and turning to the left or right. However, when you are poling downstream, a quick application of the pole can swiftly turn the canoe up to 20 degrees while only slightly checking forward progress.

TANDEM POLING

Double poling can be divided into two areas, the relaxed double stroke and the double power method. The easy double stroke consists of two canoeists proceeding slowly upstream or snubbing downstream through a rapid in order to avoid the main current, risky paddling, tracking, lining, or portaging. The two polemen slowly and methodically probe their way as they maneuver through and around boulders, logs, or other obstructions, many times starting and stopping as they gradually make forward progress. The relaxed stroke can best be per-

formed by two experienced polers in the standing position. However, it can also be performed by two polemen of less experience with the bowman kneeling or sitting with a paddle or a pole and the sternman standing with a pole. The most difficult problem for the beginner is to keep from knocking his partner off balance with a sudden or unexpected thrust when both are standing.

From the kneeling or sitting position, the center of gravity is lower, and it is far more difficult to be thrown off balance. Whether the bowman is standing, sitting, or kneeling, the sternman is in a position to see and anticipate the bowman's pole or paddle thrusts that can result in the sternman's being thrown off balance. An attempt should be made to coordinate the poling thrusts so that both poles strike the river bottom at the same time. However, in tight maneuvering situations, this coordination may not be possible, and the two canoeists will find themselves jabbing alternately. Such alternate thrusting may be done only if progress is slow and the thrusts are gentle, but it will depend on the exact degree of difficulty and the experience of the people involved.

The double power method may be used by two experienced polemen for the same purpose as the double dawdle, but its main purpose is to attain a high rate of speed. It is also used for poling up through stiff rapids that offer no alternate or easy way. It is highly recommended that only experienced polemen attempt the double power method in difficult rapids.

In order to attain the highest degree of power, both polers stand facing the same side of their canoe. They use the basic hand-over stroke at the start, and both poles are thrust at the same time and in a coordinated manner.

If a high degree of speed is desired, a straight-jab stroke is used. That is, the poles are thrust into the water at the same time, but the hand-over stroke is not used. The poles are held at a length where they will strike the river bottom. Unlike the action in the quick-jab strokes, the poles are not swept straight forward but are quickly lifted out after each powerful jab. However, if the polers find themselves moving slowly against a powerful current they may revert back to the hand-over stroke.

In the process of using the fast straight-jab stroke, the polers do not utilize the full length of the pole; therefore, there is no danger of one poler's accidentally striking his partner during the swift application of this stroke. Again, it is the sternman's responsibility to anticipate the bowman's strokes and to see to it that his pole strikes the bottom at the same time as the bowman's pole. This coordination allows both polers to develop rhythm, thus anticipating and easily absorbing any jarring movements. If the bowman wishes to change speed or direction or wishes to stop, he should do so, not suddenly but over several strokes. This transition will give the sternman the chance to follow suit. It will help if the bowman calls out a signal prior to any change in the poling rhythm, speed, or direction. Signals are especially important in a difficult rapid where many stops and turns are attempted.

COMPETITIVE POLING

Competitive poling is a suspense-filled sport for both contestants and observers. At the starting line, the poler stands with his canoe in readiness, pointing upstream. At a signal, a stopwatch is started, and he proceeds up through the course. The poler continues upstream, maneuvering around buoys. When he reaches the top of the course, or the last upstream buoy, he must then pole his canoe back downstream, snubbing or setting down, while maneuvering around other downstream buoys. Then, as his canoe's bow passes the finish line, the watch is stopped. The poler's elapsed time plus penalty points make up his score. Competitive poling tests the poleman's artistry and maneuverability as well as his speed. Besides providing action and excitement, the poler, standing in his canoe, generates intense suspense as he moves slowly upstream over the drop-offs, haystacks, and boils, seemingly in a constant state of peril.

Since the advent of competitive poling in 1965 at Times Beach, Missouri, much has been learned about the art of poling. The poling rules were designed to challenge the poler's judgment as well as his ability to maneuver to maintain a high rate of speed. The result has been a continual improvement in technique due to the numerous situations experienced.

A poling event can be set up in Class I, II, or possibly III rapids; however, the difficulty must be carefully chosen to match the experience of the participants involved. (For beginners, an event set up on slow water can also prove interesting.) When the buoys, lines, and weights have been obtained, a poling course can be set up in from 30 minutes to an hour. The

course is usually from 50 to 100 yards long, with from 12 to 16 buoys placed along its length. The color of each buoy tells the poler whether he must pole to the left, pole to the right, circumnavigate, etc. Poling events are usually held in water with a depth of from 4 inches to 4 feet; however, in some places the course may have a depth of 6 or more feet.

The National Poling Championship is held every year and is sanctioned by the American Canoe Association (ACA). A free copy of the rules, entry data, and other poling information may be obtained by writing to the ACA.

POLING ON ICE

During the winter, when the rivers are frozen over, you do not have to give up canoeing. You can canoe on ice. If you use

a pole with a steel point attached to the shoe, you may be surprised to discover the delights and the speeds that can be obtained by poling on ice. The activity is much safer than skating,
since the weight is distributed over a wider area, and if the ice
should break, you are in the canoe. If you have enough experience, you can pole directly from the ice into the water or
from the water onto the ice. However, make sure that both the

entry and the exit from the ice are made straight on and not at an angle. If the canoe is angled, you may find yourself swimming in icewater. It is certainly safer for the winter canoeist, suddenly confronted with ice, to pole onto it from his canoe than to attempt to lead the canoe onto the ice by the painter.

14

CANOE SAILING

In addition to its adaptability for cruising, wildwater sport, flatwater racing, and camping, the canoe makes an exciting sailboat when properly rigged and balanced. Sailing a canoe involves the same principles that are used in other small boat sailing. It is desirable, however, for the prospective sailor to become a competent canoeist before attempting to sail, even with prior experience in other small sailboats. The canoe is far less stable than most sailboats and could surprise a sailor who has not first become familiar with its unique characteristics. It is suggested that the prospective canoe sailor complete the American Red Cross Basic Canoeing and Basic Sailing courses. In these courses, all fundamental handling techniques are covered, and those who complete the courses are ready to branch into canoe sailing safely and with confidence.

Sailing techniques are not covered in this chapter, except those canoe sailing techniques that differ from small boat sailing techniques.

Canoe sailing can be divided into two classifications: general sailing for pleasure and competitive sailing.

Several canoe manufacturers today produce sailing equipment that can be fitted to their canoes. This equipment is suitable for general pleasure sailing or cruising. These rigs, in some cases, are designed so that they can be dismantled and stowed in the bottom of the canoe when not in use, thus maintaining the versatility of the canoe. The canoe can be adapted for both cruising and camping if you have a sail rig available for covering broad expanses of water or just for pleasure sailing from the camp. Since sailing equipment for a canoe is relatively simple, much of it can be home constructed. The sail itself, however, should be purchased from a sailmaker, because few home builders could design and manufacture an efficient sail for anything other than a lateen rig.

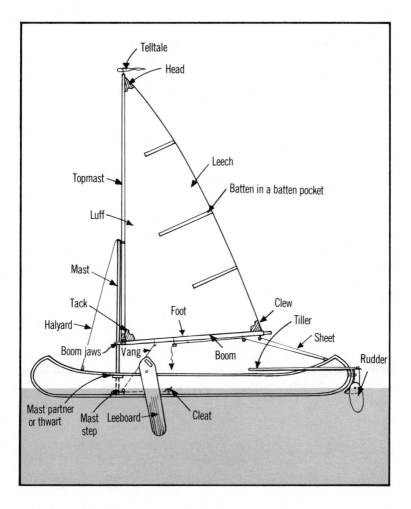

SAILING RIG

The following information should be helpful in constructing a reasonably simple, suitable rig, as shown, for pleasure and competitive sailing. A canoe sailing rig consists of the sail and appropriate spars, leeboards, and, if you like, a rudder. (The canoe can be sailed reasonably well if you use a paddle to steer with instead of a rudder.)

Class C Rig

Most canoes manufactured and used today are from 16 to 18 feet long and about 35 inches wide. The example shown on page 391 is one of the sail rigs being used in sailing competition by the American Canoe Association. This is called Class C and is designed for canoes within certain specifications. It is the most popular class. The preceding illustration shows various parts of the Class C sailing rig. The one advantage of this rig is that it is easily handled by one person. A short stub mast is used, so that the entire sail may be hoisted and lowered by one halyard (line). This design is very safe, since the sail can be quickly lowered if the wind becomes too strong for easy handling of the canoe.

As indicated in the preceding illustration, the mast and vertical spars are aluminum, but the mast could be constructed of wood. If wood is used, the mast diameter should be increased to $2\frac{1}{2}$ inches at the mast partner or thwart and tapered at the heel and to $1\frac{1}{2}$ inches at the head. The boom can also be made of wood.

On boats from 17 to 18 feet in length, the mast is stepped at the stern thwart and the canoe is sailed stern first. Whether the mast is stepped at the stern or bow, the middle thwart should be removed, thus permitting the sailor and any crew to sit at about the center of the canoe, so that the canoe can be trimmed level fore and aft. Bow- or stern-heavy canoes will be out of balance and will not sail well.

Another Common Rig

The rigging of the Class C canoe is only one of many rigs. By using the ideas and suggestions mentioned for the Class C canoe, you should be able to adapt methods and materials for attaining other combinations, such as the lateen rig. Undoubtedly, the lateen rig is the simplest to build and use. The sail itself can be made by anyone with a sewing machine. It is a flat, triangular-shaped sail with the addition, if desired, of a roach and appropriately placed batten pockets. The mast is stepped similarly to that of the Class C canoe. The halyard is also rigged similarly and hoists a gaff of the same dimensions as the boom.

Lines

The three primary lines used with the sail are the halyard, the sheet, and the boom vang.

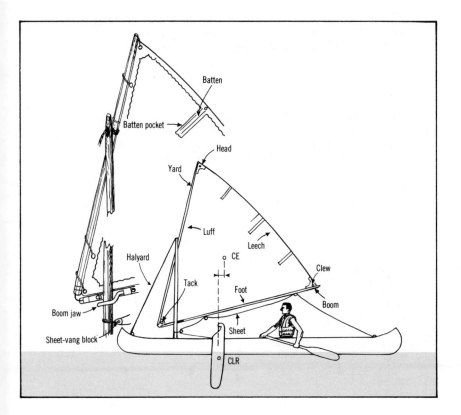

The halyard is used to raise and lower the sail. It should be secured to a quick-release type of cleat in the center of the canoe for easy access while under sail. Dacron is excellent for use as a halyard because it will not stretch under tension, as will nylon.

The sheet is the line that controls the sail with respect to the wind. It is generally of ¼-inch line and should be held in your hand at all times as a safety precaution. Perhaps the best all-around line for this purpose is made of nylon or dacron and is braided.

The boom vang is a line that keeps the boom from lifting while the canoe is running with the wind. It improves the set of the sail and also prevents an uncontrollable jibe. The vang is made fast to the boom an appropriate distance from the mast along the boom. The vang leads from the boom through a block at the mast step and back to the center of the canoe to a sturdy cleat.

Leeboards

Leeboards are another necessary item. They provide resistance to sideslipping (leeway), as does the centerboard, daggerboard, or fixed keel of a sailboat. In this way, the canoe may be sailed to within 45 degrees of the eye of the wind.

The diagram shows the construction details of the leeboard. The board can be made from ¾-inch stock, although increasing the thickness to 1 inch will make a stiffer board. Any clear,

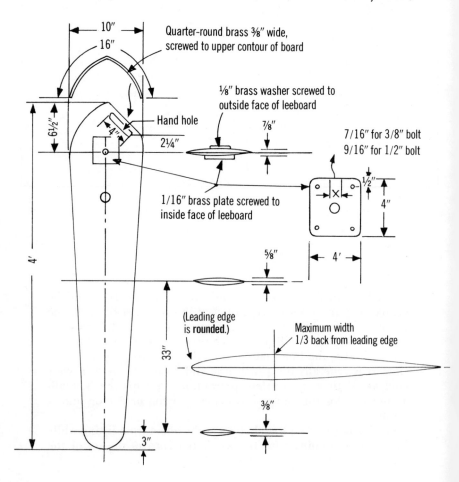

Quarter-round brass ⅜″ wide, screwed to upper contour of board

⅛″ brass washer screwed to outside face of leeboard

Hand hole

7/16″ for 3/8″ bolt
9/16″ for 1/2″ bolt

1/16″ brass plate screwed to inside face of leeboard

(Leading edge is **rounded**.)

Maximum width
1/3 back from leading edge

straight-grained wood can be used (mahogany is favored). Also, the cross section of the leeboard should be efficiently designed (streamlined), with fairly sharp edges.

When two boards are used and when you are sailing close hauled, the board on the lee side of the canoe (the side away from the wind) should be down in approximately a vertical position. When the boat changes tack, you should drop the opposite board to the vertical position, since it will then be the *lee* board. Then raise the other board to reduce drag.

Leeboard Thwart

The illustration on the following page shows how the leeboard thwart is secured to the canoe. It is designed so that it can be moved along the gunwale to balance the leeboard's center of lateral resistance with the sail's center of effort. The thwart can also be used for hiking out if you brace one or both of your feet under it while you are lying out across the gunwale.

Leeboard Position

Once you have decided where the mast will be stepped, you can roughly determine the proper location of the leeboards on the canoe with relation to the sail. This relationship is extremely important to the balance and the sailing ability of the canoe. The following steps will help in getting a rough balance:

1. Find the center of effort of the sail and mark it on the sail. This is a point on the surface of the sail where all the wind pressure theoretically centers. You can find it by drawing a line from the head of the sail (top) to the midpoint of the foot (the bottom of the sail). Draw a second line from the clew (outermost corner) to the center of the luff (side of the sail next to the mast). The point where the two lines cross is the center of effort (CE). Drop a perpendicular from this point.

2. Place the leeboard thwart so that it is centered on the perpendicular and clamp it to the boat. With the sail rigged and with the leeboards in temporary position, you are now ready to sail. Minor adjustments in the balance of the center of lateral resistance (CLR) in relation to the CE can be made by swinging the leeboard fore or aft of its fixed position.

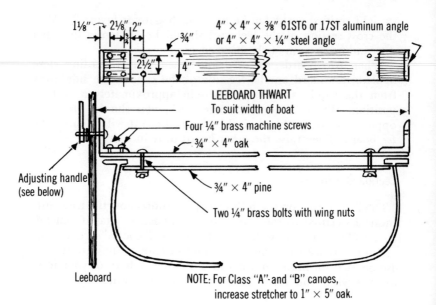

1⅛″ 2⅛″ 2″   ¾″   4″ × 4″ × ⅜″ 61ST6 or 17ST aluminum angle
                                  or 4″ × 4″ × ¼″ steel angle

2½″   4″

LEEBOARD THWART
To suit width of boat

Four ¼″ brass machine screws

¾″ × 4″ oak

Adjusting handle
(see below)

¾″ × 4″ pine

Two ¼″ brass bolts with wing nuts

Leeboard   NOTE: For Class "A"·and "B" canoes,
                            increase stretcher to 1″ × 5″ oak.

ADJUSTING HANDLE

⅛″ × ¾″ × 4″
brass strip
brazed to
hex nut

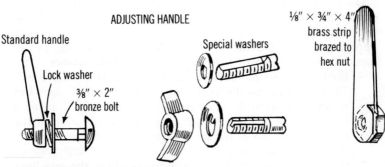

Standard handle   Special washers

Lock washer
⅜″ × 2″
bronze bolt

(A ½″ bolt is recommended for leeboards
longer than 3 feet. Use a lock washer or
a special washer to keep handle from loosening.)

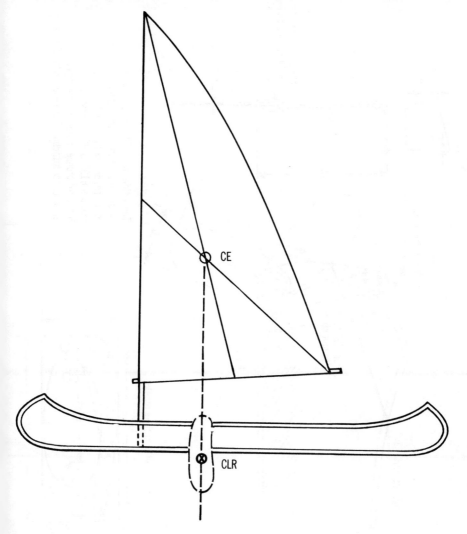

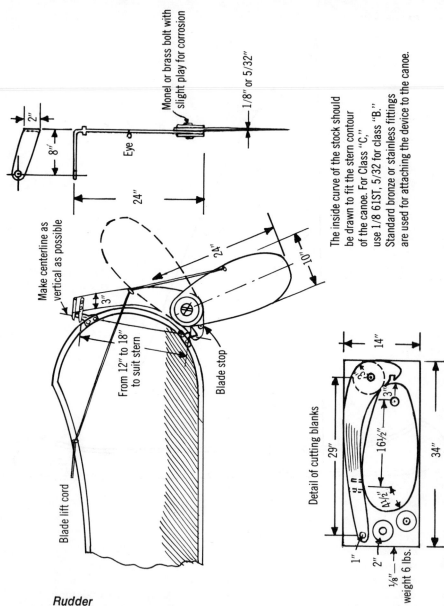

Monel or brass bolt with slight play for corrosion

Eye

1/8" or 5/32"

Make centerline as vertical as possible

From 12" to 18" to suit stern

Blade stop

Blade lift cord

The inside curve of the stock should be drawn to fit the stern contour of the canoe. For Class "C," use 1/8 61ST, 5/32 for class "B." Standard bronze or stainless fittings are used for attaching the device to the canoe.

Detail of cutting blanks

weight 6 lbs.

Rudder

The rudder assembly shown is perhaps one of the better configurations to be used. By following the diagrams and using materials similar to those used in constructing the leeboards, you can make a durable rudder and tiller.

The following four illustrations show variations in tiller arrangements.

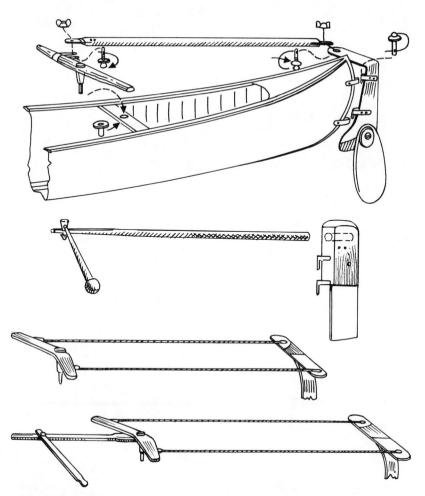

What Rig Is Best

Prospective canoe sailors should be encouraged to build or purchase rigs that fall within one of the American Canoe Association's nationally established racing classes. They should use recognized competitive rigs for at least one particular reason: over the years, these classes have been chosen to combine a reasonable sail area and configuration for handling by competent paddlers; there is always the possibility of racing, whether you do it at present or not, and the resale value of a recognized competitive rig is much higher than other types of rigs.

The rig that you choose should be one that will meet your basic needs. For example, if you plan on sailing alone most of the time, your canoe should be outfitted to reflect one-man operation.

READYING THE CANOE FOR SAILING

Before sailing, put on an approved lifejacket. For details on lifejackets, see chapter 3.

The canoe should always be positioned with the bow pointing into the wind while you are rigging and unrigging. Also, while the canoe is afloat, the leeboards should be in the down position to help keep the canoe headed into the wind while you are raising or lowering the sails.

With the mast stepped in its normal upright sailing position and the halyard rigged, the sail and the boom (or lugs, sprits, gaffs, etc.) should rest on the thwarts of the canoe. Paddle the canoe out from shore and head up into the wind. Lower the leeboards and clear the sheet so that it is free to run and will not tangle. You are now ready to hoist the sail. Once the sail is up, secure the halyard in such a way that it can be released quickly.

SAILING TECHNIQUES

With the sail up, with the leeboards down, and with the boat heading into the wind, grab the sheet. With the paddle, sweep the canoe away from the wind and begin to trim the sail by hauling in on the sheet so that the sail just fills with air. The canoe will begin to sail forward and will have a tendency to head up into the wind to a luffing position. To overcome this tendency and to continue to sail forward, place the paddle in the water on the *lee* side of the canoe, near the stern. Then, maintaining pressure on the paddle by pulling the grip toward you slightly, keep the canoe moving on a straight course with the sail filled. When you release the paddle pressure, the canoe should again tend to turn into the wind. This condition is called *weather helm*. If, when the sail is hauled in, the boat turns away from the wind and begins to sail out of control, the condition is called *lee helm*. Lee helm is an undesirable condition that could lead to a capsize. To correct a lee helm, move the leeboards forward toward the mast and try again. If the canoe wants to turn strongly into the wind and is hard to hold off, move the leeboards aft. A balance can be struck by trial until the canoe sails with moderate weather helm or no weather helm at all in light airs. (If a rudder is used, a very mild lee helm can be tolerated in light airs.) Fine adjustments can be developed by swinging the leeboard fore or aft until the canoe will sail with little paddle pressure, except in heavy breezes. The canoe will then be balanced and will sail with little effort and a great deal of enjoyment by the sailor.

If, on your first trial, you have allowed the sail to fill with the wind coming over the right side of the canoe from the bow, you are sailing to windward on the starboard tack. To have the canoe come about to the port tack, pull the paddle from the water on the lee side. The canoe should automatically round up into the wind and fall off with the sail filling on the port tack (wind coming over the left side of the canoe) . If the sail does not fill, a sweep of the paddle will help bring the canoe about. Again place the paddle on the lee side.

It is best to sit in the center of the boat with the paddle in one hand and the sheet in the other. If wind velocity increases, it may be necessary to sit up on the gunwale to keep the canoe sailing as flat as possible. If there is a marked increase in wind speed (more pressure on the sail), it may be necessary to let the sail out to spill some of the wind, hauling it in again as the pressure decreases. It is important, however, to always keep the canoe moving. If the canoe stalls dead in the water, it cannot be steered. A sudden puff in this case can catch you unaware and can cause a capsize.

Steering

In your initial attemps to sail a canoe by steering with a paddle, it will soon be evident that with the paddle on the lee side of the canoe, a canoe with weather helm can be held off the wind and on course. Another reaction should be evident: with the paddle, you can steer only in the direction that is away from the wind. To head into the wind, you must release the paddle pressure, and the weather helm will turn the canoe in this direction. You can produce additional turning movement into the wind by either heeling the boat smartly to leeward or moving your weight forward in the canoe, or both. You can use the paddle to sweep the bow of the canoe in either direction by utilizing sweep strokes or reverse sweeps. However, in competitive sailing, no forward sweeping movements are allowed.

The paddle used for sailing should be longer than the one used for paddling, since at times, when sitting on the windward gunwale for balance, you would have difficulty in reaching the water far enough aft on the lee side with a shorter paddle. It is also suggested that a lightweight paddle with a "T" grip be used for steering, since it is easier to hold onto and to lift out of the water. *Always* carry a spare paddle.

A rudder will make controlling the canoe much easier and is less difficult for the novice to use. With a rudder, the handling of a sailing canoe is much like the handling of any other small sailboat.

Sailing Practice

Canoe sailing is like any other sailing, except when the canoe is steered with a paddle. It is best to begin sailing in rather light air conditions (wind from 4 to 10 miles per hour) until you learn good control of the craft. It is a good idea to practice sailing around a triangular course so that you can learn basic sailing positions: beating into the wind, reaching across the wind, and running with the wind. It is also important to practice jibing, landing, and taking off. Refer to the Red Cross textbook *Basic Sailing* (Stock No. 321143) for detailed instructions about small boat sailing.

SAILIING CANOE SAFETY

Capsizing Precautions

There is always the possibility of capsizing a sailing canoe, as with any light, small boat. It is important to wear a lifejacket, even if you are a strong swimmer. A lifejacket must be available for each passenger under the Federal Safe Boating Act of 1971. Weak swimmers or nonswimmers should *wear* a personal flotation device (PFD) as a matter of personal safety. Capsizing is generally caused by lack of vigilance with regard to sudden changes in wind velocity or direction. You can usually see a change of wind velocity by watching the water surface ahead when you are going to windward and by watching astern while you are sailing before the wind. The surface of the water develops patches and streaks of dark ripples, contrasting with the rest of the water surface. This change on the surface indicates either higher wind velocity or abrupt changes in direction, or both, and you should be ready to instantly let the sail luff to avoid a near capsize or worse. Maintain pressure by luffing the sail. The majority of sailing canoe capsizes that result from broaching are from the running position.

A capsize usually occurs rather slowly, and if you are sailing properly and sitting on the windward side of the canoe, there is little danger of your being entangled in the sheet. After a capsize, simply hold onto the canoe and rest a moment. If you have your lifejacket on, it will help support you during the self-rescue. If you do not have it on, put it on, and recover the paddles and other equipment. Drop the sail and roll it around the boom or the boom and gaff. Take the mast out, right the canoe (it will, of course, be full of water), put all equipment in the submerged canoe, and paddle to shore. Very often, other boats will come to your rescue. Warn them to keep clear until you are ready for their help.

In all cases of capsizing, stay with the craft unless adverse conditions exist. It is important to practice a capsize in shallow water and then in deep water, until you know *exactly* what to do and how to do it.

Weather Safety

One mistake some beginners make is to sail in weather conditions that are beyond their ability. Winds from 15 to 18 miles per hour (the beginning of whitecaps) are too strong for most new sailors. An experienced canoe sailor can "feather" a canoe through much heavier wind velocities, but doing so takes experience. Getting a weather forecast should be on every sailor's agenda prior to setting sail.

If you are caught out in a sudden squall and cannot reach safety in time, drop the sail, take out the mast, if possible, and place all equipment in the bottom of the canoe or lash it to the thwarts. Then sit on the bottom of the canoe and allow the canoe to run with the wind by steering it. Keep the leeboards down.

COMPETITIVE SAILING

As mentioned earlier, competitive sailing is sponsored in the United States by the American Canoe Association. Complete information can be supplied by this organization on the specifications of canoes sailed in each class as well as on the racing rules currently being observed.

Classes

Described below are the six recognized classes of sailing canoes, three of which are in general use.

Cruising Class

Any standard canoe used for general cruising with a maximum length of 18 feet (no minimum length specified) is permitted to compete in the cruising class. The sail area is a basic 40 square feet for a canoe 16 feet in length and with 30 inches of beam. For each inch of length over 16 feet, the allowable sail area is *decreased* by $\frac{1}{3}$ square foot. The sail must be raised and lowered by a halyard; no stationary sail rigs are allowed. The sail cannot extend more than 13 feet 6 inches above the keel for 16-foot canoes; 1 inch may be added to the sail height for each additional

inch of canoe length. No supporting stays or shrouds are allowed. The canoe is normally steered by paddle throughout the race. *No rudder is allowed.* One noted competitor was known to steer his canoe without a paddle at all, simply by shifting his weight.

Class A

Class A is generally inactive at the time of this printing. Specifications are as follows:

    Length—18½–21 feet
    Beam—36 inches
    Steering—rudder or paddle
    Sail area—135 square feet
    Sail height—20 feet above keelson
    Crew—minimum three

Class B

Class B is generally inactive at the time of this printing. Specifications are as follows:

Length—17–18½ feet
Beam—34 inches
Steering—rudder or paddle
Sail area—105 square feet
Sail height—18 feet above keelson
Crew—minimum two

Class C

The C class is most popular. A maximum of 55 square feet of sail can be used with canoes of this class. The canoe must be a stock model open hull that measures from 16 feet minimum to 18½ feet maximum in length. The sail may extend 16 feet above the keel, and the mast may be supported by stays. Either a paddle or a rudder is permitted for steering. This class has no limitations on number of crew other than the skipper. Within the required sail area and height, many different and effective sailing rigs have been developed.

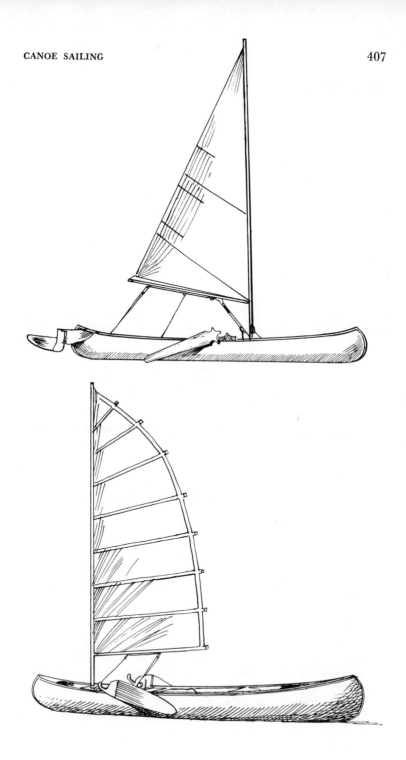

Dixie Class

The dixie class is designed for use in areas of high wind velocity or for beginning sailing. The sail area has a maximum of 30 square feet, and the sail can be hoisted a maximum of 11 feet from the keel. Either a rudder or a paddle may be used for steering.

Decked Sailing Canoes

The decked sailing canoe is used in international sailing competition. This canoe is approximately 17 feet long and approximately 40 inches abeam. It is equipped with a centerboard, sliding hiking boards, a rudder, and highly developed full-batten sails. It is decked over, it is self-bailing, and it can be quickly righted if capsized. A one-design hull has been adopted by the

International Canoe Federation. This canoe is the fastest single-hull, one-man boat so far developed.

Learning Competitive Sailing

Competitive canoe sailing is similar to any small sailboat competition. The same right-of-way rules and procedures are used. Sailing tactics are similar to those used in small boat competition. There are some sailing characteristics, however, that are particularly applicable to canoes:

• Canoes are generally much lighter than other sailing craft of the same length and therefore will not sail as efficiently to windward in- heavy weather. Since wave action has a tendency to stop the light hull, the canoe is first sailed off the wind to gain speed before quartering into the waves.

- A properly balanced canoe will sail extremely well when reaching and running before the wind. Also, if seas are not too heavy, the canoe will sail very close to the wind in windward courses.
- When the canoe is running before the wind, you must take care to prevent an accidental jibe or a broach. Capsizes are more frequent off the wind than when beating into it, since you have better control of the canoe while sailing to windward. It is harder to maintain control while you are sailing with the paddle alone, especially when you are running and reaching.
- The trim of the canoe is extremely important, both laterally and fore and aft. You must spend a great deal of time learning where your weight is most effective for the course being sailed. The bow-heavy canoe may have a tendency to increase its weather helm (rounding up into the wind) .

  A stern-heavy canoe will have a tendency to fall off the wind, thus producing a lee-helm condition. It is best to start sailing with the canoe trimmed flat fore and aft, thus producing the greatest overall waterline length. The longer the waterline, the greater the potential speed, other things being equal. This means that the weight of the crew and the skipper must be concentrated amidships. Sometimes it helps to move slightly aft, since pressure on the sail has a tendency to drive the bow of the canoe down, thus increasing the tendency of the boat to round up or even to broach.
- It is necessary for the sailor, by trial and error, to find the best athwartship (side-to-side, or lateral) balance of the canoe on *all* points of sailing. In beating to windward, it is important for you to sail the boat with minimum heel, trying at all times to keep the boat on its designed waterline. Excessive heel can cause the boat to drift to leeward by reducing the effectiveness of the leeboards. It also causes a reduction of sail area efficiency. However, heeling in very light airs may improve the shape of "soft" sails; also, heeling may produce a weather helm, which would otherwise be nonexistent. Heeling requires practice and vigilance in watching water surfaces for changes in wind velocity so that you can be ready to hike out and maintain good lateral balance.
- If you observe small craft racing, you will notice that while the boats are going to windward, their sails seem to be trimmed flat and over the gunwale of the boat. In windward canoe sailing, however, you should not trim the sail too close to the centerline of the craft. Trimming a sail in this way would result in leeway and in a stalling of forward momentum.

It is better, generally, not to sail too close to the wind, so as to make better speed over the bottom. A properly cut sail, producing a good airfoil, will increase the angle at which the canoe can sail to windward. It is good to follow the general rule of having the sail as far out as possible from the centerline of the boat for the course sailed, but just in from the luff. (This provides for maximum efficiency of the entire rig in most cases.)

• Since the leeboards are adjusted with relation to the center of effort on the sail, you can adjust their position by swinging them fore and aft for better balance of the helm. Pressure on the rudder can be reduced by adjusting the leeboards while the canoe is underway. This adjustment, of course, increases speed due to the reduced drag (braking effect) of the rudder, which would be constantly crosswise while correcting the canoe's heading. Again, you must practice on a variety of courses and wind velocities in order to learn the appropriate board adjustment and boat balance. You will find that most of the sailing techniques used in small boat racing and sailing are also usable in competition sailing. Remember, however, that the canoe is much more sensitive to weather than other sailboats of equal length because of its construction and narrow beam.

15

KAYAKS AND RAFTS

KAYAKS

It is well beyond the scope of this book to treat kayaks and kayaking in detail, but these sporty little craft are very much a part of the overall canoeing scene and, as such, deserve at least a brief mention here. This information will center on the whitewater kayak, since it is most common.

The modern version of the Eskimo kayak is of two types, the rigid and the collapsible. The collapsible kayak, or foldboat, consists of a framework of wood or tubular metal that is assembled at the water's edge and fitted into a rubberized canvas skin. (Some kayaks are inflatable.) Most of today's folding kayaks are fully decked, fore and aft and along the sides, with an appropriate opening left for the paddler.

Folding kayaks are especially popular in Europe and among large-city apartment dwellers and are available in sizes to accommodate more than one person. Also, they can be equipped with a sailing rig. Another feature of this type of craft is that it may be carried collapsed in the trunk of an automobile (even on a bus, train, or bicycle), thus eliminating the need for a cartop carrier. However, folding kayaks are less durable and less maneuverable than the rigid models made of fiberglass or other plastics.

The rigid kayak, because of its design, is able to reach a point of maximum refinement. As the needs and purposes change, so the design changes. Kayaks of wildwater designs show radical changes over those kayaks used in river slalom competition. The wildwater and slalom kayaks differ in the following ways: One of

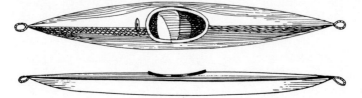

the most distinguishable differences is that of the keel line. With
the wildwater boat, the keel line is reasonably flat from end to
end, but with the slalom kayak, (see illustration, page 412), there
is a rise from the center to each end, in the form of a gentle curvature. The shape is termed the *rocker* of the craft and allows for
considerable maneuverability of the kayak.

In Olympic flatwater racing there are several highly specialized
kayaks that are designed purely for speed on flatwater. They include the single-seater (K-1), a two-seater (K-2), and a four-
seater (K-4).

Other specialized kayaks include "bat" boats, which are stubby
little craft that are slow but turn easily. They are used for playing kayak polo, often in an indoor swimming pool.

Still another type is the surf kayak, which is very flat on the
bottom and short in length, with a bow like a duck's bill.
The paddler sits well aft of center, and the craft rides the ocean
breakers much as a surfboard does.

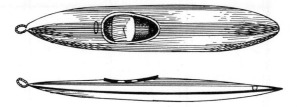

Often, canoes and kayaks will be seen in the same group on
the water. Most of the basic canoe strokes can also be applied to
kayak techniques: stern rudder, back stroke, forward stroke,
sweep, etc. Also, everything said about canoe safety applies just
as well to the kayak. Moreover, many active kayakers were once
canoeists who became attracted to the possibilities of greater precision in boat handling and quicker maneuverability, particularly
with the versatile slalom-style kayak (closed-boat construction).

Paddles

The basic means of propulsion for all kayaks is the double-bladed paddle. In contrast to the canoe paddling position, the kayak paddler sits rather than kneels. The sitting position has the advantage of lowering the center of gravity, but it also has the disadvantage of limiting the paddler's range of body movement.

The double-bladed paddle has a variety of configurations and sizes. The principles for selecting a kayak paddle are much the same as those for the canoe paddle, which are mentioned in chapter 3. The paddle used by an average paddler has about a 4-foot shaft and is about 6 feet 9 inches in length.

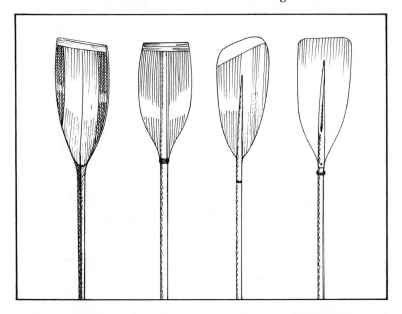

Kayak paddles are available either unfeathered (both blades in the same plane—rarely seen nowadays) or feathered, with the blades offset 90 degrees. Feathered paddles that have spoon blades can be offset 90 degrees clockwise for left-hand control or 90 degrees counter-clockwise for right-hand control. With offset flat blades, either face of the blade can be used as the primary power face. The unfeathered paddle is not as efficient as the feathered paddle and is therefore not preferred.

The solid-shaft paddle is preferred over the two-piece paddle owing to a possible weakening at the ferrule joint of the latter.

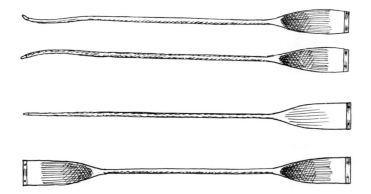

However, the two-piece paddle can be an excellent second, or spare, paddle because of storage possibilities.

Getting In and Out

Getting in and out of a kayak, with its tiny, restricted cockpit, poses a little more of a challenge than getting in and out of a canoe.

To get into a kayak, if it is resting in the water next to shore, squat down next to the cockpit, on land, facing the bow. Rest the paddle across the kayak, just behind the cockpit, with one of

the paddle blades lying flat on the shore for support. With your
hand that is nearer the boat, grip the paddle shaft *and* the rear
of the cockpit to keep the boat steady. With the other hand, grip
the paddle shaft near the blade that is resting on shore. Place
your leg that is nearer the boat into the kayak, directly in front
of the seat and slightly to the outside of the centerline of the
hull. Follow it with the other leg and place that leg next to the
first, then lower yourself into the seat. In the process, you must
slip your legs forward. By feeling with your feet, you can engage
the foot braces, then the knee braces, to secure a firm fit in the
kayak.

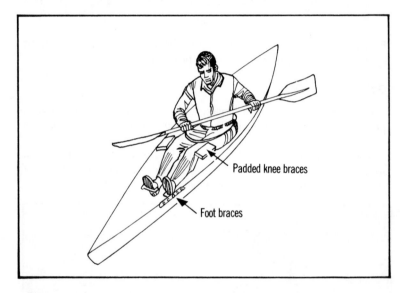

Padded knee braces

Foot braces

You exit from a kayak in a similar manner: by placing the
paddle behind you, with one blade resting on shore, and raising
yourself from the seat, drawing first one leg and then the other
from the cockpit.

An important safety measure for the kayak beginner is to practice what is commonly known as the wet exit. In shallow water,
with safety close by, purposely tip the kayak over and then carefully drop out of the cockpit to prove to yourself that you are not
trapped in the boat. You should do this first without the spray
cover on, then with it on.

When practicing with a spray cover, do not attempt to wriggle
out of it. Instead, after you capsize, slowly and carefully remove

the spray cover and exit with it still on. In an emergency, you should be able to get out of the spray cover.

Basic Strokes

After getting accustomed to the kayak, you should learn the various strokes used in kayaking as well as the Eskimo roll.

The strokes mentioned here are fundamentally the same as those mentioned in chapter 6. Only the purposes of the strokes and the differences from canoeing strokes (if any) will be mentioned.

NOTE. Since the kayak paddle is double-bladed, controlling the angle of each blade will come with practice. Also, each stroke mentioned should be practiced forward and backward and right and left.

The sweep is the first turning stroke to be learned. The draw strokes used in kayaking are the same as those in canoeing.

The sculling draw is a continuous draw.

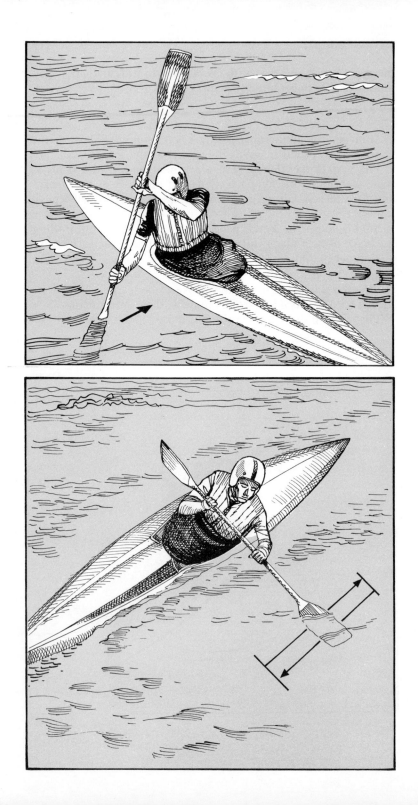

Skills

Blade Control

Blade control is a definite skill that must be learned. Since the feathered, spoon-bladed paddles are preferred because of their efficiency, a method of controlling the paddle so that the power face of each blade catches the water properly must be employed. To make this method work, you must choose either the right or left hand as the control hand. This hand maintains a firm grip on the shaft while the other hand permits the shaft to rotate in it momentarily, to facilitate proper blade angle entry into the water.

Forward Stroke

The mechanics of the kayak forward stroke are similar to the canoe forward stroke, except that both your arms should be trained to apply the necessary power and leverage to keep the kayak on course.

Back Stroke

The back stroke is applied in reverse of the forward stroke; however, the blades are *not* reversed.

Braces

The braces used in kayaking are both high and low brace techniques and are often combined with a sweeping or sculling action. The braces used, in addition to the forward brace, are the back brace and the side brace.

Duffek

The duffek is a turning stroke, which incorporates an element of bracing with a draw.

Course Corrections

Small course corrections can be accomplished by using the paddle as a rudder. However, this rudder has little effect for making major changes in course. The pry and the cross draw are not used in kayaking.

All of the principles expressed in Chapter 10, "River Canoeing," apply to the kayak as well as the canoe and therefore should suffice for a discussion on kayaking on rivers or in whitewater.

Activities

Activities involving kayaks provide challenges and thrills, as well as excellent training. Two activities are described below.

Kayak Surfing

Kayak surfing has really caught on along coastal waters, and special designs of kayaks have evolved through necessity. Surf kayaks are designed with a flat bottom and a broad bow, with the seat well aft of amidships. Slalom and wildwater kayaks should not be used for surfing because of their tendency to bury the bow. If you must use a river kayak, the best choice would be a slalom boat.

Any person wishing to learn kayak surfing should search out and befriend those with experience. This is perhaps the safest way to learn, but you must also remember the following points:

- Do not attempt surf with breakers greater than 8 feet high. If you have doubts, stay ashore!
- Never surf alone, even if your companion is only someone standing on shore. Always *wear* a lifejacket and a helmet.
- Stay away from swimmers. Being a relatively new activity, kayak surfing will draw spectators, and they will invariably get in the way.
- Do not surf at an unknown beach or near docks, jetties, or breakwaters.

The Kayak Roll

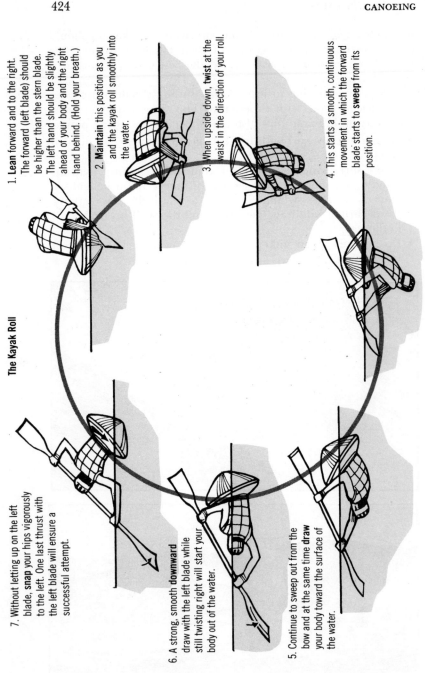

1. **Lean** forward and to the right. The forward (left blade) should be higher than the stern blade. The left hand should be slightly ahead of your body and the right hand behind. (Hold your breath.)

2. **Maintain** this position as you and the kayak roll smoothly into the water.

3. When upside down, **twist** at the waist in the direction of your roll.

4. This starts a smooth, continuous movement in which the forward blade starts to **sweep** from its position.

5. Continue to sweep out from the bow and at the same time **draw** your body toward the surface of the water.

6. A strong, smooth **downward** draw with the left blade while still twisting right will start your body out of the water.

7. Without letting up on the left blade, **snap** your hips vigorously to the left. One last thrust with the left blade will ensure a successful attempt.

Kayak Polo

Kayak polo is becoming an excellent training opportunity during the "off" season as well as becoming a popular, organized sport. The game provides participants with the elements of team play and with practice in general boating skill. Its appeal stems from combining most of the qualities of lacrosse, field hockey, and soccer, as well as traditional polo.

The game can be played indoors in a swimming pool or outdoors on an appropriate flatwater area. There are two teams of from two to six players each. The players try to hit a ball (volleyball or water polo ball) with their paddles through the opponent's goal while playing on an oblong area. Goal tending of the 3-foot-by-6-foot goal is not permitted.

Kayak polo, although not a sanctioned American Canoe Association activity, is a well-defined game with definite rules. The rules are designed to eliminate injury to players and prevent damage to equipment.

Copies of the rules for kayak polo can be obtained by writing to R. J. Evans, 11 Cottage St., Belchertown, Mass. 01007. The rules also appear in *Fundamentals of Kayaking*, by R. J. Evans, a publication of the Ledyard Canoe Club.

This chapter exposes only the "tip of the iceberg" in kayaking but will perhaps clear up some of the misconceptions that exist about this fine sport. To properly learn the skills presented here, you should contact local paddling or outdoor clubs or organizations. By practicing with such groups, you would be developing your own abilities as well as helping others to develop theirs.

RAFTS

Rafts are inflatable, bulky craft and come in a variety of sizes, depending on their intended use and the number of people using them. Shown in the illustration is a four-man raft especially constructed for river rafting. Such rafts are usually constructed of some combination of canvas, nylon, vinyl, neoprene, and rubber.

As with any other sport, rafting should not be attempted prior to getting specialized training in safe handling. Since most of the safety information in this text applies to rafting as well as canoeing, no expanded section on rafting will be found in the text.

GLOSSARY

Abeam—Directly to the side (90 degrees from ahead) of the craft.

Aft—Toward the stern (or rear) of the craft.

Ahead—Forward of or in advance of the craft.

Air tank—See *Buoyancy chamber.*

Amidships—In, or toward, the middle of the craft with regard to length or breadth.

Astern—Behind the craft.

Athwartship—Directly across the craft (90 degrees from the keel line).

Ballast—Weight concentrated on the bottom of the craft to increase stability by lowering the center of gravity of the craft.

Bang plate—A strip of corrosion-resistant metal attached to the leading edge of the stem (or the cutwater if the canoe has one) bow and stern, to protect the hull.

Bank—To tip the craft so that its bottom is presented to opposing currents while making a sharp turn.

Beam—The width of a craft at the widest point.

Bilge—The curved part of a craft's hull where the sides and the flat bottom meet.

Bilge keels—Usually found only on large freight canoes, fitted at the bilges to provide structured support and protection to the bottom of the canoe.

Blade—The flat section of a paddle.

Boil—A "mound" of water caused by the current's being deflected toward the surface by an underwater obstruction. Sometimes called a pillow.

Bow—The front end of a craft.

Bracing stroke—A stroke used to counter the capsizing moment when a paddler leans far out over the gunwale in order to bank the canoe into a sharp turn.

Bracket—A temporary device used to attach a small outboard motor to a double-ended canoe.

Breasthooks (breast plates)—Small triangular pieces of wood found above the bow and stern of wooden canoes. They are an important structural part of the canoe and are subject to considerable stress. They are often called a deck and are flush with the top of the gunwales.

Bridle—A span of rope secured at both ends. Used for tying down craft or as a means of towing another canoe.

Broaching—To be thrown broadside-on by differential currents or wind.

Buoyancy chamber—The airtight chamber or chambers that hold highly buoyant material to float a swamped or capsized craft. Located along the sides of sponson canoes and in the ends of most other craft.

Channel—A supposedly navigable route through obstructions in a section of river.

Chute—A narrow channel between obstructions that is faster and steeper than the surrounding water.

Cleat—A fitting of wood or metal with horns, used for securing lines.

Coaming—The raised lip around the cockpit of a closed (decked) canoe or kayak that holds the spray skirt on.

Deck—This term used with canoes or kayaks is more akin to a covering over the hull to prevent water from entering than to a structural support, although any deck does provide support.

Depth of canoe—The distance from the bottom of the craft vertically to the gunwale line.

Difficulty rating (class of river) —A classification of a section of river that describes its navigability.

Dock—A platform built on the shore or out from the shore; a wharf or pier. Also understood to be the area of water between two piers.

Draft—The vertical distance from the bottom of the craft to its waterline.

Drop—A steep, sudden slope down as compared to the surrounding water; a pitch.

Eddy (and eddy line or wall)—The area behind or downstream of an obstruction, which the currents swirl upstream toward the obstruction. The eddy is defined by a line separating the downstream current from the upstream current and can be either vague or well defined.

Falls—A drop over which the water falls free vertically at least part of the way.

Fastwater—Generally meant to refer to rapids but can mean swiftly flowing water without obstructions.

Feather—To recover the paddle upon completion of a stroke by leading with one edge, thus reducing the drag caused by air or wind.

Ferry—A maneuver in which the paddler uses the force of the current to move his craft laterally across the current.

Flatwater—Lake water or river current where no rapids exist and eddys are slight.

Floorboards—Temporary slats placed in the bottom of a craft to protect the ribs and planking and to distribute weight more evenly.

Freeboard—The vertical distance from the waterline to the lowest part of a craft's gunwale. The draft plus the freeboard should equal the craft's depth.

Full deck—Decking covering the entire hull, with appropriate openings for the paddlers.

Grip—The end of the canoe paddle opposite the blade and tip, shaped to comfortably and securely fit the paddler's hand.

Gunwales—Structural supports for the sides of a canoe. Located at the uppermost portions of the sides and extending from stem to stern on both sides. Held together at the ends by the breasthooks.

Hanging stroke—A high, bracing stroke.

Haystacks—Large standing waves at the base of a chute or other fast-flowing water as it enters relatively still water.

Heavy water—A great volume of water in a rapids section creating greater-than-average turbulence. Also, lake surface in a strong wind where wave action is great.

Heel—To list over; tip to the side.

Hull—The body of a craft.

Hydraulic—See *Hydraulic jump.*

Hydraulic jump—A physical phenomenon caused by a descent of water flowing over an obstacle, resulting in standing waves, haystacks, rollers, stoppers, souse holes, and/or reversals.

Inwale—The inside gunwale.

Keel—A strip running from stem to stern along the bottom of a canoe to protect the bottom of the craft and, in some instances, to prevent sideslipping. The keel is often termed the backbone of a craft and is its main structural member.

Keeper—A manifestation of a hydraulic jump, which will have the tendency to hold you and your boat in the keeper's recirculation of water.

Lash—To securely tie an object down with rope or cordage to prevent loss.

Ledge—A projecting stratum of rock that restricts or partially dams a stream flow.

Lee (or leeward) —Sheltered from the wind; the downwind side.

Lining—A method of working a craft downstream from shore by using rope.

Mold (or form)—A specially prepared, shaped form in which a "plastic" boat is layed up.

Nonpower face—The face of a paddle blade opposite the power face; back face.

Outer stem—A piece of wood attached to the stem outside the hull, forming the cutwater (the foremost part of the stem that cuts the water as the boat passes through it).

Outwale—The outside of the gunwale.

Painter—A line attached to the bow and/or stern of a craft.

Pier—A dock that extends from shore.

Pillow—See *Boil*.

Pitch—See *Drop*.

Planking—Broad strips of wood used to cover the sides of a craft.

Port—Toward the left of the craft when facing forward.

Portage—To carry a canoe and its supplies around a river obstruction or overland between two waterways.

Power face—With the forward or power stroke used as a reference, the power face is the face of the blade that bears against the water. The back stroke uses the back face of the blade to bear against the water.

Rapids—A section of river characterized by a steepening of terrain, increased water speed, obstructions, and turbulence.

Ribs—The athwartship frame of the craft extending from gunwale to gunwale and forming the shape of the hull.

Riffles—A shallow section of river flowing across a gravel or sand bottom, creating small waves; also known as a gentle rapids.

Rocker—Upward, gentle curvature of the keel line of the craft from the center toward both ends. Very characteristic of slalom boats.

Rudder—A steering device used to direct a craft on a desired course. Found on flatwater kayaks and some sailing canoes; also the paddle when used to steer a sailing canoe.

Setting—A term used in describing a controlled descent down a stream using a pole; also means to ferry with bow downstream; back ferry.

Shaft (loom)—The handle of a paddle between the blades of a double-bladed paddle or between the blade and the grip.

Shakeout—A method for the paddler to use when emptying a swamped canoe while in deep water.

Sheer—The longitudinal upward curvature of the gunwales or sides of the hull toward the ends.

Shoe keel—A wide, shallow keel used for structural support and protection. It offers minimal resistance to sideward movement and is good for river canoes.

Slack water—Stream flow without rapids or riffles.

Slalom—A series of predetermined maneuvers in a stretch of rapids defined by numbered gates and used for competition. Can be set up on flatwater also.

Snubbing—Used in setting; slowing or stopping a canoe's forward momentum while running downstream.

Souse hole—A variety of white eddy in a powerful current, characterized by foamy backflow and a surface level lower than that of the surrounding water.

Sponson—A buoyant chamber; a bulge in the side or an attachment of buoyant material just beneath the gunwale of a canoe to assist in improving athwartship stability.

Spray skirt—A waterproof fabric cover designed to close the space between the paddler and the cockpit coaming of a canoe or kayak.

Standing wave—A wave that accompanies the deceleration of a current; a haystack.

Starboard—Toward the right side of the craft, facing forward.

Stem—The curved piece of wood at the extreme ends of the craft to which the gunwales, planking, keel, ribs, and breasthook are attached; also the bow.

Stern—The rear or back end of a craft.

Stopper—A manifestation of a hydraulic jump, which has the tendency to stop your forward momentum downstream.

Stow—To put in place, out of the way.

Swamp—To sink by filling with water.

Sweep boat—The last boat down a stretch of river. A safety measure to make sure no boats are left behind on the course.

Tip—The extreme end of a paddle at the blade end.

Throat—The section of the paddle shaft that flares to form the blade.

Thwart—Transverse braces from gunwale to gunwale.

Towing shackle—A piece of hardware attached low on the stem or the cutwater, used to connect a line for the purpose of towing the craft.

Tracking—A method for towing a canoe upstream by hand, using lines.

Trim—The fore-and-aft angle in which a canoe rests or moves on water—for example, a craft can be stern-heavy or down at the stern as opposed to being evenly trimmed.

Trip leader—The qualified canoeist in charge of a group of canoes and canoeists on a trip.

Trough—The hollow or depression between two waves.

Tumblehome—The amount of inboard curvature of a canoe's sides from the bilge to the gunwale.

Waterline—A line reached by the water on the craft when the craft is carrying a normal load and is evenly trimmed.

Weir—A low-level dam on a river. Characterized by a uniform, smooth flow over the dam and a rather innocent-appearing backflow beneath it. *Very* dangerous.

White eddy—The eddy formed by water that is flowing *over* an obstruction, characterized by a marked and highly aerated (bubble-filled) backflow at the surface.

Whitewater—Rapids with a great deal of aeration.

Wildwater—Long stretches of untamed whitewater; also a type of race.

Windward—Toward the wind; the direction from which the wind is blowing.

Yoke (portage)—A padded shoulder rest attached to the canoe for carrying the canoe long distances.

SELECTED REFERENCES

Publications

Periodicals

American Whitewater, official journal of the American White-water Affiliation. For information: *American Whitewater,* P.O. Box 321, Concord, N.H. 03301

Canoe, official publication of the American Canoe Association. For information: *Canoe* magazine, P.O. Box 487, Marble-head, Mass. 01947.

Downriver. For information: *Downriver,* P.O. Box 366, Mountain View, Calif. 94040.

Oar and Paddle. For information: *Oar and Paddle,* P.O. Box 621A, Idaho Falls, Idaho 83401.

Whitewater Program, publication of the U.S. International Slalom Canoe Association. For information: United States International Slalom Canoe Association, P.O. Box 45, Elwyn, Pa. 19063.

Wilderness Camping, official magazine of the United States Canoe Association, in which appears *Canoe News,* official publication of the American Whitewater Association. For information: *Wilderness Camping* magazine, 1597 Union Station, Schenectady, New York, N.Y. 12309.

Books

Bark Canoes and Skin Boats of North America, by Adney and Chapella. Smithsonian Institution, Washington, D.C.

Basic River Canoeing, by Robert E. McNair. American Camping Association, Martinsville, Ind.

Boatbuilders Manual, by Charles Walbridge. Wildwater Designs, Inc., Penllyn, Pa.

Canoe Camping, by C. W. Handel. A. S. Barnes and Company, New York, N.Y.

Canoe Poling, by Al, Syl, and Frank Beletz. A. C. McKenzie Press, St. Louis, Mo.

Canoeing, Merit Badge Series, Boy Scouts of America, North Brunswick, N.J. 08902.

From Start to Finish, by George G. Siposs. "Haystackers," Glendale, Calif.

Fundamentals of Kayaking, by Jay Evans. Ledyard Canoe Club, Dartmouth College, Hanover, N.H.

Introduction to Canoeing, by Angier and Taylor. Stackpole Books, Harrisburg, Pa.

Kayaking, by Jay Evans. Stephen Greene Press, Brattleboro, Vt.

Malo's Complete Guide to Canoeing and Canoe Camping, by J. W. Malo. Quadrangle Books, Chicago, Ill.

Pole, Paddle, and Portage, by Bill Riviere. Van Nostrand Reinhold Company, New York, N.Y.

River Running, by Verne Huser. Henry Regnery Co., Chicago, Ill.

A Whitewater Handbook for Canoe and Kayak, by John T. Urban. Appalachian Mountain Club, Boston, Mass.

Whitewater Rafting, by William McGinnis. Quadrangle—The New York Times Company, New York, N.Y.

Wilderness Canoeing, by J. W. Malo. Macmillan Company, New York, N.Y.

Associations and Organizations

American Association of Health, Physical Education, and Recreation
    1201 16th Street, N.W.
    Washington, D.C. 20036

American Camping Association, Inc.
    Bradford Woods
    Martinsville, Ind. 46151

American Canoe Association
    4260 East Evans Ave.
    Denver, Colo. 80222

American Whitewater Affiliation
    P.O. Box 321
    Concord, N.H. 03301

Boy Scouts of America
  North Brunswick, N.J. 08902

Canadian Canoe Association
  333 Vanier Road
  Ottawa, Ontario, Canada

U.S. Canoe Association
  6338 Hoover Road
  Indianapolis, Ind. 46260

United States Coast Guard Office of Boating Safety
  U.S. Coast Guard Headquarters
  400 Seventh Street, S.W.
  Washington, D.C. 20560

INDEX